3

KING SOLOMON

AND

HIS FOLLOWERS

N. Y.

A VALUABLE

AID TO THE MEMORY

STRICTLY IN ACCORDANCE
WITH THE
LATEST REVISIONS
1917

ALLEN PUBLISHING COMPANY
John and Dutch Streets
NEW YORK, N. Y.
1917

4-3

5-3 —: INDEX :— Page

To the Complete Book.

ORDER OF BUSINESS

1 Opening the Lodge.
2 Calling the roll of officers.
3 Reading minutes of last communication.
4 Sickness and distress; report of visiting committee.
5 Reports on petitions previously referred.
6 Balloting on petitions.
7 New petitions for membership.
8 Reports of committees, regular and special.
   Annual Election of Officers.
9 Unfinished business.
10 New business, communications etc.
11 Work—Conferring degrees.
12 Reading minutes of present communication.
13 Closing.

OPENING

(*An ofc or b, whn adrsd, shd cm t ○ by rsg @ gvg* +| *§ % fidlty, wh is by plc* +| *r h on* +| *l b, @ respond.*)

Ⓣ ◓- Ofs, tk ur rsptv sts @ plcs; Ɔn, b cld. * Ɔr ⌡ Ɒ.

⌡ Ɒ- (℞*s @ gv* §.) Ⓣ ◓.

Ⓣ ◓- Th f g c % ◓s wn cvd.

⌡ Ɒ- ∓ c tt th r dl td.

Ⓣ ◓- Ⱥtn t tt du @ inf +| ∓ tt I m ab t o — ::, ɳ–, o +| t ° % ◓y; dr hm t tk du ntc thr% @ gvn hms ac.

⌡ Ɒ- (*Spkg thro op d.*) Ɔr ∓.

∓- Ɔr ⌡ Ɒ.

⌡ Ɒ- I am dr t inf u tt +| Ⓣ ◓ is ab t o — ::, ɳ–, on +| th ° % ◓y; tk d nc thr% @ gvn urs ac. (*Cls dr.*) *** ·(∓- ***) Ⓣ ◓.

Ⓣ ◓- Ɔr ⌡ Ɒ.

⌡ Ɒ- Ⓣe r dl td.

Ⓣ ◓- ♓w r w td. 7–3

⅃ Ͽ- Ͽy a ⊥ ⊥ wth, ard wh ⊣ ppr im % hs of.

⊤ ⊥- ♓s dt th.

⅃ Ͽ- T obs ⊣ aph % cns @ evds, c tt nn p o rp xcp sh as r dl ql @ hv prms fm ⊣ ⊤ ⊥.

⊤ ⊥- Ͽr ≀ ⊤.

≀ ⊤- (R @ §.) ⊤ ⊥.

⊤ ⊥- ℞ al prs ⊥ ⊥s.

≀ ⊤- I wl asrtn thr m ppr ofcr @ rpt. Ͽr ⅃ Ͽ.

⅃ Ͽ- (*Tks stf @ stps in ft % ⊣ ≀ ⊤ @ rspns.*) Ͽr ≀ ⊤.

≀ ⊤- ℞ al pr ⊥ ⊥s.

⅃ Ͽ- (*Ps ard on ⊣ ♌ sd % ⊣ ∷. If thr b any prs unkn t hm, he wl paus in frnt % ⊣ strngr @ rprt:*) Ͽr ≀ ⊤.

≀ ⊤- Ͽr ⅃ Ͽ.

⅃ Ͽ- ♓r is a gtlm fr whm I cnnt vh as a ⊥ ⊥.

≀ ⊤- ♀s ⊣ gm t rs.

⅃ Ͽ- (*To ⊣ str:*) ℘ls rs.

≀ ⓣ- ⓣl ny br prs vh fr ths gm as a ⓐ ⓐ. (*If vhd fr:*) Th vhr is acptd. (*If nt vhd fr; trns t stngr:*) ♆ls rtr fr a fw mts untl a cmt cn b aptnd t xm u.

J Ͽ- (*In* ǂ ⓣ.) Ͽr ≀ ⓣ.

≀ ⓣ- Ͽr J Ͽ.

J Ͽ- Δl pr r ⓐ ⓐs.

≀ ⓣ- ⓣ ⓐ. (J Ͽ *tks hs plc.*)

ⓣ ⓐ- Ͽr ≀ ⓣ.

≀ ⓣ- Δl pr r ⓐ ⓐs.

ⓣ ⓐ- As fth evd tt a pr r ⓐ ⓐs, rc ǂ p-w fm ǂ ≀ @ J Ͽs, wh wl obt it fm ǂ bn on ǂ r @ l, @ cm it in ǂ Є.

≀ ⓣ- Ͽs, apr ǂ ⓣ. (*Th shd mt* ⓣ *%* Δ *@ prcd tgthr.*) Gv m ǂ p-w % ⓐ ⓐ. (*Dn.*) Nw obt i fm ǂ bn o ǂ r @ l, @ cmc it t ǂ ⓣ ⓐ in ǂ Є.

Ͽs- (*Prcd, ech on his rsp sd %* ǂ ::. *If thr r ny wtht* ǂ *ps-w thy wl paus as bfr @ rpt:*) ⓣ ⓐ.

(⊤) (⊥)- Ↄr ≀ (*or* J) Ḋ.

Ḋ- Thr i cnfs in ⊣| cft.

(⊤) (⊥)- (⊤)t i ⊣| cs % ⊣| cnf.

Ḋ- A br wtho ⊣| p-w.

(⊤) (⊥)- Cs ⊣| br t rs.

Ḋ- (*To* ⊣| *br:*) Ꝑls rs.

(⊤) (⊥)- (⊤)l ny br prs vh fr ths br as a (⊥) (⊥) in gd stndg. (*If vhd fr:*) Th vhr is acptd. (*To* ⊣| Ḋ :) Invst hm wh ⊣| p-w @ rc it fm h. (*If nt vhd fr,* ⊣| (⊤) (⊥) *wl ask hm t rt fr a fw mnts, @ apnt a cmt t xmn hm.*)

Ḋs- (*Prc @,* ≀ Ḋ *thn* J Ḋ, *cmc* ⊣| *pw t* ⊣| (⊤) (⊥) *in* ⊣| Є.)

(⊤) (⊥)- Ↄr ≀ (⊤).

≀ (⊤)- (⊤) (⊥).

(⊤) (⊥)- Th pw is rt @ dl rcd in ⊣| Є. ℞ u a (⊥) (⊥). (Ḋ*s trn t plcs.*)

≀ (⊤)- I a.

(⊤) (⊥)- (⊤)t indcd u t bcm a (⊥) (⊥).

≀ (⊤)- Tt I mt obt ⊣| (⊥)st wd, trv in frn cntrs, wk @ rc (⊥)st wgs @ b thrby btr enbld t suprt ms @ fml @

cntrbt t ⫲ rlf % dstrsd wrthy (⊥) (⊥)s, thr wds @ orps.

(⊤) (⊥)- (⊤)t ms u a (⊥) (⊥).

≀ (⊤)- (⊥)y o.

(⊤) (⊥)- (⊤)hr wr u m a (⊥) (⊥).

≀ (⊤)- (⊤)th ⫲ bd % a js @ dl cstd :: % (⊥) (⊥)s, asm i a pl rpstg ⫲ unfs ≀ ≀ % Ꝗ ≀ ∓, fur wh ⫲ ⋊ ϶, ≀ @ Ꝗ̵s, tgth wh a Ꝗ̵hrt or ⟩ spntn fm sm gr bd % cmp jrs mprg it t wk.

(⊤) (⊥)- ⋊w mn cmps a (⊥) (⊥)s ::.

≀ (⊤)- T or m.

(⊤) (⊥)- (⊤)n cmps % sv, % whm ds it cnst. (*Fv ma b usd, omtg ∓rs @ ≀ ec.*)

≀ (⊤)- Th (⊤) (⊥), ≀ @ ⌡ (⊤)s, ∓rs, ≀ ec, @ ≀ @ ⌡ ⟩s.

(⊤) (⊥)- Th ⌡ ⟩s plc i ⫲ ::.

≀ (⊤)- At m r.

(⊤) (⊥)- ** (*Ofs rs*) ϶r ⌡ ⟩.

⌡ ⟩- (§) (⊤) (⊥).

(⊤) (⊥)- Ur dts. (*Fr shrt fm omt dts.*)

⌡ ⟩- T cr msgs fm ⫲ ≀ (⊤) in ⫲ (⊤) t ⫲ ⌡ (⊤) in ⫲ ≀, @ lsw ab ⫲ ::

as h ma drc; atd t lms at ǂ ot dr, rpt ǂ sm t ǂ ⊙ ⦾; als t c tt w r dl tl.

⊙ ⦾- Th ≀ Ḍs plc.

J Ḍ- At ǂ rt % ǂ ⊙ ⦾ in ǂ Є.

⊙ ⦾- Ↄ̇r ≀ Ↄ̇. (§) ⊙ ⦾. Ur dts.

≀ Ḍ- T cr ○s f ǂ ⊙ ⦾ in ǂ Є t ǂ ≀ ⊙ in ǂ ⊙, @ lsw abt ǂ :: as h ma drc; wlcm @ clo vsg br, atd t als at ǂ in dr, als t rc @ cn cs.

⊙ ⦾- Th Scs plc.

≀ Ḍ- At ǂ l % ǂ ⊙ ⦾ in ǂ Є.

⊙ ⦾- Ↄ̇r Sec. (§) ⊙ ⦾. Ur dts.

≀ c- T obs ǂ prcdgs % ǂ ::, mk a fr rcrd % al thgs ppr t b rtn, rc al mny du ǂ ::, pa ǂ s t ǂ ∓, @ pfm sh oth dts as m b prscbd by ǂ cnstn % ǂ ₲d ::.

⊙ ⦾- Th ∓s plc.

≀ c- At ǂ r % ǂ ⊙ ⦾ in ǂ Є.

⊙ ⦾- Ↄ̇r ∓rs. (§) ⊙ ⦾. Ur dts.

∓r- T rc al mns fm ǂ ≀, kp a js @ acrt ac % ǂ sm, pa i ot by ○

%. ⊣| :: wn sgnd b ⊣| (T) (⊥), @ prf sh oth dts as m b prscbd b ⊣| cnstn % ⊣| ȼd ::.

(T)(⊥)- Th ȷ (T)s st.

∓r- In ⊣| ≀.

(T)(⊥)- Ↄr ȷ (T). (§) (T) (⊥). Ur dts.

ȷ (T)- T obs ⊣| ≀ at mr, wh is ⊣| gl @ b % ⊣| d; cl ⊣| cf fm ŧb t rfs, sptnd thm dr ⊣| hs thr%, crfly t obsv tt ⊣| mns % rfs r nt prvtd t intmprc or xcs; @ c tt thy rtn to thr ŧb in du ssn, tt ⊣| (T) (⊥) ma rc hn @ th pls @ prf thby.

(T)(⊥)- Th ≀ (T)s st.

ȷ (T)- In ⊣| (T).

(T)(⊥)- Ↄr ≀ (T). (§) (T) (⊥). (T)h in ⊣| (T).

≀ (T)- As ⊣| ≀ is in ⊣| (T) at cls % da, so stds ⊣| ≀ (T) in ⊣| (T) t ast ⊣| (T) (⊥) i op @ cls ⊣| ::; pa ⊣| cf thr wgs, if an b d, tt nn ma g aw dsfd, hrmy bn ⊣| sp % al ins, espcly ths % ors.

⊙ ⌓- Th ⌓st st. In ⫲ Ͼ. ⊙h in ⫲ Ͼ.

≀ ⊙- As ⫲ ≀ rs in ⫲ Ͼ t op @ gvn ⫲ da, so rss—

⊙ ⌓- *** (*Rs.*) —

≀ ⊙- T ⊙ ⌓ in ⫲ Ͼ t op @ gv ⫲ ::, @ st ⫲ cft at wk, gvg thm ppr instcn fr thr ƀ.

⊙ ⌓- Ͽr ≀ ⊙, it is m ○ tt — ::, ŋ –, b nw o on ⫲ t ° % ⌓y, @ st o fr ⫲ trnsn % sh bs as ma rgly @ cnstly b br bf it; ths cmc t ⫲ ⌡ ⊙ i ⫲ ≀, @ h t ⫲ bn prs, tt hvg du ntc th% th ma gv ts ac.

≀ ⊙- Ͽr ⌡ ⊙.

⌡ ⊙- (§) Ͽr ≀ ⊙.

≀ ⊙- It is ⫲ ○ % ⫲ ⊙ ⌓ tt — ::, ŋ –, b nw o on ⫲ t ° % ⌓y, @ st op fr ⫲ trns % sh bs as m rgl @ cnstl b bt bf it; ths cmc t ⫲ bn prs, tt hvg d ntc thr% th m g t ac.

⌡ ⊙- Ͽn, (*Bn shd gv § % fdlt, by plcg rt hn on lf br.*) it is ⫲ ○ % ⫲

⊙ ⊙, cmcd t m thro ⊣⊢ ≀ ⊙ in ⊣⊢ ⊙, tt — ::, ℞ –, b nw op on ⊣⊢ t ° % ⊙y, @ st o fr ⊣⊢ trnsn % sh bs as m rg @ cnstly b bt bf it. I cmc ⊣⊢ sm t u, tt hv d ntc thr% u m g ursls ac.

⊙ ⊙- ⊃n, at t g ⊣⊢ §s; obs ⊣⊢ Є.

Al- (*Gv §s, tkg tm fm* ⊣⊢ Є.)

⊙ ⊙- ** * ≀ ⊙- ** * | ⊙- ** *

Org or ⊙ ⊙- ⊃n wl pls sng ode—

(*Music and Singing.*)

⊙ ⊙- ⊃n, gv ur atn t ⊣⊢ Çhp.

PRAYER

Çhp- ⊙st hly @ gls ∟d Ç, ⊣⊢ Ç A % ⊣⊢ U, ⊣⊢ Çvr % al gd gfts @ gracs, Tho hst prms tt "wh t oř thr gth tgh in Th nm, Tho wlt b i thr mdst @ bls thm." In Th nm w hv asmbld, @ i Th nm w dsr t prcd i al o dngs.

Çrnt tt ⊣⊢ sblm prnc % F⊙y ma s subd ev dscrdt pssn wthn us, so hr- monz @ enrh ou hrts wth Thin own lv @ gdns, tt ⊣⊢ ::, at ths tm, m hmbl reflc tt ○ @ buty wh rgn frevr bfr Thy thrn. Amn. (*Or.*)

(Ma ⫲ fvr % Ꞡ, rfshg as ⫲ dw % ⋊r, @, as ⫲ dw tt dscd up ⫲ mts % Zi, abid wth @ gvn us i a our prcdngs. Amen. (*Or.*)

(Ma ⫲ fvr % ⋊v ɒ up ths mtg; @ as it is hply bgn, my it b cdtd wth ○ @ clsd in hmny. Amen. (*Or.*)

[Ꞡrt ⩜ % ⫲ U! in Th nm w dsr t prcd in al our dngs. Ꞡrnt tt ⫲ sublm prns % F ⊙y ma s subd ev̇ dscrd psn wthn us, so harmonz @ enrch ou hrts wth Thn own lv @ gdns, tt ⫲ ::, at ths tm, m hmbl reflc tt ○ @ bty wh rn frv bf Th thrn. Amn.]

⩜l- S mt i b.

⊙⊙- ⊖r ≀ ⊖.

≀ ⊖- ⊙ ⊙.

⊙⊙- ⩜tn at ⫲ ⩜ @ dsp ⫲ t g ls in ⊙y.

≀ ⊖- (*Gs to* ⊙ *%* ⩜, *gs § % fdlt, dsps lts @ rts t hs pl.*)

⊙ ⌓- I nw dcl ⫲ :: dl o @ i O fr bs, at ⫲ sm tm stc fbdg al idl, imr, o oth unmc cdt, whrb ⫲ hrm % ⫲ sm m b dstrbd, undr n ls a pn thn ⫲ b-ls prsc o a mj % ⫲ br prs c cs t in. ⊃r ⌡ ⊃. ⊙ ⌓. Inf ⫲ ∓.

⌡ ⊃- *** (∓- ***) ⊃r ∓.

∓- ⊃r ⌡ ⊃.

⌡ ⊃- Th :: is op o ⫲ thd °. ⊙ ⌓.

⊙ ⌓- ⊃r ⌡ ⊃.

⌡ ⊃- Th ∓ is inf.

⊙ ⌓ If thr r prst any ₲d :: ofs o ⌓sts % ::s, thy r crdly @ frtrnly invtd t a st in ⫲ ⋲. * (*Or*).

If thr r prs ny prs or ps ₲ :: ofcrs, prs or pst ⌓sts, thy r crdl @ frtrnly invtd t a st in ⫲ ⋲. * 3

—o—

Sc- (*Cls rl % ofs, whr sh i dn, to b ansd by ≀ Ↄ stdg, or by ⫲ ⊤⃝ ⊥⃝.*)

⊤⃝ ⊥⃝- Ↄr Sc.

Sc- (℞*s*, @ §.) ⊤⃝ ⊥⃝.

⊤⃝ ⊥⃝- I wl thk u t rd ⫲ mnts % o lst sta cmc.

Sc- (*Rds mts.*)

⊤⃝ ⊥⃝- Ↄn, ths r ⫲ mts % o lst std cmc; th wr thn rd, apvd, @ r nw rd fr ur infm. (*Mnts % spcl or Emrgnt com, if any r rd.*) Undr Sickns @ dstrs. Ↄr ≀ ⊤⃝.

≀ ⊤⃝- (*Rs* @ §) ⊤⃝ ⊥⃝.

⊤⃝ ⊥⃝- ♓v u ant t rp. 18–3

≀ ⊤⃝- Ɲth i ⫲ ⊤⃝.

⊤⃝ ⊥⃝- Ⱥnth i ⫲ ≀, Ↄr ⌡ ⊤⃝.

⌡ ⊤⃝- (*Rs* @ § .) Ɲthg i ⫲ ≀.

⊤⃝ ⊥⃝- Ↄs any br prs k % a br i sk or ds, or i nd % ou ad @ smpthy

(*Reports if any.*)

⊤⃝ ⊥⃝- Ͽr Sc, hv u any rprts on ptns fr mbrshp.

Sc- I hav a fav (*or* unfv) rpt upn +| aplcn % ⊥⃝r Ѧ Ͽ.

⊤⃝ ⊥⃝- Ͽrn, wt is ur pls in refrnce to ths rprt.

Ͽr Ѧ Ͽ- ⊤⃝ ⊥⃝.

⊤⃝ ⊥⃝- Ͽr Ѧ Ͽ.

Ͽr Ѧ Ͽ- I mv tt +| rpr b rcd, +| com dschd @ +| cdt bltd fr.

⊤⃝ ⊥⃝- If th b no ob it is so ○d. (*or*) If thr is n obj, +| rpt wl b rcd, +| com dschd, @ +| Ç blotd fr. Thr bng nn, i i s od. Ͽr ≀ Ɖ, prp +| bl.

≀ Ɖ (*Taks up bx @ pts it in* ○.)

⊤⃝ ⊥⃝- Dsp it ≀, ⊤⃝ @ Є. (*Dn @ +|* ⊤⃝ ⊥⃝ *tks +| bx.*) Ͽn, w r ab t bl upn +| apln % ⊥⃝r Ѧ Ͽ, on whm ou comt hv rpd fvbly (*or* unf); a w b elcs; a b bl or cu rjcts. (*Deps hs bal @ hds bx t* ≀ Ɖ.) Cr it t +| ≀ @ ⌡ ⊤⃝s fr thr blts, bal ursf @ plc it on +| Ѧ fr +| blts % +| bn. (*Dn.*) Ͽn, prc t b, cmc on m lf. (*or*) in du fm; (*wh is by gv* ⫲ *d* @ § % ⊥⃝ ⊥⃝, *in frt* % ⫲ Ą.)

⊤⃝ ⊥⃝- Ↄr ⌡ ⊤⃝,

⌡ ⊤⃝- (℞ @ §.) ⊤⃝ ⊥⃝.

⊤⃝ ⊥⃝- Ӿ al b i ⫲ ≀.

⌡ ⊤⃝- Ąl in ⫲ ≀.

⊤⃝ ⊥⃝- Ↄr ≀ ⊤⃝.

≀ ⊤⃝- (℞ @ §.) ⊤⃝ ⊥⃝.

⊤⃝ ⊥⃝- Ӿ al b i ⫲ ⊤⃝,

≀ ⊤⃝- Ąl in ⫲ ⊤⃝.

⊤⃝ ⊥⃝- Ąnd al in ⫲ ∈; I thrfr dcl ⫲ bl clsd. * (≀ Ð *clos bal bx.*)

⊤⃝ ⊥⃝- Ↄr ≀ Ð.

≀ Ð- ⊤⃝ ⊥⃝.

⊤⃝ ⊥⃝- Ȼry ⫲ bal ≀, ⊤⃝ @ ∈ fr insp. *Dn.* ⊤⃝ ⊥⃝ *insps* ⫲ *bal* @ *rtns* ⫲ *box t* ⫲ ≀ Ð.) Ↄr ⌡ ⊤⃝.

⌡ ⊤⃝- (℞ @ §.) ⊤⃝ ⊥⃝.

⊤⃝ ⊥⃝- Ӿw sts ⫲ bl in ⫲ ≀.

⌡ ⊤⃝- Ȼlr (*or* cldy) in ⫲ ≀.

⊤⃝ ⊥⃝- Ↄr ≀ ⊤⃝.

≀ ⊤⃝- (℞ @ §.) ⊤⃝ ⊥⃝.

⊤⃝ ⊥⃝- Ӿw in ⫲ ⊤⃝.

≀ ⊤⃝- Clr (*or* cldy) in ⫲ ⊤⃝.

⊙ ⊙- A̸nd cl (*or* cldy) in ǂ Є; acl I dc ⊙r A̸ Ͽ dly elctd t bc a mbr % ths ::. (*or*) I dcl ǂ aplcn % ⊙r A̸ Ͽ rjcd. Ͽr ≀ c, u wl s infm hm, (*if rjctd*) @ rtn hs ptn fe.

⊙ ⊙- Ͽr ≀.

Sc- (℞ @ §.) ⊙ ⊙.

⊙ ⊙- ⋊v u any ptns on ur dsk.

≀ ec- I hv. (*Reads petin.*)

⊙ ⊙- Ͽn, wt s ur pl wh ths ptn.

Ͽr A̸ Ͽ- (℞*s* @ §.) ⊙ ⊙.

⊙ ⊙- Ͽr A̸ Ͽ.

Ͽr A̸Ͽ- I mv tt ǂ ptn b rcd @ rfd t a cmt fr nvstgn.

Ͽr Ͽ Ȼ. (*Ris.*) I sec ǂ mo.

⊙ ⊙- A̸l bn i fr % ǂ mo wl mk i k b ǂ anc § % a ⊙. (*Dn.*) Al wh r op, b ǂ sm §. * It is s ○d. (*Or, bfr ǂ vot tkn.*) If thr is n objn, it wl b so ○d. * (*or*) If thr is no obj, it wl tk ǂ usl crs * I wl apt o tt cm, Ͽrs A̸ Ͽ, Ȼ Ḋ, @ Є Ŧ.

(*Rpts % Comt, Reg @ Spcl. Unfsd Bsns. New Bsns, etc.*)

INITIATION

⊙⊙- Ͽr ⌡ Ͽ.

⌡ Ͽ- (℞ @ §) ⊙ ⊙.

⊙⊙- Ѧsrt if ny cs r in wtg. If s, thr nms @ fr wt °.

⌡ Ͽ- (*Obtns crd wh nm % c fm* ⊣ ∓ @ *rprts.*) ⊙ ⊙.

⊙⊙- Ͽr ⌡ Ͽ.

⌡ Ͽ- ⊙r Ѧ Ͽ, s i wtg fr ⊣ f °.

⊙⊙- Ͽn, ⊙r Ѧ Ͽ is i w fr ⊣ f ° % ⊙y.)(hvg bn dl acptd, if thr is n objn, I shl cnf ⊣ ° upn h. (*Pauses.*) Thr bn n obj, I wl prcd. * Ͽr ≀ @ ⌡ ⊙s%c.

≀ ⊙%c- (*Both rs.*) ⊙ ⊙.

⊙⊙- Hw shd a Ȼ b prp fr ⊣ fst ° % ⊙y. 22–3

≀ ⊙%c- Ͽy bn dvs % al mtc sbts, nth n nr cthd, bf nr sh, lf k @ bs br, hw @ a ct abt hs n.

⊙⊙- ℞pr t ⊣ prp r, whr ⊙r Ѧ Ͽ

is i wtg. T⃝n ths prpd. cs hm t mk +| usl al at +| inr dr. Ↄr Sc, acmp thm.

Sc @ ⊥⃝s%c- (*Rpr t* +| *Ճ; Sc btwn ⊥⃝s % c, slt, fc* ≀ *, f* T⃝, *f* Ŋ, *f* T⃝, *mch t prp rm.)*

T⃝ ⊥⃝- * Ↄr ⌡ T⃝.

⌡ T⃝- (℞*s* @ §.) T⃝ ⊥⃝.

T⃝ ⊥⃝- Ƣl +| crf fm ℔ t rfs, t rsm ℔ at +| sd % +| gv n +| Ͼ.

⌡ T⃝- *** Ↄn, (*Bn, gv* § % *fdlt.*) it is +| ○ % +| T⃝ ⊥⃝ tt u b cld f ℔ t rfs, t rs ℔ at +| sd % +| g n +| Ͼ. *

Sc- (*Or oth ofc or mbr, m ask.*) [Is ths ur ptn @ sig.] (*Beng satfd, he contu:*) (⊥⃝r Ճ Ↄ, smwht % ur motvs n aplyg fr admsn int ou an @ hnbl Fty, w hv lrnd f +| dclrn, ov ur sgntr, cntnd n ur ptn; bt, in ○ tt u ma nt b msld as t +| chrtr or +| prps % +| crms n wh u r abt t eng, +| :: adrss t u thes prelmnry wds % advc.

(F ⊙y is fr rmvd fm al tt is trvl, slfh @ ungdly. Its struct i blt upn ⊣⊢ evrlstg fndtn % tt ₲d-gvn lw, ⊣⊢ ⊖rhd % mn in ⊣⊢ fmly whs Fthr i ₲. Our anc @ hon Fty wlcms t its drs @ admts t its prvlgs wrthy mn % al crds @ % ev rce, bt it insts tt al mn shl stnd upn an exact eqlt @ rc its instns in a sprt % du humlt, emphszg, i demr, in cndc, in cmny, @ in lng, ⊣⊢ hlpls, gropng natr % mn at hs brth, @ hs nd % relinc upn ⊖vn guidnce thro al ⊣⊢ trnsctns % lf.

(U wl hr b tgt t divst ur mnd @ cnsce % al ⊣⊢ vcs @ supflts % lf, @ ⊣⊢ :: int wch u r nw t b adm expcs u t divs ursl % al thos wrldly dstctns @ eqipmts wch r nt in kpng wth ⊣⊢ hmbl, revnt, @ chldlk atud it is nw ur dty to asum, as al hv dn wh hv gn ths wa bfr u.)

Sc- ⊖o u declr, upn ur hnr, tt, unbisd b ⊣⊢ impr solictn % fds, @ uninflcd b mrcny motvs, u frl @ vln ofr urs a Ç fr +| msts % ╤ ⊙y. Ç-I d.

≀ c- Do u dcl, upn ur hnr, tt u r prmptd to solic +| prvlgs % F ⊙y b a favrbl opn cncvd % +| instn, a dsr fr knlg, @ a sincr wsh % beng srvcbl t ur flo crtrs. Ç-I d.

Sc- ⊃o u dcl, upn ur hnr, tt u wl chrfly cnfrm to al +| anc usages @ estbshd cstms % +| Fty. Ç-I d.

Sc- (*Colcts bal % +| in fe, rtns to* ⊙ % +| ⩞.)

⊙⊙- * (*Cls +| :: t* ○.)

Sc (§) ⊙ ⊙.

⊙⊙- ⊃r ≀.

Sc- ╤h Ç hs ansd +| usl qs in +| afmt @ pd (+| bl %) hs in fe.

⊙s%c- (*Prp cdt, @ whn rdy cs hm t mk +| al.*)

—O—

⊙ ⊕- * ⊃r ⌡ ⊃.

⌡ ⊃- ⊙ ⊕.

⊙ ⊕- ∓h ls as wl as f g c % ⊕s wn cnvd.

⌡ ⊃- ∓ c tt th r dl td.

⊙ ⊕- Ѧt t tt dt, @ inf ⫲ ∓ tt I am abt t dspns wth ℔ in ⫲ t ° fr ⫲ prps % o ⫲ :: on ⫲ f, fr wk @ inst; dr hm t tk d ntc thr% @ g hms ac.

⌡ ⊃- *** (∓- ***) ⊃r ∓.

∓- ⊃r ⌡ ⊃.

⌡ ⊃- ∓h ⊙ ⊕ is ab. t ds wh ℔ in ⫲ t ° fr ⫲ prps % o ⫲ :: on ⫲ f, fr wk @ ins. ∓k du nt thr% @ gvn urs ac. (*Cls dr.*) ⊙ ⊕.

⊙ ⊕- ⊃r ⌡ ⊃.

⌡ ⊃- ∓h ∓ is nfd. 26–3

⊙ ⊕- *** I nw dc ℔ dspd wh in ⫲ t °. ⊃r ⌡ ⊃, nf ⫲ ∓.

⌡ ⊃- *** (∓- ***) ⊃r ∓.

∓- Ͽr ⌡ Ͽ.

⌡ Ͽ- Lb is nw dspd wh in ⫲ t °.

(*Cls dr.*) Ⓣ ⌓.

Ⓣ ⌓- Ͽr ⌡ Ͽ.

⌡ Ͽ- ∓h ∓ is infd.

Ⓣ ⌓- * (*Sts* ⫲ ::.) Ͽr ≀ Ⓣ.

≀ Ⓣ-(℞*s* @ §.) Ⓣ ⌓.

Ⓣ ⌓- Ⓣhc c u.

≀ Ⓣ- Fm a :: % ⫲ ♓ ≀s ⌡ % ⌡.

Ⓣ ⌓- Ⓣt cm u h t d.

≀ Ⓣ- Ln t sb m ps @ im ms i ⌓y.

Ⓣ ⌓- ∓hn u r a ⌓, I prs.

≀ Ⓣ- I am s tk @ ac am bn @ fls.

Ⓣ ⌓- Ⓣt mks u a ⌓.

≀ Ⓣ- ⌓y o.

Ⓣ ⌓- Ⓣhr wr u m a ⌓.

≀ Ⓣ- Ⓣthn ⫲ bd % a j @ d cns :: % ∓ @ ⩚ ⌓s, asmd i a pl rpstg ⫲ ₲r ∓ % Ʀ ≀ ∓, fshd wh ⫲ ♓ Ͽ, ≀ @ ₵s, tgh wh a ₵h o Ͽ spn fm sm ₲ Ͽ % cmpt jsdn emp it t wk.

Ⓣ ⌓- ♓w mn cmps an ⋲ ₰ ::.

≀ Ⓣ- ≀ or m.

⊤⃝ ⊥⃝- ⊤⃝n cmps % s, % whm ds i cn.
≀ ⊤⃝- ∓h ⊤⃝ ⊥⃝, ≀ @ ⌡ ⊤⃝s, ∓, ≀, @ ≀ @ ⌡ Ɗs. (*Fr fl fm, see pg 11.*)
⊤⃝ ⊥⃝- ∓h ⌡ Ɗs pl i ╫ ::.
≀ ⊤⃝- Ⱥt m rt.
⊤⃝ ⊥⃝- ** (*Ofs rs*) Ɗr ⌡ Ɗ.
⌡ Ɗ- (§) ⊤⃝ ⊥⃝.
⊤⃝ ⊥⃝- ∓h ≀ Ɗs pl.
⌡ Ɗ- Ⱥt ╫ r % ╫ ⊤⃝ ⊥⃝ i ╫ Ͼ.
⊤⃝ ⊥⃝- Ɗr ≀ Ɗ.
≀ Ɗ- (§) ⊤⃝ ⊥⃝.
[⊤⃝ ⊥⃝- ∓h ≀ cs pl.
[≀ Ɗ- Ⱥt ╫ l % ╫ ⊤⃝ ⊥⃝ i ╫ Ͼ.
[⊤⃝ ⊥⃝- Ɗr ≀.
[≀ c- (§) ⊤⃝ ⊥⃝.
[⊤⃝ ⊥⃝- ∓h ∓s pl.
[≀ ec- Ⱥt ╫ r % ╫ ⊤⃝ ⊥⃝ i ╫ Ͼ.
[⊤⃝ ⊥⃝- Ɗr ∓.
[∓rs- (§) ⊤⃝ ⊥⃝.]
⊤⃝ ⊥⃝- ∓h ⌡ ⊤⃝s st.
∓rs- In ╫ ≀.
⊤⃝ ⊥⃝- Ɗ ⌡ ⊤⃝. ⊤⃝ ⊥⃝. ∓h ≀ ⊤⃝ st.
⌡ ⊤⃝- In ╫ ⊤⃝.

⊙ ⊙- ⅁r ≀ ⊙. ≀ ⊙- (§) ⊙ ⊙. ∓h ⊙sts st.

≀ ⊙- In ⊣⊢ ∈.

⊙ ⊙- ⊙h i ⊣⊢ ∈.

≀ ⊙- Ꜿs ⊣⊢ ≀ rs i ⊣⊢ ∈ t o @ gv ⊣⊢ d, so rss—

⊙ ⊙- *** (*Rs.*)

≀ ⊙- ⊣⊢ ⊙ ⊙ i ⊣⊢ ∈, t op @ gvn ⊣⊢ ::, @ st ⊣⊢ cf at wk, gvg thm pr ins fr thr ℔.

⊙ ⊙- ⅁r ≀ ⊙, it i m ○ tt ⊣⊢ :: b nw o on ⊣⊢ f ° fr wk @ ins. ∓hs cmc t ⊣⊢ ⌡ ⊙ n ⊣⊢ ≀ @ h t ⊣⊢ bn ps, tt hv d ntc thr% th m gv ths ac.

≀ ⊙- ⅁r ⌡ ⊙.

⌡ ⊙- (§) ⅁r ≀ ⊙.

≀ ⊙- It is ⊣⊢ ○ % ⊣⊢ ⊙ ⊙ tt ⊣⊢ :: b nw op on ⊣⊢ f ° fr w @ nstn. ∓hs cm t ⊣⊢ bn prs, tt hv du ntc thr% th ma gv ths acdy.

⌡ ⊙- ⅁n, (*Bn gv* ⊣⊢ § *%fdlt.*) it s ⊣⊢ ○ % ⊣⊢ ⊙ ⊙, cm t m thr ⊣⊢ ≀ ⊙ in ⊣⊢ ⊙, tt ⊣⊢ :: b nw o on ⊣⊢ f °

fr w @ nst. I cmc ǂ sm t u, tt hv d nc thr% u m gv urs ac.

T⃝ ⊥⃝- Ͽn, atn t gv ǂ §s; obs ǂ Ͼ. (*§s % Ͼ Ⱥ r gvn, tkg tm fm* ǂ Ͼ. T⃝ ⊥⃝- * ≀ T⃝- * ⌡ T⃝- *) Ͽr ≀ ⋑, atn at ǂ Ⱥ.

≀ ⋑- (*Gs t* T⃝ *%* ǂ Ⱥ, *gs* § *% fdlt dsps ls @ rts t hs pl.*)

T⃝ ⊥⃝- I nw dc ǂ :: d op on ǂ f °. Ͽr ⌡ ⋑. T⃝ ⊥⃝. Inf ǂ ∓.

⌡ ⋑- *** (∓- ***) *Ops d*) Ͽr ∓.

∓- Ͽr ⌡ ⋑.

⌡ ⋑- ∓h :: is o on ǂ f °. (*Cls dr.*) T⃝ ⊥⃝.

T⃝ ⊥⃝- Ͽ ⌡ ⋑. ⌡ ⋑- ∓h ∓ i nfd. *

Ȼd- *** (≀ ⋑ *rs* @ §). T⃝ ⊥⃝.

T⃝ ⊥⃝- Ͽr ≀ ⋑.

≀ ⋑- ∓h i an a at ǂ nr d.

T⃝ ⊥⃝- Ⱥtn t ǂ a @ asrtn ǂ cs.

≀ ⋑- ***

≀ ⊥⃝%c- *

≀ ⋑- (*Ops dr.*) T⃝h cs hr.

≀ ⊙%c- ⊙r Ⓐ ⊙, a pr bl cd, wh is dsrs % hv @ rcg a pt n ǂ rts, lt @ bfs % ths wfl ::, erc t ⊕ @ dc t ǂ my % ǂ ℋ ≀ s ⅃, as al bn @ fls hv d wh hv gn ths wa bf h.

≀ ⊙- ⊙r Ⓐ ⊙, is ths an ac % ur on f w @ ac.

Çd- It s.

≀ ⊙- ⊙r ≀ ⊙%c, is h wh @ wl q.

≀ ⊙%c- ℋ is.

≀ ⊙- ⊙l @ t pd.

≀ ⊙%c- ℋ is.

≀ ⊙- ⊙ wt fh r ds h xp t obtn ths mp pv.

≀ ⊙%c- ⊙n a m, fr b, % l ag @ w rcmd.

≀ ⊙- ≀nc ǂ Ç is i psn % al ths nsc qlfs, lt h (*or* thm) wt ntl ǂ ⊙ ⊙ cn b nfd % h (*or* thr) rqs @ hs ans rt. (*Cls dr @ rts t* Ⓐ.) ⊙ ⊙.

⊙ ⊙- ⊙r ≀ ⊙.

≀ ⊙- ⌈hr is wto, ⊙r Ⓐ ⊙, a pr b cd, wh s dsrs % hv @ rcg a pt in ǂ

rs, lt @ bfs % ths wfl ::, erc t ₲ @ dc t ⊣ my % ⊣ ӿ ≀ s ⌡, as al bn @ fls h dn wh hv gn ths w bf h.

ⓣ ⓛ - Is it an ac % hs ow f w @ a.

≀ Ꭰ - It is.

ⓣ ⓛ - Is h wh @ w q.

≀ Ꭰ - ӿ is. Ꭰ l @ tr pd. ӿ is.

ⓣ ⓛ - Ꭰ wt fh rt ds h xp t obt ths mpt prv.

≀ Ꭰ - Ꭰn a mn, fr bn, % lfl ag @ wl rcmd.

ⓣ ⓛ - ≀ nc ⊣ cd is in psn % a ths nscr qlfns, lt hm nt ths wfl :: in ⊣ n % ₵, @ b rc i d @ an f.

≀ Ꭰ - * (*Ops dr.*) Lt h nt ths wfl :: i ⊣ n % ₵, @ b rc i d @ a f.

ⓣ ⓛ - ***

Ȼd- (*Is cdc nt* ⊣ :: @ *rc i ft* % ⊣ ≀ ⓣ, *fcg* ⊣ Ⓔ.)

≀ Ꭰ - ⓛr Ⓐ Ꭰ, I am cmd t rc u on ⊣ pt % a s ns pc ur n l b, (*Plc Ȼs.*) wh is to th u tt as ths is an ns % tr t ⊣ fl, s sd ⊣ rcltn thr% b t ur mn @ cns shd u ev rvl +| scs % F (⊥)y nlf.

(⊥)*usic. Ode.*

(T) (⊥)- *

Ȼdr- (*Tks Ȼ by r rm @ sts* ɛ *on n sd % +| ::. +| ≀ Ↄ @ Mar shd wk tgh, folwd by +| (⊥)s%c, a br ldng eh Ȼ @ Stds n +| rr.*)

(T) (⊥)- * Lt n m ntr up any gt o mpt undtkg wth fst inv +| ad % Ↄ. Ↄr ≀ Ↄ.

≀ ⊃- (§) (T) (⊥).

(T) (⊥)- Ȼdc +| c to +| cntr % +| :: @ cs hm t k fr +| bf % pr.

Ȼh or (T) (⊥)- (*Pls. hd o cs h.*) ∀hsf ∓hn ad, Ⱥlmt ⊤ % +| U, to ths or prs cnvn, @ gt tt ths c fr (⊥)y ma dct @ dvt hs lf to ∓hy srv, @ bc a tru @ fhfl br amg us. ɛndu hm wh a cmpc % ∓hy dv wsdm, tt, by +| inflc % +| pu prncpls % or Fty, h ma b btr enab t ds +| bs % hlns, t +| hon % ∓h hl n. Amn.

Ⓓn- (*Rsp.*) ≀ mt i b.

ⓎⒶ- Ⓐr Ⱥ Ⓓ, i whm d u p ur t.

Ҫd- I Ⓖ.

ⓎⒶ- Ur tr bn i Ⓖ, ur fh is w fdd. (∓*s c by* ⊣⊢ *r h.*) ℞s, flw ur cdr @ fr n d. (*Rts t* Ⓔ.) *

≀ Ⓓ- (*Lds* Ⓔ *on* Ɲ *sd @ cntus ar* ⊣⊢ ::. Ⱥ*s th ps —*)

⌡ Ⓨ- *

Ҫhp- "Ⓓhld, hw gd @ h pls i s fr bn t dw tg i unt.

≀ Ⓨ- *

Ҫhp- "It is lk ⊣⊢ prs oi up ⊣⊢ hd, tt rn dn up ⊣⊢ bd, ev Ⱥrs bd, tt wnt dn t ⊣⊢ sks % hs gmts;

ⓎⒶ- *

Ҫhp- "Ⱥs ⊣⊢ dw % ⋊rmn, @ as ⊣⊢ d tt dcnd up ⊣⊢ mts % Ʒi: Fr thr ⊣⊢ Ld cmd ⊣⊢ bls, ev lf frvmr."

≀ Ⓓ- (*In* ⊣⊢ ≀.) ***

⌡ Ⓨ- * (*Rs.*) Ⓨh cs hr.

≀ Ⓓ- Ⓐr Ⱥ Ⓓ, a pr bl c, wh is dsrs % hv @ rcg a pt i ⊣⊢ rs, lt @ bfs

% ths w ::, er t ₲ @ dc t ⊣| my % ⊣|)(≀ s ⌡, as a bn @ fls hv dn wh hv g ths w bf hm.

⌡ ⊙- ⊖r ∆ Ↄ, is ths n ac % ur ow f w @ a.

₵d- It is.

⌡ ⊙- Ↄr ≀ Ↄ, is h wh @ w q.

≀ Ↄ-)(is.

⌡ ⊙- Ↄl @ tr pd.

≀ Ↄ-)(is.

⌡ ⊙- Ↄ wt f rt ds h xp t ob ths mp prv.

≀ Ↄ- Ↄn a mn, f bn, % lfl a @ wl rcm.

⌡ ⊙- Snc ⊣| c is in ps % a ths ncs qlfs, cdc hm to ⊣| ≀ ⊙ in ⊣| ⊙, fr hs x.

≀ Ↄ- (*In* ⊣| ⊙.) ***

≀ ⊙- * (*Rs.*) ⊙h cs h.

≀ Ↄ- ⊖r ∆ Ↄ, a pr bl c, wh is dsrs % hv @ rcg a pt i ⊣| rs, lt @ bfs % ths w ::, er t ₲ @ dc t ⊣| my % ⊣|)(≀ s ⌡, as al bn @ fls hv dn wh hv gn ths wa bf h.

≀ ⊙- ⊚r Ⱥ Ͽ, is ths an a % ur ow f w @ ac.

Ȼd- It is.

≀ ⊙- Ͽ ≀ Ͽ, is h wh @ wl q.

≀ Ͽ-)(is. Ͽl @ tr pd.)(is.

≀ ⊙- Ͽ wt f r ds h xp t ob ths mp pv.

≀ Ͽ- Ͽn a m, fr b, % lfl a @ wl rcm.

≀ ⊙- ≀nc ⊣| c is in psn % a ths nsc qlfs, cdt hm t ⊣| ⊙ ⊚ in ⊣| Є, fr h xm.

≀ Ͽ- (*In* ⊣| Є.) ***

⊙⊚- * ⊙h cs h.

≀ Ͽ- ⊚r Ⱥ Ͽ, a pr bl c, wh is ds % hv @ rcg a pt i ⊣| rts, lt @ bfs % ths w ::, er t Ȼ @ ddc t ⊣| my % ⊣|)(≀s ⌡, as a bn @ fls hv dn wh hv gn ths wa bf h.

⊙⊚- ⊚r Ⱥ Ͽ, s ths an a % ur ow f w @ ac.

Ȼd- It is.

⊙⊚- Ͽr ≀ Ͽ, is h wr @ w q.

≀ ⦘- ♓ is. ⦘l @ tr pd. ♓ is.

⦶ ⦵- ⦘ wt fth r ds h x t ob ths mpt pv.

≀ ⦘- ⦘n a m, f bn, % lfl ag @ wl rcm.

⦶ ⦵- ⦶hc cm u, @ wth r u tv.

≀ ⦘- Fm ⫲ ⦶, tv ⋲.

⦶ ⦵- ⦶h dd u lv ⫲ ⦶, @ tv ⋲.

≀ ⦘- In sh % l i ⦵y.

⦶ ⦵- Snc ⫲ c is in psn % al ths ncr qlfs, @ i sh % l i ⦵y, rcdt hm t ⫲ ≀ ⦶ in ⫲ ⦶, wh wl th h hw t ap ⫲ ⋲ i d @ an fm.

≀ ⦘- (*Rcd c, mrh on ≀ sd % ⫲ ::, l fc, mh ⋲, l f, mh ₽, l fc, mh to ⦶ % ⫲ ⩓, hlt, fc ⫲ ≀ ⦶.*) ⦘r ≀ ⦶.

≀ ⦶- ⦘r ≀ ⦘.

≀ ⦘- It is ⫲ ○ % ⫲ ⦶ ⦵ tt u th ths c hw t ap ⫲ ⋲ in d @ an f.

≀ ⦶- Cs ⫲ c t fc ⫲ ⋲.

≀ ⦘- (*Cs c t fc ⋲.*)

≀ ⦶- ⦵r ⩓ ⦘, adv o ur l f; (*Dn.*) bg ⫲ h % ur r nt ⫲ hl % u l, thby fmg

⊣⊢ ng % a ob, bd er, fcg ⊣⊢ ∈. (*Dn.*)
⊙ ⊝, ⊣⊢ c is i ○.

⊙⊝- ⊝r Ⱥ ∋, bf u cn pr f n ⊤ ⊝y, it wl b nsc f u t tk a s ob aprt t ⊣⊢ ° % ∈ Ⱥ, @ I, ⊝st % ⊣⊢ ::, asu u tt thr is nhg thrn wh wl cnf wh ur mrl, scl, or cvl dts r prv, b th wt th ma. ⊙th ths asrnc, r u wl t tk ⊣⊢ o.

Ҫd- I m.

⊙⊝- Thn adv t ⊣⊢ scd Ⱥ % ⊤ ⊝y @ k o ur n l k, ur r fmg ⊣⊢ ng % a s; ur l h spg @ r rst upn ⊣⊢ ⋊ ∋, ≀ @ Ҫs. Ҫond or ≀ ∋ - (*Plcs c.*)

≀ ∋- ⊙ ⊝. ∋ ≀ ∋. Th c i i d f.

⊙⊝- ***

∋rn- (*⊤m eql lns dressng t ⊣⊢ Ⱥ.*)

⊝s%c- (*Stratn ⊣⊢ lns as th pas insd @ fm arch at ⊣⊢ ∈.*)

⊙ds-. (*⊙h escrt, ps insd % ⊣⊢ lns @ tk thr stns undr ⊣⊢ rch.*)

≀ ts- (*Ma fm rh ov ⊝r ⊙ % ⊣⊢ Ⱥ.*)

⊙⊙- (*Dcnds t ⩓.*) ⊙r ⩓ ⊙, if u r stl w⟩ t t ⫞ o, sa I, (*Dn.*) pr ur nm in fl (*Dn.*) @ rp af m: Of m o fw @ a, i pr % ⩓ ⊙ ₲ @ ths w :: % ∓ @ ⩓ ⊙s, er t ₲ @ ddc t ⫞ my % ⫞ ⋊ ≀ ts ⌡, d hb @ hn sl @ s p @ s tt I w k @ c @ nv r, a % ⫞ sc rt or rs, pr o ps, pt o ps, % ⫞ hdn ms % ⩓ ∓ ⊙y wh I h rc, am ab t r, or ma hf b nst i, t an prs, nls it sh b t a wh b ⋹ ⩓, or whn ⫞ bd % a j @ d cnst :: % sh; @ nt un hm o th whm I sh hr s t b, bt un h @ th onl whm I sh f s t b, af d tr, st xm or lfl ⊙c nfm.

(2) ∓m, I d p @ s tt I w n wr, in, pr, p, st, st, hw, ct, c, mk o ng ⫞ s up nthg, mv or imv, whb or whn ⫞ lst w, s, l or crc ma bc lg or int t ms or ant, whb ⫞ ss % ∓ ⊙y m b unlfy ob thr m unw.

∓o al % whch I d sl @ sn p @ s, wtho an hstn, mn rs or sc ev % md i m wtev, bdg ms un n l a p thn tt % hv m t ct ac, m t t ot @ bd i ⊣ sd % ⊣ s at l w m, wh ⊣ t ebs @ fls † i twf hs, shd I e, kly or wl, vl ths m s o % ⊖ Ⱥ. ≀ hp m ₲, @ mk m stf t kp @ pf ⊣ s.

In tstm % ur snc, k ⊣ ⋈ Ↄ up wh ur h rsts—fst rmv ur hd. (*Dn.*) Ↄr ≀ Ↄ, rmv ⊣ ct. (*Dn. Al lts ot xcp t at* Ⱥ.) ⏀y br, i ur prs situn, wt d u m ds.

Ȼd- (*Prmptd b* ≀ Ↄ.) L i ⏀y.

⊙⏀- Ↄn, st fh ur hs @ ast m i br ths nly md b t tr ⏀c lt. "In ⊣ bg ₲ cr ⊣ ⋈ @ ⊣ ⊖. An ⊣ ⊖ ws wth fm @ vd; @ dks ws upn ⊣ fc % ⊣ dp. Ⱥ ⊣ ≀ p % ₲ mvd upn ⊣ fc % ⊣ wts. Ⱥ ₲ sd, L t b lt; @ thr ws l." In hm cm % tt aug ev, I n sa ⏀cl, "Lt thr b l."

⊙⏀- Ↄ Ⱥ Ↄ, on bg bt t l in ⏀y, u bh ⊣ t g ls b ad % ⊣ rps % ⊣ t lsr.

∓h t gt ls in ⊙y r +| ♓ Ͽ, ≀ @ Çs, @ r ths xpld. Th ♓ Ͽ is gv us as +| r @ g fr ou fh @ prc; +| ≀, t sq ou acs; @ +| Çpses t crcmscb.ou dsrs, @ kp ou psns i d bds wh al mk, esp +| bn.

∓h t ls lts r +| ≀, ⊙n, @ ⊙st % +| ::, @ r ths xpld: Ⱥs +| ≀ rls +| d @ +| ⊙n gvs +| nt, s shd +| ⊚ ⊙, wh eq rglt, rl @ gv +| ::.

∓h rpsts % +| t l lts r t brn cdls, o tps, plcd up cdlsts o pdsts, situ Є, ⊚, @ ≀. (*Lsr trnd on.*)

(I prtcly drct ur atn to +| ¢t Lt in ⊙y, +| ♓ Ͽ. ♓wsev mn dffr i crd o theolg, al gd mn r agrd tt wthn +| cvrs % +| ♓ Ͽ r fd thos prncpls % mrlt wh la +| fndtn upn wh t bld a ritous lf. ∓ ⊙y, thrf, opns ths Ͽk up its Ⱥs, wth +| cmnd t eh % its votrs tt h dlgntly stdy thrin t lrn +| wa t evlst lf. Ⱥdpg n ptclr crd, frbdg sctarn dscssn wthn its :: rms, encrgg eh t b stdfs in ǂ fh % hs acptnc, Ŧ ⊙y tks al gd mn b ǂ hnd, @, ldg thm t its A̧ls, pnts t ǂ opn Ͽ thrn, @ urges upn eh tt h fthfly drc hs stps thro lf b ǂ Lt h thr shl fnd @ as h thr shl fnd it.

(lf, fm ou sac A̧lts, ǂ aths, ǂ nfdl, ǂ irlgs mn, or ǂ lbrtn, shd ev b abl to wrst ths Ͽk % ≀ acrd Ls, @ ths rmv, or evn obscr, ǂ grtst Lt in ⊙y, tt lt wh fr centurs hs bn ǂ rul @ gd % Ŧ ⊙s, thn cld w n lngr clm fr ousls ǂ grt rnk @ titl % Ŧ @ A̧ ⊙s; bt, so lng as tt ≀ c Lt shns upn ou A̧s, so lng as it ilumnts ǂ pthwa % ǂ Çfmn b ǂ gldn ras % trh, s lg, @ n lng, cn Ŧ ⊙y lv @ shd its bnefct inflc upn mnkn. Ȼrd thn, tt Ͽk % sac @ imutbl lw as u wd gd ur vry lf. Ͽ fnd it as u wd ǂ flg % ur cnty. Lv acrdg t its dvn thgs, wh its evlstg asurnc % a blsd imrtlt.) (*Stps bk @ advncs.*)

≀ Ð- (*Adrsg* ⫲ *c.*) Ɔhld ⫲ ⊤⃝ ⊥⃝ apr fm ⫲ Є, on ⫲ st, (*tkn.*) und ⫲ dg, (*gvn.*) @ §, (*gvn.*) % Є ⩕.

⊤⃝ ⊥⃝- ⊥⃝y br, an Є ⩕ advs on h l f, (*Adv.*) bg ⫲ h % h r nt ⫲ ho % hs l, (*Dn.*) thb fg ⫲ ag % an o. Ths i ⫲ dg, (*Gs it.*) @ al t ⫲ psn % ur hs wl tg ⫲ ob; ths is ⫲ §, (*Gs it.*) @ al t ⫲ p % ⫲ o. Ths dg @ ths § r alw t b gv as a sln t ⫲ ⊤⃝ ⊥⃝ on ntg o rt f an Є ⩕ ::. (*Adv t* ⫲ ⩕, *acmpd b* ≀ @ ⌡ ⊤⃝*s.*) I nw prs m rt h, i tk % fsh @ b l, @ wl inv u w ⫲ g @ wd, bt as u r unins, h wh hs htht ans fr u wl at ths tm. Ɔr ≀ Ð.

≀ Ð- ⊤⃝ ⊥⃝.

⊤⃝ ⊥⃝- I h. ≀ Ð- I c. ⊤⃝t d u c.

≀ Ð- ⩕l ⫲ s % a ⊥⃝ i ⊥⃝y t wh ths tk als. (*Plcs cs hd.*)

⊤⃝ ⊥⃝- (*Gs gp also.*) ⊤⃝t i t.

≀ Ð- ⩕ g. ○ w. Є ⩕.

⊤⃝ ⊥⃝- ⋊s i a n.

≀ Ð- It h.

ⓣ ⓛ- ⓣl u g i t m.

≀ Ɗ- I dd nt s r i, nth w I s i i.

ⓣ ⓛ- ӿw w u ds % i.

≀ Ɗ- L o h i. L i @ bg. U b.

ⓣ ⓛ- Ɗb u. (ⓣ*d gvn.*) – is ⊣| n % ths g, @ shd alw b gv i ths cts mnr, b l or hg. ⓣn ltrg, al c wh ⊣| l – (*Aids cdt.*) Rs, sl ⊣| ⌡ @ ≀ ⓣs @ sf thm tt u r i ps % ⊣| st, dg, §, g @ w % Ɛ ⅄. Ofs rsm u sts. (*Rts t* Ɛ.) *

ⓣds- (*As* ⊣| ⓣ ⓛ *passes, rsme thr sts, flwd b* ⓛs % c.)

Ɗrn- (*1k thr sts.*)

≀ Ɗ- (*Cds c drc t* ⌡ ⓣ*s s on* ⊣| *st %* Ɛ ⅄.) ***

⌡ ⓣ- * (*Rs.*) ⓣh cs h.

⅄ dl in Ɛ ⅄. ӿw m I k h t b sh.

Ɗ crt §s @ a tkn. ⓣt r §s.

℞t ngs, hrs @ prp. ⅄d a §.

(≀ Ɗ @ Ȼ *gv d.*) ӿs tt an als.

It h, t ⊣| ps % m hs w t ⊣| o.

ӿv u a fr §. I h. (≀ Ɗ @ *c gv* §.)

ӿs tt a al. It h, t ⊣| pn % ⊣| o.

☉t is a tn.

≀ ◗- Ⱥ cr fdl or bl g whb on ⊙s m k anth i ⊣⊢ d as i ⊣⊢ l.

⌡ ☉- Ⱥd @ gv m a tn.

≀ ◗ @ ₵- (*Adv on ⊣⊢ stp % Ͼ Ⱥ @ gv g; caus cs t gv i t eh oth.*)

⌡ ☉- ☉t i t. ≀ ◗- Ⱥ g. ⌡ ☉- ○f w

≀ ◗- Ͼ Ⱥ. ⌡ ☉- ♓s i a n. It h.

⌡ ☉- ☉l u g i t m.

≀ ◗- I dd n s rc i, nth w I s i i.

⌡ ☉- ♓w w u ds % i.

≀ ◗- L o h i. ⌡ ☉- L i @ b. U b.

⌡ ☉- ⊝ u. (*Gvn.*) I am sfd.

≀ ◗- (*In ☉, c on stp % Ͼ Ⱥ.*) ***

≀ ☉- * (*Rs.*) ☉h cs h. Ⱥ dl in Ͼ Ⱥ.

♓w m I k h t b sh. ⊝ cr §s @ a tn.

☉t r §s. ℞t ngs, hrz @ prpl.

Ⱥd a §. (≀ ◗ @ ₵ *gv dg.*)

♓s tt an a. It h, t ⊣⊢ p % m hs w tg ⊣⊢ o.

♓ u a fr §. I h. (≀ ◗ @ *c gv* §.)

♓s tt a al. It h, t ⊣⊢ pn % ⊣⊢ o.

☉t s a tk.

≀ Ð- Ⲁ crt fdl o bl g whb on ⍝s m k anth i ⊣ d a i ⊣ l.

≀ Ⓣ- Ⲁd @ g m a tk.

≀ Ð @ Ç- (*Adv o ⊣ st % Ͼ Ⲁ @ g g; caus cs t gv i t eh oh.*)

≀ Ⓣ- Ⓣt i t. ≀ Ð- Ⲁ g. ○ w.

≀ Ð- Ͼ Ⲁ. ≀ Ⓣ- ♓s i a n. It h.

≀ Ⓣ- Ⓣl u g i t m.

≀ Ð- I dd n s rc i, nth w I s i i.

≀ Ⓣ- ♓w w u ds % i.

≀ Ð- L o h i. ≀ Ⓣ- L i @ b. U b.

≀ Ⓣ- Ͽ u. (*Gvn.*) I a sfd.

(*or short form.*)

Ⓣ ⍝- Ͽr ≀ Ⓣ, r u stsf tt ⊣ bn r dly i Ͼ Ⲁs @ as sh r i psn % ⊣ stp, dg, §, gp @ w.

≀ Ⓣ- I m.

Ⓣ ⍝- Ͽr ʃ Ⓣ, r u stfd.

ʃ Ⓣ- I m.

Ⓣ ⍝- Ofs, tk yr sts.

≀ Ð- (*Cds c Ͼ, on n sd % ⊣ ::. Ⓣhn nr ⊣ Ⲁ.*)

⊙⊙- * (*Gos t c.*) ⊙y b, I nw prs u wth a l-s o wt lth apn. It is an mbm % inc @ ⊣⊢ bg % a ⊙, mr anc thn ⊣⊢ ȼl ⊤l o ℞m ⋴, mr hnbl thn ⊣⊢ ≀ tr @ ȼr, wn wthly wr.

[It ma b tt, i ⊣⊢ cmg yrs, upn ur h wl rst ⊣⊢ lrl wrth % vctr; fm ur brs m hng jls fit t grc ⊣⊢ didm % an estrn potnt; na, mr thn thes, wth lt ad t ⊣⊢ cmg lt, ur amb ft ma tred rnd aft rnd % ⊣⊢ ldr tt lds t fm i ou mystc crcl, @ evn ⊣⊢ prpl % ⊣⊢ frtnty ma rst upn ur hon shlds; bt nvr ag fm mrtl hns, nv agn untl ur enfrnch sprt shl hv psd upwd @ inw thro ⊣⊢ prl gts, shl any hnr s dstg, so emblc % purt @ al prfcns, b cnfrd upn u as ths wh I n bsto. It is urs; urs to wr thro an honb lf, @ at ur dth t b dps upn ⊣⊢ cfn wch shl incls ur lfls rmns, @ wth thm ld bn ⊣⊢ cls % ⊣⊢ vl.]

(Lt its pu @ sptls srfc b t u an ev-prs rmdr % a "℟rt % lf @ rctd % cdc," a nvr-end argmt fr nblr dds, fr hi thts, fr gtr achvmts. An whn at is ur wr ft shl hv cm t +| end % thr tolsm jr, @ fm ur grsp shl fal frev +| w tls % lf, ma +| rcrd % ur lf @ acns b as wh @ sptls as +| emblm wch I plc in ur hnd t-nt; [@ wn ur trmlg sol shl std nkd @ aln bfr +| gr wt thrn, thr t rc jgmt fr +| dds dn whl hr in +| bd,] ma i b ur prtn t hr fm h wh sith as +| ⌡g ≀ u +| wlc wds: "ⓣl dn, gd @ fthf svt. [∓ho hs bn fthf ovr a fw thgs; I wl m u rlr ovr mn thgs.] ϵntr tho int +| jy % thy Ld.")

Ꞔar i t +| ≀ ⓣ in +| ⓣ, wh wl th u hw t wr i as ϵ Ⱥ.

≀ ⓟ - (*Cs c t* +| ⓣ, *nr* ≀ ⓣ.) ⓟ ≀ ⓣ.

≀ ⓣ - ⓟr ≀ ⓟ.

≀ ⓟ - It is +| ○ % +| ⓣ ⓐ tt u th ths b hw t wr hs a as ϵ Ⱥ.

≀ ⓣ - (*Rcvs a @ ts i on* Ꞔ.) ⓟr Ⱥ ⓟ, at +| bld % Ʀ ≀ ∓ +| df bnds % wkm wr dstghd by +| mnr in wh th wr thr aps. ⋲ Ⱥs wr thrs wh +| fl td up, t prv slng th clths; ⊙cly, t prv dbg wh untmpd mrt; thus wr urs ntl fr advd.

≀ ⊃ - (*Cds c to* +| ⋲ .)

⊙ ⊙ - ⊃r Ⱥ ⊃, agrbl t an an est estm, adpd i ev rg @ wl gvd ::, it bcs m du, at ths tm, t dm % u sm mtl sbst; nt s mh on ac % its intrc v, as tt i ma b dpsd i +| achvs % +| ::, as a mmrl tt u wr a ths t @ pl md a ⊙. Any mtc sb u ma hv, +| ≀ c wl rc.

· ɲthg, nt ev a p, t cmrat on % +| ms mpt evts % ur l.

⊙ br, ths is t th u tt shd u ev mt a mbr % +| hmn fml, espcly a br ⊙, in a lk dstu situ, it wd b ur dt t cntrbt to hs rl as lbrl as hs ncsts mt rq @ ur ablt prmt. 3

⊃r Ⱥ ⊃, as u r nw clthd as ⋲ Ⱥ, I prs u, mblmcly, +| wk ts, wh r +| ∓fi ₲ @ +| Ꞔm ₲, @ r ths xplnd:

∓h ∓fi ₲ is an inst usd b oprtv ⊙s t msr @ la ou thr wk; bt w, as

∓ @ Ạ ⊖s, r tt t us it fr ⊣ mr nb @ gls prs % dvdg ou tm. It hg dv nt tf eq pts, s mblcl % ⊣ tfr hs % ⊣ da, wh w r tgt t dvd nt th eq pts, whb r fd e hs fr ⊣ srv % ₲ @ a dst wth br, e f o usl vcns, @ e f r @ sl.

∓h Çm ₲v is an ins usd b opt ⊖s t bk of ⊣ crnrs % rh sts, ⊣ btr t ft thm f ⊣ blds us; bt w, as ∓ @ Ạ ⊖s, r tg t us it f ⊣ m nb @ gls pps % dvstg ou hrts @ cnscs % al ⊣ vcs @ sprflts % lf, thb ftng ou mds, as lv sts, fr tt sprl bldg, tt hs nt md wh hds, etr in ⊣ ḥvs.

⊙⊖- ⊖r ≀ ⊖, cdc ⊣ br to ⊣ ṇ ⊖ Ç % ⊣ ::.

≀ ⊖- (*Cds ⊣ b as ○, plcg hm o ⊣ st % ⊖ Ạ; bd er, f ⊣ ⊙ ⊖.*)

⊙⊖- ⊖r Ạ ⊖, u thr std an upr m @ ⊖, @ I gv it u str i chg ev t wk @ act as sh bf ₲ @ m. I als prs u a nw nm, wh is Ç. It ths u t b cts ov al ur ws @ acns, espcly on ⊣ sb % ∓ ⊖y wn in prs % its enms. [⊖r ≀ ⊖.

≀ Ͽ- [(⊤) (⊥).

(⊤)(⊥)- [Cnd ⊣| br to ⊣| ⩞.]

(⊥)s%c- (*Prcd t ⊣| ⩞, stg aprt.*)

≀ Ͽ- (*Plcs c bt thm @ tks hs pl.*)

Ͽrn- (*Slt as th hv bn instd.*)

(⊤)(⊥)- ℞cd ⊣| br t ⊣| plc whc h cm, nvst hm wh tt % wh h hs bn dvs, @ rtn hm t ⊣| :: fr fh nst.

Ҫ @ (⊥)s%c- (*Slt; l fc, mh t pr rm; invs cdt @ whn rdy gv alm.*)

(⊤)(⊥)- * Ͽr ⌡ (⊤).

⌡ (⊤)- (⊤) (⊥).

(⊤)(⊥)- Ҫl ⊣| cft fm ŧb t rf, t rsm ŧb at ⊣| sd % ⊣| g n. ⊣| Є.

⌡ (⊤)- *** Ͽn, (*Ͽn gv § % fd.*) it is ⊣| ○ % ⊣| (⊤) (⊥) tt u b cld fm ŧb t rfs, t rsm ŧb at ⊣| sd % ⊣| g in ⊣| Є. *

At refreshment.

—○—

SECOND SECTION

⊙s%c- (⊙*hn cs r rdy.*) ***

⊙ ⊙- * (*Çls* ⫲ :: *t* ○.)

≀ ⦘- ⊙ ⊙, thr is an al at ⫲ in d.

⊙ ⊙- At t ⫲ alm.

≀ ⦘- (○*ps dr, fnds* Ç *rdy to rtn @ cnds hm t th* Ą. ⊙*%c folo @ all slt.*)

⊙s%c- (*¢o drc t thr plcs.*)

≀ ⦘- (Ç*dcs c t* ⫲ ⋲*: sts hm i fr %* ⫲ ⊙ ⊙ *@ tks hs plc.*)

⊙ ⊙- ⊙y br, ⫲ snd sctn % ths ° ratnly acnts fr ⫲ fms @ crms thro wh u hv psd.

∓hs sctn is cmpsd % a lctu % tw pts, ⫲ fs treg ths fms @ crms, ⫲ scd xplg ⫲ rsns thrf. 52–3

(⊤)(⊥)- Ↄr ≀ Ð. ≀ Ð- (⊤) (⊥).

(⊤)hc c u.

Ŧ a :: % ⫣ Ӿ ≀t ⌡ % ⌡r.

(⊤)t c u h t d.

Ln t sb m ps @ im m i (⊥)y.

ǂhn u r a (⊥), I prsm.

I˙a s tk @ ac am bn @ fs.

(⊤)t ms u a (⊥). (⊥) o.

(⊤)hr wr u m a (⊥).

(⊤)thn ⫣ bd % a j @ d cns :: % Ŧ @ Ⱥ (⊥)s, asmb i a pl rpst ⫣ ₵ Ŧ % Ʀ ≀ ǂ, frshd wh ⫣ Ӿ Ↄ, ≀ @ Çses, tgh wh a Çhtr o Ð spsn f sm ₵ Ↄ % cmp jrs emp it t w.

Ӿw d u k us t b a (⊥).

Ӿvg bn tr, nv dn, @ am rdy t b td ag.

Ӿw m I k u t b a (⊥).

Ↄy crt §s, a tkn, a w @ ⫣ pf pts % m ntrc. 53–3

(⊤)t r §. Ɽt ngls, hrzs @ pdlrs.

Ⱥdv a §. (≀ Ð @ Ç *gv dg.*)

♓s tt an al.

It h, t ǂ psn % m hs wl tk ǂ o.

♓v u a f §. I hv. (*Gvs* §.)

♓s tt an alsn.

It hs, t ǂ pn % ǂ o. ⊙t i a tkn.

Ⱥ crt frn or brl g, whb on ⊜ ma kn anth i ǂ dk as i ǂ lt.

Ⱥdv @ g m a tkn. ≀ Ð @ Ç- (*Gv gp.*)

⊙t i tt. Ⱥ g. ○ w. Ͼ Ⱥ.

♓s it a n. It h. ⊙l u g i t m.

I dd nt s rc i, nth wl I s i i.

♓w w u ds % i. L or h i.

L i @ b. U b.

Ↄg u. ≀ Ð - (*Bgs: wd gvn.*)

⊙hr wr u fs ppd t b m a ⊜.

In m h. ⊙hr nx.

In a r adjng ǂ bd % a j @ d cns :: % Ŧ @ Ⱥ ⊜s.

♓w wr u pd.

Ð vsd % a mtlc sbs, nth n n clthd, bf n shd, l k @ br b, hw @ a c ab m n; i wh cnd I ws cdc t a dr % ǂ :: @ csd t gv t ds ks, wch wr ans b t wthn.

☉t ws sd t u f wthn. ☉h cs h.

Ur ans.

Ⱡ pr b c, wh is ds % hvg @ rcvg a prt i ╫ rts, l @ bfs % ths wf ::, er t ¢ @ dc t ╫ mm % ╫ ⋊ ≀s ⌡, as al bn @ fs hv dn wh hv gn ths wa bf m.

☉t wr u th skd.

If it w an ac % m o f w @ ac, if I ws wy @ w q, dl @ t pd; al % wh bng nsd i ╫ aftv, I ws skd b w fh rt I xp t ob ths im prv. Ur ans.

Ɔng a m, fr b, % lf ag @ wl rcmd.

☉t wr u thn tld.

≀ nc I ws in psn % a ths ncs qlfns, I shd w unt ╫ ☉ ⊙ cd b nfd % m rqs @ hs ans rtd.

☉t ws h a wr rtd.

Lt h en ths wf :: i ╫ n % ¢, @ b rc i d @ a fm. ⋊w wr u r.

On ╫ p % a sh in pc m n l b.

⋊w wr u th dsp %.

Çdcd t ╫ cn % ╫ ::, @ csd t k f ╫ bf % p.

Ⱥft p w wr u skd.

In whm I p m tr.

Ur a. In ₵. (⊤)t wr u thn tl.

(⊥)y tr bn i ₵, m fh ws wl fdd; I ws tn b +| r h, ○d t rs, fl m cdtr, @ fr n dgr.

)(w wr u thn ds %.

Ҫdd onc rg arn +| :: @ t +| ⌡ (⊤) i +| ≀, wh +| sm qs wr skd @ ans rtd as at +| d.

)(w dd +| ⌡ (⊤) ds % u.

Ϸrd m t b cdct t +| ≀ (⊤) in +| (⊤). wh +| s qs wr sk @ ans rt as bf.

)(w dd +| ≀ (⊤) ds % u.

Ϸr m t b cdc t +| (⊤) (⊥) in +| Є, wr +| s q w sk @ ans rtd as b; who als dmd wnc I cm @ whtr tv.

Ur a. ⊤m +| (⊤), tv Є.

(⊤)h dd u lv +| (⊤) @ tv Є.

In sh % l i (⊥)y.

)(w dd +| (⊤) (⊥) ds % u.

○d m rcdtd t +| ≀ (⊤) i +| (⊤), wh tg m hw t ap +| Є in d @ a f.

Ⓣt ws tt d @ a f.

Ⱥdvg on m l f, bg ⊣ h % m r int ⊣ hol % m l, thb fmg ⊣ ng % an ob, bd erc, fcg ⊣ Ⓔ.

Ⓣt dd ⊣ Ⓣ ⊙ thn d w u.

⊙ m a ⊙.

♓. In d f. Ⓣt w tt d f.

Ꝁng o m n l k, m r fg ⊣ ng % a s, m l h spt, m r rst up ⊣ ♓ Ɔ, ≀ @ Ȼs; i wh d f I tk ⊣ s o % Ⓔ Ⱥ.

♓v u ⊣ o. I h. Ꞧp i.

I, Ⱥ Ɔ, % m o f w @ a, i p % Ⱥ ₲ @ ths wf :: % Ŧ @ Ⱥ ⊙s, er t ₲ @ dc t ⊣ my % ⊣ ♓ ≀ s ⌡, d hb @ hn s @ s p @ s tt I w k @ cn, @ n r, ny % ⊣ s ar o ats, pr o ps, pt o ps, % ⊣ hd ms % Ⱥ Ŧ ⊙y wh I h rc, am ab t r, or ma hf b ins i, t an prs, nls it sh b t a wy b Ⓔ Ⱥ, or wthn ⊣ b % a j @ d cns :: % sh; @ nt un hm o thm whm I sh h s t b, bt un h @ th onl whm I sh f s t b, af d t, st xmn or lf ⊙c inf.

(2) ∓m, I d p @ s tt I w n wr, ind, pr, pa, st, sta, hw, ct, c, mrk or eng ⊣ sm up nthg, mvb or imv, whb or wn ⊣ lst w, s, l or cr ma bc lg or intl t ms or anth, whb ⊣ ss % ∓ ⊙y ma b unlfy obt thr m unwtns.

∓ a % wh I d s @ s p @ s, wtho ny hstn, m rsv or s ev % m i m wtev, bdg ms un n l a p th tt % hv m t c ac, m t t o @ br i ⊣ sd % ⊣ s at l w m, whr ⊣ t ebs @ fs tw i tf hs, shd I ev, kn or wlf, vl ths m s o % ⓔ Ⱥ.
≀ hp m ₲, @ mk m stf t k @ p ⊣ sm.

Ⱥf ⊣ o, wt wr u a. ⊙t I m ds.

Ur a. L i ⊙y. ⊳d u r i.

I d, by ○ % ⊣ ⊙ ⊙, wh ⊣ astc % ⊣ bn.

○n bg br t l, wt d u bh.

∓h t gt ls i ⊙y by ad % ⊣ rpsts % ⊣ t lsr.

⊙t r ⊣ t g ls i ⊙y.

∓h ⋊ ⊙, ≀ @ ₵ses.

⋊w r th xp.

∓h ♓ ⊝ is gn us as ⫲ r @ g fr ou fth @ p, ⫲ ≀ t s ou ac, @ ⫲ Çs t crcmscb ou drs @ kp ou ps in d bds wh al mk, es ⫲ bn.

Ⓣt r ⫲ t l ls. ∓h ≀, ⍜ @ ⍜ % ⫲ ::.

♓w r th xp.

Ⱥs ⫲ s rls ⫲ d, @ ⫲ m gvns ⫲ n, s sh ⫲ Ⓣ ⍜, wh eq rg, r @ g ⫲ ::.

Ⓣt r ⫲ rps % ⫲ t ls ls.

∓ bng cdls or tps, plcd up csts or pdsts, situ Ͼ, Ⓣ @ ≀.

Ⓣt dd u nx bh.

∓h Ⓣ ⍜ aph f ⫲ Ͼ, on ⫲ s, un ⫲ d @ § % Ͼ Ⱥ, wh prs h r h in tn % fdsh @ b l, nvstd m wh ⫲ g @ w; ○d m t r, sl ⫲ ⌡ @ ≀ Ⓣs, @ sfy thm tt I w i psn % ⫲ s, d, §, g @ w % Ͼ Ⱥ.

Ⓣt dd u nx bh.

∓h Ⓣ ⍜ aprhg f ⫲ Ͼ a sc tm, wh prstd m wh a l-s or wh lr ap, @ nfd m it ws an mbm % noc @ ⫲ bg % a ⍜; ○d m t cr it t ⫲ ≀ Ⓣ i ⫲ Ⓣ, wh tgt m hw t wr i as Ͼ Ⱥ.

Ӿw shd an Ͼ Ѧ wr h a.

ⓣh ⫞ fl tr up, t prv sl hs cls; ⓐcl, t prv db w untp mtr.

ⓣt ws thn dmd % u.

≀ m mtlc subst; nt s mh o ac % its intrc v as tt it m b dps in ⫞ rchvs % ⫞ ::, as a mmrl tt I w at tt t @ pl md a ⓐ; bt on st srh I f ms ent ds.

ⓣh wt wr u th prsntd.

∓h w ts % Ͼ Ѧ, wh r ⫞ ∓fi ₲ @ Ҁ ₲. Ӿw r th xp.

∓h ∓fi ₲ is an ins usd by op ms t msr @ la ot thr w; bt w, as ∓ @ Ѧ ⓐs, r tg t us it f ⫞ m nbl @ gls pps % dvg ou t. It bg dv nt tf eq pts is mbcl % ⫞ tf hs % ⫞ d, wh w r tg t dv nt t eq ps, wb r fd e hs f ⫞ srv % ₲ @ a dst wr b, e f ou usl vocns, @ e f rf @ sl.

∓h Ҁ ₲ i an ins usd b op ms t br o ⫞ crns % rh sts, ⫞ btr to ft thm f ⫞ blds us; bt w, as ∓ @ Ѧ ⓐs, r tg t us i f ⫞ mr nb @ gls prps % dvstng ou hts @ cns % al ⊣| vs @ sprflts % l, thb ftg ou mds, as lvg sts, f tt sprl blg, tt h nt m wh hs, etrl i ⊣| hvs.

ℋw wr u th ds %.

Ꝑlcd i ⊣| Ŋ ϵ Ç % ⊣| ::, bf ⊣| ⊙ ⊙,
wh nfd m tt I thr st an upr m @ ⊙, @ gv it m stl in chg ev t wk @ a as sh bf ȼ @ m.

⊙th wt w u th prsd.

Ѧ nw n, wh i Ç. It ths m to b cs ov al m ws @ acns, esp on ⊣| sbj % ⊤ ⊙y, wn in prs % it nms.

ℋw wr u th dsd %.

Ɍc t ⊣| p whc I cm, nvstd wh tt % wh I hd bn dvsd, @ rtd t ⊣| :: f fh ins.

϶r Ѧ ϶, I wl apt a cm to nst u in ⊣| lc tt hs js psd bt ⊣| ≀ ϶ @ ms, as it w b ncs f u to cmt hs ans to mry bf u cn b psd t ⊣| ° % ⊤c.

—○—

ⓨⓐ- Ǝr ≀ Ǝ. ≀ Ǝ- ⓨ ⓐ.

ⓨy wr u dvs % a mc sb wn m a ⓐ.

Ŧr t rss; fs, tt I mt cr nh of or df int ∤ ::; sc, at ∤ bld % ⨳ ≀ + thr ws nt hd ∤ sd % x, hm, or oth mt t.

⋌w cld so stpnds an edfc hv bn erc wtho ∤ sd % mtl ts.

+h sts wr hn, sqd, @ nmbd i ∤ qs whr rsd; ∤ tmb, fld @ prpd in ∤ frst % Lbn, cnvd by s, in flts, to J, thnc b ld t J, whr th wr st up b ∤ ad % wdn instmts ppd fr tt prps, @ wn ∤ bldg ws cmpl, ev pt thr% ftd wh sh xct ncty, tt i rsm mr ∤ hndiwk % ∤ ≀ Ⱥ % ∤ U thn tt % hm hds.

ⓨy wr u nth nk nr clhd.

ⓐy rgds no m on ac % hs wrldl wlh or hns; it is ∤ intrnl, @ nt ∤ xt, qlfs tt rcmd a m t ⓐs.

ⓨy wr u nth b n shd. 62–3

[Ạgrbly t an anc Isrltsh cstm adptd amg ⦹s.] Ⓣ rd i +| bk % ℞th cncrg thr mnr % chngg @ rdmg, tt, "∓o cnfm al thngs, a mn plkd off hs sho @ gv i t hs nghbr." ∓t ws tstmny in Isrl. ∓hs, thfr, w do, tstfyg thrby in +| strngst mnr pssbl +| sncty % our intntns in +| wk in wh w r engd.

Ⓣy w u hw @ hd a ct ar ur n.

Ŧr t rsns: f, tt m hr mt cncv bf m es bhld +| bts % ⦹y; sc, as I ws i dkns, it ws t th m t k +| whl wld s rspg +| ss % Ŧ ⦹y, xc fm sh as wr a jsl entld t rc +| sm as I ws abt bcmg; th, hd I nt cnfmd t +| crmons % m ntn, thrb rndrg msl nwthy to b tk by +| h as a ⦹, I mgt, by ad % +| ct, hv bn l ot % +| :: wto hvg bhld ev +| f thr%.

Ⓣy wr u csd t gv thr ds ks.

∓ al +| ::, @ inf +| Ⓣ ⦹ tt a pr b c crvd adm.

∓ wt dd +| t ks al.

Ⱥ crtn psg % ≀ cp, wh rds: "Ⱥsk, @ it sh b gv u; sk, @ ye shl fd; kn, @ it shl b op unt u."

⋊w dd u fd tt psg vrifd b ur situn in ⊙y at tt t.

I skd % a fd ⊣⊢ rcmndtn t b m a ⊙; thro hs rcmdn I sgt ini; I knd, @ ⊣⊢ dr % ⊙y ws op unt m.

⊙y wr u rc o ⊣⊢ p % a sh ins p u n l b.

∓o th m tt as tt ws an ins % trt t ⊣⊢ fls, s shd ⊣⊢ rcltn thr% b to m md @ cnc shd I ev rv ⊣⊢ ss % ∓ ⊙y nlfy.

⊙y wr u cdc t ⊣⊢ cnt % ⊣⊢ :: @ csd t k fr ⊣⊢ bf % pr.

⊙fr ntrg up an gt or imp ndtkg, w ot alws t nvk ⊣⊢ ad % ⊙.

⊙y wr u skd i wh u pt u t.

Ⱥgrbly t or an lw, n athst cn b m a ⊙; it ws thrf ncs tt I shd xprs a blf i ⊙, othrws n o wd hv bn rgrd as bndg.

⊙y wr u tn b ⊣⊢ r h, ○d t rs, fl ur cdtr @ f n dgr.

Ⱥs I ws i dks, @ cd nth frs nr av dng, it ws t th m tt I ws in ⫲ hs % a fl fd, in whs fdlt I mt wh sft cnfd.

⊙y wr u cdc onc rg ar ⫲ ::.

∓t ⫲ ⊙ ⊚, ⊙s @ Ͽn mt c tt I w d @ t ppd.

⊙y wr u csd t mt wh ⫲ svl obsts on ur psg ar ⫲ ::.

∓hs @ ev rg @ w gvd :: is, or ot t b, a crct rpstn % Ꝁ ≀ ∓, wh hd grds statd at ⫲ ≀, ⊙ @ Є gts t prv an fm ps r rps xc sh as wr d q @ hd prm fm Ꝁ ≀; it ws thrf ncsy tt I shd mt wh thos svrl obsts @ b at eh % ths sts dl xmd.

⊙y wr u csd t k o ur nkd l k, @ nt ur r or bh.

∓h l sd hs ev bn dmd ⫲ wks pt % ⫲ hm bd; it ws thrf t th m tt I ws ab tkg upn ms ⫲ wks pt % ⊚y, bg tt % Є Ⱥ onl.

⊙y dd ur r h rs up ⫲ Ӿ Ͽ, ≀ @ Çs, @ nt u l or bh.

∓h rt h, by or an bn, ws dmd ⊣ st % fdlt: ⊣ ans wrshpd a ⋑ nmd ∓ides, smtms rpstd b tw r hs jnd, at oths, b t hm figrs hldg eh oth b ⊣ r h. Th r, thfr, we us i ths gt @ impt undtkg, tstf thb in ⊣ stgs mnr psbl ⊣ fdlty % ou prpses i ⊣ wk i wh w r engd.

⊙y wr u prs wh a ls or wt l ap.

∓h l, in al ags, hs b dmd an mb % inoc. ∓h ls ws, thrf, to rmd m % tt prty % lf @ cndc so essntly ncy to my gng adm int ⊣ Ҁlstl :: ab, wh ⊣ ≀ A % ⊣ U prsds.

[⊙y ws a dmd md % u fr sm mtlc sbc.

[∓o th m tt shd I ev mt a mbr % ⊣ hmn fml, espc a b ⊙, in a lk dst situ it wd b m dt t cntrb t hs rlf as lbl as hs ncs mt rq @ m ab pmt.

[⊙y wr u pld in ⊣ ᑎ ⋐ Ҁ % ⊣ ::.

[In ⊣ ercn % pb bldgs, esp ths % ⊙c fm, ⊣ f st is, or ot t b, ld in ⊣ ᑎ ⋐ Ҁr; I ws thrf plc i ⊣ ᑎ ⋐ Ҁ % ⊣ :: t rc m f insts whrn t bld m fut mr @ ⊙c efdc.]

THIRD SECTION

∓hs brgs us t ⊣ t @ ls sctn % ⊣ °, wh xplns ⊣ natr @ prcpls % ou cnstn. ♓r, t, w rc instn rltv t ⊣ fm, spts, cvrg, frntr, ornmts, lts, @ jwls, % a :: ; hw i shd b situd, @ t whm ddc. [U r tgt, b ⊣ ad % imprsv smbls, t dschrg wth prpty ⊣ duts tt devlv upn u as a mn @ ⊙.]

LODGE

∆ :: ma b dfind as a crtn nmb % ∓ @ ∆ ⊙s, dl asmb; frnshd wth ⊣ ♓ ⊖, ≀, @ Çs, tghr wh a chtr o dspn fm sm ₲ ⊖ % cmpt jrsdc mprn i t wk.

CHARTER

∓h ♓ ⊖, ≀, @ Çs hv b prvsly xpld t u; ⊣ Çhrtr hs nt. It plesd ⊣ ₲r :: % ∓ @ ∆ ⊙s % ⊣ ≀t % ℞ Y, ov wh bdy ⊙ ⊙ —, ₲r ⊙, at prs prsds, t grnt t ths :: ⊣ Çhrtr nw i its possn, mprng i t cnfr ⊣ thr °s % ⊙y, wh pwr w r nw prtly xrcsng. 67–3

[It is signd by ⊣ ₲r ○fs, wh ⊣ s % ⊣ ₲r :: atchd @ cntns al ⊣ ncsry instns fr retaing ⊣ sm.]

LODGES HELD

○r anc bn hld thr ::s on hi hls or in lo vls, ⊣ btr t obsrv ⊣ aprh % cwns @ evsdps, asndg or dsndg. Lg mtgs, at ⊣ prs da, r usly hld in upr chmbrs, prbl fr ⊣ btr scrty wh sh plcs afd.

(∓h custm ma hv hd its orgn in a prctc obsvd by ⊣ anc ⌡ws wn bldng thr tmpls, schls, @ syngs, on hi hls, a prctc wh sms t hv mt ⊣ aprbtn % ⊣ Ⱥlmt, wh sd unt ⊣ Ᵽrpht Ɛzkl, "Upn ⊣ top % ⊣ mntn, ⊣ whol limit thr% rnd abt shl b most holy.")

FORM

∓h form % a :: is ob, in lngh fm est t wst, in brdth bet nth @ sth, as hi as hv @ as dp as fm ⊣ srfc t ⊣ cnt.

It is sd t b thus extnsv t denot ⊣ unvslty % ∓⊙y, @ ths tt a ⊙s chrt shd b eqly xtnsv.

SUPPORTS

Ⱥ :: is suprtd b thr grt plrs, denmd ⓣsd, ≀ t, @ ϶t; fr thr shd b wsd t cntrv, str t supt, @ bty t adrn al grt @ imprt undrtkgs. ∓h r rpsntd b ⫲ thr prcpl ofcrs % ⫲ ::, ⫲ plr ⓣsd, b ⫲ ⓣ ⍝ in ⫲ Ͼ, wh is prsumd t hv ws to opn @ gvn ⫲ :: ; ⫲ plr ≀ tr, by ⫲ ≀ ⓣ i ⫲ ⓣ, whs dty it i t ast ⫲ ⓣ ⍝ in ⫲ dschg % hs ards dts; @ ⫲ plr ϶ty, by ⫲ ⌡ ⓣ in ⫲ ≀, whs dty it i t cl ⫲ cft fm ℔ t rfs, suprntd thm drng ⫲ hrs thr%, crfly t obs tt ⫲ mns % rfsmt r nt prv t intprc or xcs, c tt th rtn t thr ℔ in du ssn, tt ⫲. ⓣ ⍝ ma rc hnr, @ thy pls @ prft thby.

COVERING

∓h covrg % a :: is n ls thn ⫲ cldd cnopy, or stry dkd hvn, whr al gd ⍝s hop at ls t arv, by ad % tt ladr wh ⌡.cb in hs vsn sw xtndd fm erth t hvn, th prncp rnds % wh r denmntd ∓th.

♓p, @ Ꞔhry, wh admsh us t hv fth i ₲, hp % imrlt, @ chrt t al mknd. ∓h grtst % ths i Ꞔhrt. Ͱr ou fth ma b ls i sgt, hp end i fruitn, bt chrt xtns bynd ⊣⊢ grv, thro ⊣⊢ bndls rlms % etr.

FURNITURE

⊖ vry rglr @ wl gvrd :: is frnsh wh ⊣⊢ ♓ ⊃, ≀, @ Ꞔs, tghr wh a Ꞔhr, or ⊃ spnsn. ∓h ♓ ⊃ is ddc t ⊣⊢ srvc % ₲, bcs i is ⊣⊢ instmbl gft % ₲ t mn, @ on it w o or nly md bn; ⊣⊢ ≀ q t ⊣⊢ ⊙st, bcs i is ⊣⊢ pr ⊙c mblm % hs ofc; @ ⊣⊢ Ꞔses t ⊣⊢ cft, fr by a du atn t thr use, thy r tgt t crcmscb thr dsrs @ kp thr pssns in d bnds.

ORNAMENTS

∓h ○rnamnts % a :: r ⊣⊢ ⊙osaic ℘vmnt, ⊣⊢ Indnt ∓ssl, @ ⊣⊢ ⊃lzg ≀ tr.

∓h ⊙saic ℘vmt is a rpstn % ⊣⊢ ₲r Ͱ % Ꝁ ≀ ∓; ⊣⊢ Ind ∓s, % tt btfl tslatd brdr or skirtng wh srndd it. Th ⊙saic ℘vmnt is mbtcl % hmn lf, chkrd wh gd @ evl; ⊣ Idnt ∓ssl, or ∓sld ⊖dr, % ⊣ mnifld blsgs @ cmfs wh cnstnly srrnd us, @ wch w hp t njy b a fm rlnc on ⊖ vn ₿rv, wh is rpsd b ⊣ ⊖lz ≀ tr i ⊣ cntr.

LIGHTS

Ⱥ :: hs thr smblc lts, sit ⊖, ⊙, @ ≀. [∓hr is nn i ⊣ N, bcs K ≀ ∓ ws sit s fr N % ⊣ eclptc tt ⊣ sun, evn at mrdn, dd nt drt its ras int ⊣ nthrn-mst prts thr%.] ∓h nth w ⊙cly trm a plc % dkns.

JEWELS

Ⱥ :: hs sx jls, thr mv @ thr imvb.

∓h imvbl jls r ⊣ ≀ q, ⊣ Lvl, @ ⊣ ₿lm. ∓hy r so trmd bcs thy r apprptd to prtclr prts % ⊣ :: whr aln th shd b fnd, ⊣ ≀ q t ⊣ ⊖, ⊣ Lvl t ⊣ ⊙, @ ⊣ ₿l t ⊣ ≀. [Ⱥltho ⊣ bn ocpyg thos stns ma fm tm t tm b chngd, stl ⊣ ⌡ls wl alws b fnd i thr rspt stns in ⊣ ::.] ∓h ≀ tchs mrlty; ⊣ Lv, eql; @ ⊣ ₿l, rctud % cndc.

∓h mvbl jls r ⊣ ℞gh Ⱥsh, ⊣ ℟rfc Ⱥsh, @ ⊣ ∓rsbd. ∓h ℞gh Ⱥsh is a stn in its rud @ ntrl stat, as tkn fm ⊣ qry; ⊣ ℟fc Ⱥsh, one prpd by ⊣ wkm, t b adj b ⊣ wkg tls % ∓ Ȼ; @ ⊣ ∓rb i fr ⊣ ⊙ wkm t dr hs dsns upn.

Ɜy ⊣ ℞gh Ⱥsh w r remdd % tt rud @ impfc stat wch is ors b ntr; b ⊣ ℟fc Ⱥsh, % tt stat % pfctn at wch w hp t arv b educn, ou own endvrs, @ ⊣ bls % Ↄ. Ⱥn as ⊣ opr wkm ers hs tmprl bldg in acdc wth ⊣ dsns ld dwn upn ⊣ ∓rsbd b ⊣ ⊙st wkm, s shd w, bth opr @ spc, ndvr t erc ou sprtl bldg in ac wth ⊣ dsns ld dn by ⊣ ≀ Ⱥ % ⊣ U in ⊣ gr bk % rvltn, wh i ou ⊙c ∓rbd.

HOW SITUATED

Ⱥ :: is siu du Ǝ @ ⊙, bcs Ʀ ≀ ∓ ws s sit. ⊙os, by dvn cmd, hvng cdcd ⊣ chldn % Isrl ot % ⊣ lnd % Ǝgp, fm ⊣ hse % bndg, thro ⊣ ℞ed ≀ e, int ⊣ wldrns, erc a ∓bcl t Ǥ, wch h sit du

Ɛ @ ⊍, to comrat t ⊣ ltst pst tt mracls Ɛ wnd wch wrgt thr mgty dlvrnc. Ʀ ≀ ∓ is sd t hv bn a rpsn % tt tbncl.

TO WHOM DEDICATED

Ldgs wr ancly ddc t Ʀ ≀, as h i sd t hv bn ou fs ⊙s Ɛ ₲ ⊙; bt spc ⊙s ddc thrs t ⊣ mmr % ≀ t ⌡ ⊣ Ɜ, @ ≀ t ⌡ ⊣ Ɛv.

(≀ nc thr tm, ther is rpstd, in evr rg @ wl gvnd ::, a ctn pt wthn a crcl, ⊣ pt rpstg ⊣ indvl br, ⊣ crcl, ⊣ bdry ln % hs cdt t ₲ @ mn, byd wch h i nvr t sfr hs psns, prjdcs, o intrsts t btry hm on any ocsn. ∓hs crc is brdd b two prpdclr prl lns rpstg thos sts @ upn ⊣ vrtx rst ⊣ ⋊ ≀ s, wch pt ot ⊣ whl dty % mn. In gng arnd ths crcl, w ncsrly tuch upn thes two lns, as wl as upn ⊣ ⋊ ≀ s, @ whil a ⊙ kps hmsf ths crcs, it i imps tt h shd mtrl er.)

PRINCIPAL TENETS

∓h prncpl tnts % ou prfsn r thrfld, ncldg ⊣ inclctn @ prctc % thos trly cmndabl vrtus, Ɜrl Lv, ℞lf, @ ∓.

BROTHERLY LOVE

Ͽy +| xrcs % Ͽrl Lv, w r tgt t rgrd +| hu rc as on fmly, +| hi, +| lw, +| rh, +| pr, wh, as cratd b on Ꭿlm ℘rnt, @ inhbtg +| sm plnt, shld ad, suprt, @ protc on anoth. ○n ths prncp, ⊙y units mn % evry cnty, sct, @ opnon, @ prmts tru frnshp amg thos who mgt othws hv rmnd prpul at a ds.

RELIEF

∓ relv +| dstrsd is a dty incmbt o al mn, prtcly upn ⊙s, who r lnkd tghr b a chan % sncr afctn. ∓ soth +| unhpy, t smpz wth thm i thr msftns, t cmpsat thr msrs, @ t rstr pc t thr trbld mds, r aims w hv in vw. ○n ths bas w fm ou frshps @ est ou cnctns.

TRUTH

∓rth is a dvn atbrut, @ +| fndtn % evr vrtu. ∓ b gd @ tru, is +| fst lsn w r tgt in ⊙y. ϰnc, whl infled by ths prcpl, hyprsy @ dect r unkn amg us; sncrty @ plndlng dstgh us; @ ⫞ hrt @ ⫞ tng jn in prmtg ech oths wlfr, @ rjcg in ech oths psprty.

⊙y br, in ○ tt u ma btr undrst wt is t fol, I wl ask ⫞ ≀ ⊳ a qs.

⊙ ⊙- ⊳r ≀ ⊳.

≀ ⊳- ⊙ ⊙.

⊙ ⊙- ⋊w ma I k u t b a ⊙.

≀ ⊳- ⊳y cr §s, a tn, a w @ ⫞ pf ps % m ent.

⊙ ⊙- ⊙y br, ⫞ §s, tn @ w hv bn xpld t u bt ⫞ pf ps % ur ent hv nt.

∓hy r fo: ⫞ ₱ctrl, ⫞ ⊙anul, ⫞ ₲utrl, @ ⫞ ₱dl. ∓hy rps ⫞ fo crdnl vrts—⊤ortud, ₱rudnc, ∓mpc @ ⌡s.

FORTITUDE

⊤rtd is tt nbl @ stdy prps % ⫞ md, whby w r enabl t undgo any pn, prl, or dngr. ∓hs vrtu is eqly dstnt frm rashns @ cowrdc, @ shd b dply imprsd upn ur mnd as a safgrd or scrity ags an atm tt ma b md, b frc or othws, t xtr fm u an % ⫞ sc wt wh u hv bn s sl intrsd. ∓hs vrtu ws emblmly rpsd upn ur fs adms int ⊣⊢ ::, whn u wr rcv on ⊣⊢ pnt % a shp ins pcg ur nk lf brs. ∓hs is ⊣⊢ pfc pt % ur ntrc, ⊣⊢ Ᵽctrl.

PRUDENCE

Ᵽrdnc tchs us t rglt our lvs @ acns agrbl t ⊣⊢ dics % ℞sn @ is tt hbt by wch w wsly jdg @ dtmn on al thgs rltv t our prs, as wl as ou fu, hpns. ∓hs vru shd b ur chrstc, nt onl in ⊣⊢ gvmt % ur cdc whl in ⊣⊢ ::, bt als whn abrd i ⊣⊢ wld. U shd b partculy cauts, in al strng @ mxd cmpns, nvr t lt fal ⊣⊢ ls §, tkn, or wd, whby ⊣⊢ scs % ⊤⊙y mgt b obtd, evr brng in rmbrc tt sl mmt, whl knlg at ⊣⊢ scd ⅄ % ⊤⊙y, wth ur l hn sptg @ rt rs upn ⊣⊢ ӿ Ͽ, ≀ @ Ꝗses, u slmy prmsd t cncl @ nv rvl any % ⊣⊢ scs % ⊤⊙y. Ths is ⊣⊢ sec per pt % ur ntrc, ⊣⊢ ⊙nul.

TEMPERANCE

∓mprc i tt du rstnt upn +| psns wch rndrs +| bd tme @ gvnbl, @ fres +| mnd fm +| alurmts % vice. ∓hs vrtu shd b ur cnstnt prc, as u r thrby tgt t avd xcs, @ +| cntrcg % any lic or vics hbt, +| indlgc % wch mgt ld u t dscls thos scs wch u hv prm t cncl @ nv rvl, +| btrl % wch wld subjc u t +| cntmp @ detstatn % al gd ⊙s, if nt t +| pn fr +| vl % ur o, tt % hvg ur th ct ac, ur tn tr ot @ br in +| sn % +| se at lo wt mk whr +| td eb @ fls twc i tw-f hrs. ∓hs i +| thd pf pt % ur ntc, +| ¢tr.

JUSTICE

J stc is tt stndrd wh enb us t rnd t ev mn hs d, wtho dstn. ∓hs vr i nt onl cns wth dv @ hu lw, bt is +| vr cmt @ sup % soc; @ as J s, in a gr ms, dstg +| gd m, s shd i b ur prc t b jst; ev rmbg whl st i +| ŋ ⊂ ₵ %

+| ::, ur ft fmg +| ngl % an ob, ur bd erc bf +| ☉ ⊙, u wr tld tt u thr st an up m @ ⊙, @ i ws gvn u stl i cg ev t wk @ ac as sch bf ȼ @ m. ∓hs is +| f pt % ur ntc, +| Ɋdl, @ al t +| psn % ur ft w st i +| ℞ ϵ Ç % +| ::.

CHALK, CHARCOAL, CLAY

ϵ Ⱥs shd srv thr ⊙sts wth frdm, fr, @ zl, wch r mblc rpsd b Çhl, Çr, @ Çl.

∓hr is nthg fr thn Çh, +| sl th % wh lvs a trc; thr is nthg mr frv thn Çr, fr t i, wn prpl igntd, +| ms obdr mtl wl yld; thr i nthg mr zl thn Çl, ou ⊙h ϵ, fr it aln % al +| elm hs nv prv unfdl t mn. ∓ho cns harsd, mr t frnsh +| lxs thn +| ncrs % lf, she nv rfs hr acs yld, strwg our pthwa wth fls @ spdg our tabl wth pl; tho she prdcs psn, stl she frnsh +| antdo, @ rtns wth intrs ev gd cmtd t hr cr. Ⱥnd whn, at ls, w r cl upn t ps thro

⊣ vl % ⊣ shd % dh, sh onc mr rc us, @ tndly nflds our rms wth hr bsm, ths admshg us tt, as fm ⊖ w cm, s t eth w ms surly rtn. (*Or.*)

(⊖ Ąs shd srv thr ⊙sts wth ∓rdm, ∓rv, @ Zl, wch r mblc rpsd b Çhl, Çr @ Çl.

(∓hr is nthg fr thn Çhl, ⊣ sl tch % wch lvs a trc; nthg mr frvt thn Çh, fr t it, whn prpl igntd, ⊣ ms obdur mtls wl yld; @ nthg mr zls thn Çl, ou ⊙thr ⊖th, whs prdc is cnstly mpld fr mns use, @ is as cnstl remdng hm tt fm eth h cm @ t eth h ms surly rtn.)

SYMBOLISM

[∓h fst, or ⊖ Ą, ° % ⊙y is intdd, smboly, t rpsnt ⊣ entrc % mn int ⊣ wld i wh h is afwds t bcm a lvg @ thkg actr. Çmg fm ⊣ igrnc @ dkns % ⊣ otr wld, hs fs crvg is fr lt—nt tt pscl lt wh sprngs fm ⊣ gt orb % da as its fountn, bt tt mrl @ intlctl lt wh emnats fm ⫞ priml ≀rce % al thgs— fm ⫞ ȼrd Ą % ⫞ U ⫞ Çre % ⫞ sn @ % al tt i ilmnats. ⋊nc ⫞ gt, ⫞ prmy objc % ⫞ fs ° is t symblz ⫞ brth % intlctul lt int ⫞ mnd, @ ⫞ Ǝ Ą is ⫞ typ % unrgnratv mn, gropg i morl @ mntl dkns, @ sekg fr ⫞ lt wh is t guid hs stps @ pnt hm t ⫞ ph wh lds t du @ t ⋊m wh gvs t du its rwd.

[∓hos arn u r ur bn, rdy t dschg al ⫞ ofcs % tt intmt rltn. ∓h nw bid u wlcm t th nmbr @ flshp, t thr afcns @ astnc, t thr prvlgs @ jys; @ thro m th prms t prtc u b thr inflc @ autht, to advs u b thr ablt @ skl, t ast ur xignce by thr libralt @ bnty, @ t chr u at al tm wth thr kdns @ lv. Ąnd u wl hv ⫞ hpns % xprncg ⫞ trth % ⫞ anct rmrk tt, "⊙s bng bn, thr xist n invids dstcn amg thm;" @ tt they "lv ech oth mtly, as hth bn sd, wh, indd, ma nt othws b. ȼd mn @ tru, kng ech oth t b sh, d alws lv ⫲ mr as thy b ⫲ mr gd."

[∓hs, br, is ⫲ bgng % our art. ⋊w sucsfl is its prgrs @ hw hapy in its nd u ma fly kn if u r bt atntv, fthfl @ wise. Ur dlgnc @ actvty in wrks, ur skl in acqrg ⫲ instcns % ur °, @ ur zl in ⫲ caus % ⊤ ⍝y wl ld u frwd t grtr hghts, t clerr vws, @ to noblr prvlgs.

[∓hs, m br, cnclds ⫲ fs ° % ⍝y, wth ⫲ xcpn % ⫲ chrg.] 3

CHARGE

⍡⍝- ⍥r, as u r nw ntdc nt ⫲ fs prcp % ⊤ ⍝y, I cngt u upn bg acpd int ths anc @ hn ⊤rty, anc as hvg subsstd fm tm imorl, @ hnrbl as tndg in evry prtclr so to rndr al mn wh wl b cnfmbl t its prcpts. Ŋo instu ws ev rsd on a btr prn, or mr sld fndtn, nr wr ev mr exclt rls @ usfl mxs ld dn thn r inclctd in ⫲ svrl ⍝c lctrs.

∓h grts @ bs % mn, in al ags, hv bn encrgs @ prmts % ⊣⊢ rt, @ hv nv dmd it drogty to thr digt t lvl thsl wth ⊣⊢ ∓rt, xtd its prvlgs, @ ptrnz its asmbls.

∓hr r thr gt dts wh, as a ⊙s, u r chrgd, t nclct, t ₲, ur nb, @ ursl. ∓o ₲ i nv mntg ♓s nm bt wth tt rvntl aw wh i du fm a crtr t hs Ͼ, impl ♓s aid i al ur ldb undtkgs, @ estmg ♓m as ⊣⊢ chf gd; t ur nbr, in actg upn ⊣⊢ sq, @ dng unt hm as u wsh h shd d unt u; @ t ursl, in avdg al irglrty @ intmpr, wh m impr ur fclts, or dbs ⊣⊢ dgt % ur prfsn. Ѧ zls ath to ths dts wl ins pblc @ pv es.

In ⊣⊢ ≀ t u r t b a qt @ pcbl citzn, tru t ur gvmt @ jst to ur cnt. U r nt t cntnc dslyl o rbln, bt patntly submt t lg auth, @ cnfm wh chrflns to ⊣⊢ gvmt % ⊣⊢ cnt i wch u lv. In ur otwd dmnr b prtcl crfl to avd cnse or reprch.

Ꜳltho ur frqt aprnc at ou reg mtgs is ernstl solctd, yt it i nt mnt tt ⊙y shd intfr wth ur ncsry vocns, fr ths r on no act t b nglc; nthr r u t sfr ur zl fr ⊣⊢ instu t led u int argmt wth ths wh, thro igrnc, ma rdcl it.

⊃rng ur lsr hrs, tt u ma mprv in ⊙c knlg, u r to cnvrs wh wl-nfd brn, who wl b alws as rdy to gv as u wl b to rc instn.

₸nly, kp sacd @ invlt ⊣⊢ mstys % ⊣⊢ ₸ty, as ths r to dstg u fm ⊣⊢ rst % ⊣⊢ cmmt @ mk ur cnsqc amg ⊙s.

If, i ⊣⊢ crcl % ur aqnc, u fnd a prs dsrs % bng initd int ⊙y, b prtc crfl nt t rcmnd hm, unls u r cnvncd tt h wl cnfm t ou rls; tt ⊣⊢ hnr, gl, @ rptn % ⊣⊢ Instn ma b frmly estab, @ ⊣⊢ wld at lrg cnvcd % its gd efcts.

(⊙⊙- ⊙y br, wtev ma hthto hv bn ur mrl atud twds ⊣⊢ ₲ % mn, u, b ur vlnty actn ths evg, hv prcld opnl ur blf tt ♓ rely is, @ rtfly ruls.

(∓h titl by wh I hv js adrsd u is ⊙cl gvn bcs % ⋊s ∓thrhd. U hv nw entrd upn a nw tie wth ⋊m; u lk up t ⋊m as ou frtys ₲. ₳s sch u hv, at yndr ₳, swr in ⋊s nm @ ask ⋊s hlp t b an uprt mn @ ⊙s. ∓t mns ur dt t hm, @ dt mns a dbt.

(I kn nt ur frmr estmtn % ⊣⊢ rvrnc du t ⋊m. I do kn tt fm ths tm fth ur oth % algnc dmds stdfs felty t ⋊s ls, @ extrm rvrnc fr ⋊s gt @ sc nm.

(∓h wrld itsl styls hm wh ks no ₲ a hthn. ⋊ is a mnac t soct @ a mrl blnk in hmsl. ∓h ⊙ wh ackl ₲ i ⊣⊢ :: rm @ ignrs o blsphs ot % it inslts ⊣⊢ cft as h violts hs oth. Ur ⊙y mst b prvn b ur rel atud tords our ≀ u ₲r ⊙st. ∓h tng wch tks ⊣⊢ obl % ⊣⊢ ⊙, shd nt dmen ⊣⊢ ⊙s ₲.

(Ꝛestrn ⊣⊢ curs agst ur ∓thr in hvn as u wd resnt a curs agst ur fthr on ⊣⊢ eth. ≀ trv t b a ⊙ who wl fashn brvly hs lyl sonshp. Ꞔare litl fr ⊣⊢ jibs % mn, bt hd ⊣⊢ sting % consc.

(₲ ot fm ths evngs crmns a lyl ⊙, a wrthy br, an Ꭿprtc etnd upn a nw field % ℔, wh a nw sns % du, @ bnd b a sl vw ev t wlk @ ac uprtl, @ spek rvntly ♓s nam befr whm al ⊙s shd hmbl, rvrntl, @ dvo bw.)

∓hs, m br, cnclds ⫞ fs ° % ⊙y; u wl st to ⫞ Ꭿ, slt @ rtr. ∓h ≀ ec wl notfi u whn t prs ursl fr ⫞ sec °.

—o—

CLOSING

CLOSING FIRST—RESUMING THIRD

⊤⃝ ⊥⃝- Ↄr ⌡ Ↄ.

⌡ Ↄ- ⊤⃝ ⊥⃝.

⊤⃝ ⊥⃝- ∓h ls as wl a f gr c % ⊥⃝s wn cnv.

⌡ Ↄ- ∓ c tt th r d td.

⊤⃝ ⊥⃝- Ⱥtd t tt d, @ inf ⊣| ∓ tt I am ab t cls ⊣| :: on ⊣| f °, fr ⊣| pps % rsmg ℔ in ⊣| thd; dr hm to tk d nt th% @ gvn hms ac.

⌡ Ↄ- *** (∓***) Ↄr ∓.

∓- Ↄ ⌡ Ↄ.

⌡ Ↄ- ∓h ⊤⃝ ⊥⃝ is ab t cls ⊣| :: on ⊣| f ° f ⊣| ps % rs ℔ in ⊣| thd; tk du nc thr% @ gv us ac. ⊤⃝ ⊥⃝.

⊤⃝ ⊥⃝- Ↄ ⌡ Ↄ.

⌡ Ↄ- ∓h ∓ is inf.

⊤⃝ ⊥⃝- *** ⊤⃝vg al §s @ crms, I nw dc ⊣| :: dly clsd on ⊣| f °, @ ℔ rsmd i ⊣| t. Ↄr ≀ Ↄ, atd at ⊣| Ⱥ. Ↄ ⌡ Ↄ, inf ⊣| ∓.

≀ ◗- (*Gs t* (T) *% Ꞩ, gs § % fdlty, dspls ls @ rts t hs pl.*)

⌡ ◗- *** (∓- ***) ◗ ∓.

∓- ◗r ⌡ ◗.

⌡ ◗- Lb i nw rsmd in +| t °. (*Cls d.*) (T) (⊥).

(T) (⊥)- ◗ ⌡ ◗.

⌡ ◗- ∓h ∓ is nfd.

(T) (⊥)- *

CLOSING THIRD

(T) (⊥)- ◗ ≀ (T).

≀ (T)- (T) (⊥).

(T) (⊥)- ♓v u anth t br bf +| :: bf || prc t cls.

≀ (T)- (*Rs.*) Ꞃth i +| (T).

(T) (⊥)- ◗ ⌡ (T). (T) (⊥). Ꞩnt i +| ≀.

⌡ (T)- (*Rs.*) Ꞃth i +| ≀.

(T) (⊥)- ♓s an br ant t bg bf +| :: bf || prc t cls. (*Ᵽaus.*) ◗ sec.

≀ ec- (T) (⊥).

(T) (⊥)- ℞ u rdy wh +| mts.

≀ ec- || am.

(T) (⊥)- Ↄn, gv ur atn t ⊣ rdg % ⊣ ms % our prs cmcn. ((⊥)*ts.*) Ↄ ≀ (T).

≀ (T)- (T) (⊥).

(T) (⊥)- Ↄo u dsc any ers or oms in ⊣ mts as r. Ŋth i ⊣ (T). Ↄr J (T).

J (T)- (T) (⊥). Ⱥn i ⊣ ≀. Ŋh i ⊣ ≀.

(T) (⊥)- Ↄs any br prs dsc any ers or oms i ⊣ ms as rd. ∓hr bng nn, || dc thm aprvd. * Ↄr J Ↄ.

J Ↄ- (T) (⊥).

(T) (⊥)- ∓h ls as wl a f g c % (⊥)s wn cnvd.

J Ↄ- ∓ c tt th r d td.

(T) (⊥)- Ⱥt t tt du, @ inf ⊣ ∓ tt || am ab t cls—::, Ŋ –, drc h t tk d ntc thr% @ gv hms ac.

J Ↄ- *** (∓- ***) Ↄ ∓.

∓- Ↄ J Ↄ.

J Ↄ- || am drc t inf u tt ⊣ (T) (⊥) is ab t cl—::, Ŋ–, tk d nc thr% @ gv urs ac. (*Cls d.*) (T) (⊥).

(T) (⊥)- Ↄr J Ↄ.

J Ↄ- (T)e r d td.

Ⓨ ⍝- ♓w r w td.

J ☽- Ͽy a ⍝ ⍝ who, ard wh ⫲ ppr m % h ofc.

Ⓨ ⍝- ♓s d thr.

J ☽- ∓ obs ⫲ ap % cs @ evs, c tt nn p or rp xc sh as r dl q @ hv prms f ⫲ Ⓨ ⍝.

Ⓨ ⍝- Ͽ ≀ Ⓨ. Ⓨ ⍝. ℞ u a ⍝ ⍝.

≀ Ⓨ- ‖ a.

Ⓨ ⍝- Ⓨt ind u t bc a ⍝ ⍝.

≀ Ⓨ- ∓t ‖ mt ob ⫲ ⍝st w, tv in frn cntrs, wk @ r ⍝st ws, @ b thrb btr enbld t spt ms @ fm @ cntrb t ⫲ rl % dst wh ⍝ ⍝s, th ws @ os.

Ⓨ ⍝- Ⓨt mks u a ⍝ ⍝.

≀ Ⓨ- ⍝ o.

Ⓨ ⍝- Ⓨh wr u m a ⍝ ⍝.

≀ Ⓨ- Ⓨthn ⫲ bd % a jt @ d cstd :: % ⍝ ⍝s, asb i a pl rpstg ⫲ unf ≀ ≀ % Ꝁ ≀ ∓m, frshd wh ⫲ ♓ Ͽ, ≀ @ Çses, tgh wh a Çhtr o ☽ spntn f sm ₵ Ͽdy % cmp jrs mpr it t wk.

Ⓨ ⍝- ♓w mn cps a ⍝ ⍝s ::.

≀ ⊙- ∓ o mr.

⊙ ⍝- ⊙n cps % f, % whm ds i cs.

≀ ⊙- ∓h ⊙ ⍝, ≀ @ ⌡ ⊙s; @ ≀ @ ⌡ Ɖ s.

⊙ ⍝- ∓h ⌡ Ɖ s plc i ⫲ ::.

≀ ⊙- Ⱥt m r.

⊙ ⍝- ** Э ⌡ Ɖ.

⌡ Ɖ- ⊙ ⍝.

⍝ ⊙- Ur d.(*Fr sht fm, omit dts.*)

⌡ Ɖ- ∓ cr ms f ⫲ ≀ ⊙ n ⫲ ⊙ to ⫲ ⌡ ⊙ n ⫲ ≀, @ elsw ab ⫲ :: as h ma dr; at t als at ⫲ o dr, rpt ⫲ sm to ⫲ ⊙ ⍝; als t c tt w r d td.

⊙ ⍝- ∓h ≀ Ɖ s pl.

⌡ Ɖ- Ⱥt ⫲ r % ⫲ ⊙ ⍝ n ⫲ Є.

⊙ ⍝- Э ≀ Ɖ. ⊙ ⍝. Ur d.

≀ Ɖ- ∓ cr ○s f ⫲ ⊙ ⍝ n ⫲ Є t ⫲ ≀ ⊙ n ⫲ ⊙, @ els ab ⫲ :: as h ma dr; wlcm @ clo vst bn, atd t al at ⫲ nr dr, als t rc @ cn cs.

⊙ ⍝- ∓h ⌡ ⊙s st.

≀ Э- ||n ⫲ ≀.

⊙ ⍝- Э ⌡ ⊙. ⊙ ⍝. Ur d n ⫲ ≀.

J ⓣ- ∓ obs ⫲ ≀ at mer, wh is ⫲ gl @ bt % ⫲ d; cl ⫲ cft f ℔ t rfsmt, sptnd thm dr ⫲ hs thr%, crfly t obs tt ⫲ ms % rfs r nt prvtd to intmprc or xcs; c tt th rt to thr ℔ in d ssn, tt ⫲ ⓣ ⓐ ma rc hnr @ th pls @ prft thby.

ⓣ ⓐ- ∓h ≀ ⓣs st.

J ⓣ- ||n ⫲ ⓣ.

ⓣ ⓐ- ⓑ ≀ ⓣ. ⓣ ⓐ. ⓣh in ⫲ ⓣ.

≀ ⓣ- Ⱥs ⫲ ≀ is in ⫲ ⓣ at cl % d, so sts ⫲ ≀ ⓣ i ⫲ ⓣ t as ⫲ ⓣ ⓐ i o @ c ⫲ ::; pa ⫲ c thr ws, if an b du, tt nn m g a dsf, hr bn ⫲ supt % al ins, es ths % ors.

ⓣ ⓐ- ∓h ⓐs s. I ⫲ Є. ⓣ i ⫲ Є.

≀ ⓣ- Ⱥs ⫲ s r i ⫲ Є t o @ gv ⫲ d; so rses—

ⓣ ⓐ- *** (*Rs.*)

≀ ⓣ- ∓h ⓣ ⓐ i ⫲ Є t o @ gv ⫲ ::, @ st ⫲ c at w, gv thm pr inst f thr ℔.

⊙ ⊚- ⊃r ≀ ⊙, it i m ○ tt — ::, Ŋ –, b nw cls, @ st c ntl its nx rg cmtn, nls spl cnvd, i wh emrg du @ tml nt w b gn. ∓hs cm t ǂ ⌡ ⊙ i ǂ ≀, @ h t ǂ bn pr, tt hv du nc thr% th ma g ths ac.

≀ ⊙- ⊃r ⌡ ⊙.

⌡ ⊙- ⊃r ≀ ⊙.

≀ ⊙- It is ǂ ○ % ǂ ⊙ ⊚ tt — ::, Ŋ –, b nw c, @ s cl ntl its nx rg cmc, nls spc cnvd, in wh emr d @ tl nc wl b g. ∓hs cmc t ǂ bn prs, tt hv d n thr% th ma gn ths ac.

≀ ⊙- ⊃n, (⊃*n cm t* ○.) it i ǂ ○ % ǂ ⊙ ⊚, cmcd t m thr ǂ ≀ ⊙ in ǂ ⊙, tt — ::, Ŋ –, b nw c, @ st c ntl its nx r cmtn, nls sp cvd, in wh em d @ tm nc wl b gn. || cm ǂ sm t u, tt hg d nc thr% u ma g us ac.

⊙ ⊚- ⊃n, at t g ǂ §s; ob ǂ Є.

** * ≀ ⊙- ** * ≀ ⊙- ** *⊃ ≀ ⊙.

≀ ⊙- ⊙ ⊚.

⊙ ⊚- ӿw sh ⊚s m. ○n ǂ l. ⊃ ⌡ ⊙.

⌋ ⊙- ⊙ ⊙. ⋇w s ⊙s ac. ⊙y ⊣⊢ pl. ⊙⊙- Ⱥnd pt up ⊣⊢ ≀. ≀ sh w, my bn, ev m, a @ p. (*Rmvs ht.*)

PRAYER.

Çhp- Ⱥlmt ⊧th, w ask ∓hy bls upn ⊣⊢ prcds % ths cmctn, @, as w r abt to sep, w ask ∓he t kp us und ∓hy prctg cr untl agn w r cld tghr. ∓ch us, ○ ₲, t reliz ⊣⊢ bu % ⊣⊢ prcpls % ou tm hon instu, nt onl whl i ⊣⊢ ::, bt whn abrd i ⊣⊢ wrl. ≀ ubdu ev dscrdt pasn wthn us, @ enab us t lv on anth i ⊣⊢ bnds % unin @ frshp. Ⱥmn. (*Or.*)

(Çhp- ≀ pm Ⱥrtc % ⊣⊢ Unvs, acpt ou hmbl thks fr ⊣⊢ mn mrcs @ bls ∓hy bnty hs cnfrd on us, @ espcly fr ths frndl @ socl intrcs.

(Ᵽardn, w besch ∓h, wtev ∓ho hast sn amis i us snc w hv bn tghr, @ cntu to us ∓hy prsnc, prtcn, @ blsg.

(⊙k us snsibl % ⊣⊢ renwd obgs w r und t lv ∓h, @, as w r ab t sepr @ rtn t ou rspctv placs % abod, wilt

∓ho b plsd s t inflc ou hrts @ mnds, tt ech one % us ma prtc, ot % ⫲ ::, ths gt ml dts wch r inclctd in it, @ wth rvc stdy @ ob ⫲ lws wh ∓ho hast gvn us i ∓h ⋊h (⊤)d. Ⱥmn.)

(⊤) (⊥) - (⊥)a ⫲ blsng % ⋊vn rs upn us @ al rgl (⊥)s. (⊥)a bly l prvl, @ ev mrl @ socl vrt cmnt us. Ⱥmn.

⊢)rn - (*Rsp.*) ≀ o m i b.

(⊤) (⊥) - ⊢) ≀ ⊨).

≀ ⊨) - (⊤) (⊥).

(⊤) (⊥) - Ⱥt a ⫲ Ⱥ @ c ⫲ g l i (⊥)y.

≀ ⊨) - (*Gs* (⊤) *%* Ⱥ, *gs § % fdlt, cl lts @ rts t hs plc.*)

(⊤) (⊥) - || nw dc ⫲ :: dl cld. ⊢)r ⌡ ⊨).

⌡ ⊨) - (⊤) (⊥).

(⊤) (⊥) - In ⫲ ∓.

⌡ ⊨) - *** (∓ - ***) ⊢) ∓.

∓ - ⊢) ⌡ ⊨).

⌡ ⊨) - ∓h :: i n c. (*Cl d.*) (⊤) (⊥).

(⊤) (⊥) - ⊢) ⌡ ⊨). ∓h ∓ i in. *

PASSING

Ⓣ⍊- Ͽr ⌡϶.

⌡϶- Ⓣ⍊.

Ⓣ⍊- Ⱥsrtn i any Ȼs r in wtg. If s, thr nms @ f wt °.

⌡϶- (*Obts card wh full nm % ch Ȼ fm ∓ @ rps.*) Ⓣ⍊.

Ⓣ⍊- Ͽ ⌡϶.

⌡϶- Ͽ Ⱥ Ͽ is i wt f ∓ s ° % ⍊y.

Ⓣ⍊- Ͽn, Ͽ Ⱥ Ͽ is i wg f ∓ s ° % ⍊y. Ӿ hvg md sutb pfc in ∓ prc °, if th is n ob, I sh cn ∓ ° up h. (*Pauses.*) ∓h bn n o, I w prc. * Ͽ ≀ @ ⌡ ⍊s % Ȼ.

≀ ⍊ % Ȼ- (Ͽ*h rs.*) Ⓣ⍊.

Ⓣ⍊- Ӿw s a b b pr f ∓ s ° % ⍊y.

≀ ⍊ % Ȼ- Ͽy bn dvs % 'al m sbs, nthr nk nr ch, bf n sh, r kn @ b br, h-w, @ a c-t twc a hs r a, c as Ͼ Ⱥ.

Ⓣ⍊- ℞pr to ∓ prr, wh Ͽr Ⱥ Ͽ i i wtg. Ⓣh ths pd, cs hm t m ∓ us a at ∓ in dr.

⊙s % Ç- (*℞pr t ⊣ Ą, slt, lf fc, mh t pp-r @ pr ⊣ c, s on r f etc.* ‖ *n ⊣ mntm ⊣ :: prcds wh rgl bsns.*)

⊙ ⊙- * ⊙ J D.

J D- ⊙ ⊙.

⊙ ⊙- ∓h l as w as f g cr % ⊙s whn cnvd.

J D- ∓ c tt th r d t.

⊙ ⊙- Ąt t tt dt, @ inf ⊣ ∓ tt ‖ am ab t ds wh ℔ i ⊣ t ° fr ⊣ prps % o ⊣ :: o ⊣ s fr w @ ins; dr hm t t d nc thr% @ gv hms ac.

J D- *** (∓- ***) ⊙ ∓.

∓- ⊙ J D.

J D- ∓h ⊙ ⊙ is ab t dsps wh ℔ in ⊣ t ° fr ⊣ prps % o ⊣ :: on ⊣ sc fr w @ ins. ∓k du n thr% @ g urs ac. (*Çls d.*) ⊙ ⊙.

⊙ ⊙- ⊙ J D.

J D- ∓h ∓ is infd.

⊙ ⊙- *** ‖ nw d ℔ dspd wh in ⊣ t °. ⊙r J D, inf ⊣ ∓.

J D- *** (∓- ***) ⊙ ∓.

∓- Ͽr ⌡ Ɗ.

⌡ Ɗ- Lb is nw dspd wh in ⫲ t °.
(Ç*ls dr.*) ⊙ ⊚.

⊙⊚- Ͽ ⌡ Ɗ.

⌡ Ɗ- ∓h ∓ is inf.

⊙⊚- * (≀ *ts* ⫲ ::.) Ͽ ≀ ⊙.

≀ ⊙- ⊙ ⊚.

⊙⊚- (℞*s*.) ℞ u a Ŧc.

≀ ⊙- || m; t m.

⊙⊚- Ͽ wt w u b t. Ͽ ⫲ s. ⊙h b ⫲ s.

≀ ⊙- Ͽcs i is an em % mrlt @ on % ⫲ w tls % a Ŧc.

⊙⊚- ⊙t is a s.

≀ ⊙- Ⱥn ng % nt °s, or ⫲ f pt % a crc.

⊙⊚- ⊙t ms u a Ŧc.

≀ ⊙- ⊚y o.

⊙⊚- ⊙hr wr u m a Ŧc.

≀ ⊙- ⊙thn ⫲ b % a j @ d cstd :: % Ŧs, asmb in a p rpstg ⫲ ⊚ Ç % Ʀ ≀ ∓, fur wh ⫲ ⊁ Ͽ, ≀ @ Çss, tgh wh a Çhtr o Ɗ spntn fm sm gr bd % cmp jrs mprg it t wk.

(⊤)(⊥)- ♓w mn cps a ∓c ::.

≀ (⊤)- ∓ o mr.

(⊤)(⊥)- (⊤)n cps % f, % wm ds it cnst.

≀ (⊤)- ∓h (⊤) (⊥), ≀ @ ⌡ (⊤)s, @ ≀ @ ⌡ ◗s.

(⊤)(⊥)- ∓h ⌡ ◗s plc i ⫲ ::.

≀ (⊤)- Ѧt m r. ** ⊖ ⌡ ◗. (⊤) (⊥).

(⊤)(⊥)- ∓h ≀ ◗s plc.

⌡ ◗- Ѧt ⫲ r % ⫲ (⊤) (⊥) i ⫲ Є.

(⊤)(⊥)- ⊖ ≀ ◗. (⊤) (⊥). ∓h ⌡ (⊤)s s.

≀ ◗- In ⫲ ≀. ⊖ ⌡ (⊤). (⊤) (⊥).

(⊤)(⊥)- ∓h ≀ (⊤)s s. || ⫲ (⊤). ⊖ ≀ (⊤).

≀ (⊤)- (⊤) (⊥). ∓h (⊥)s st. In ⫲ Є.

(⊤)(⊥)- (⊤)h i ⫲ Є.

≀ (⊤)- Ѧ ⫲ ≀ rs i ⫲ Є t o @ g ⫲ d; so rses—

(⊤)(⊥)- *** (℞s.)

≀ (⊤)- ∓h (⊤) (⊥) i ⫲ Є, t o @ g ⫲ ::, @ st ⫲ cf at w, gvg thm pr inst fr thr ℔.

(⊤)(⊥)- ⊖ ≀ (⊤), it i m ○ tt ⫲ :: b nw o on ⫲ s ° fr w @ inst. ∓hs cmc t ⫲ ⌡ (⊤) i ⫲ ≀ @ h t ⫲ bn ps, tt hvg d nc thr% th ma gv ths ac.

≀ ⊙- ⋺r ⌡ ⊙.

⌡ ⊙- ⋺r ≀ ⊙.

≀ ⊙- ||t is ⫲ ○ % ⫲ ⊕ ⊕ tt ⫲ :: b nw o on ⫲ s ° fr w @ ins. Ths cmc to ⫲ bn prs tt hvg d nc thr% th m gvn thms ac.

⌡ ⊙- ⋺n, (⋺*n gv* § % *fdlt.*) it is ⫲ ○ % ⫲ ⊙ ⊕, cmc t m thr ⫲ ≀ ⊙ in ⫲ ⊙, tt ⫲ :: b nw op o ⫲ s ° fr wk @ instn. || cmc ⫲ sm t u, tt hvg d nc thr% u m gv urs ac.

⊙ ⊕- ⋺n, at t gvg ⫲ §s; ob ⫲ ⋲.
(§s % ⋲ ⩓ @ ∓c, *tk tm f* ⫲ ⋲.) **

≀ ⊙- ** ⌡ ⊙- **

⊙ ⊕- ⋺r ≀ ⊅, at at ⫲ ⩓.

≀ ⊅- (*$s t* ⊙ *%* ⩓, *gs* § *% fdlt, dspls ls @ rts t hs pl.*)

⊙ ⊕- || nw dcl ⫲ :: dl o on ⫲ s °. ⋺ ⌡ ⊅, inf ⫲ ∓.

⌡ ⊅- *** (∓- ***) ⋺ ∓.

∓- ⋺ ⌡ ⊅.

⌡ ⊅- ∓h :: is o on ⫲ s °. (*₵ls d.*) ⊙ ⊕. ⋺ ⌡ ⊅. ∓h ∓ is inf.

⊙ ⊚- * (≀ *ts* ǂ ::.)

(∓*h* :: *ma b cld fm* ħ *to rfsmt.*)

⊙ ⊚. * Ɔr ⌡ ⊙.

⌡ ⊙- (℞*s.*) ⊙ ⊚.

⊙ ⊚- Çl ǂ crf fm ħ t rff, t rsm ħ at ǂ sd % ǂ gv n ǂ Є.

⌡ ⊙- *** Ɔn, (Ɔ*n, gv* § %*fdl.*) it is ǂ ○ % ǂ ⊙ ⊚ tt u b c f ħ t rfs, t rs ħ at ǂ sd % ǂ g n ǂ Є. *

Ɔr A̧ Ɔ- *** ⊙ ⊚ *

A̧ll (Ç*m to* ○.)

≀ Ↄ- (℞*s.*) ⊙ ⊚.

⊙ ⊚- Ɔr ≀ Ↄ.

≀ Ↄ- ∓hr i an al a ǂ inr d.

⊙ ⊚- A̧t t ǂ a @ asctn ǂ cs.

≀ Ↄ- ***

≀ ⊚%Ç- *

≀ Ↄ- (○*ps d.*) ⊙h cs h.

≀ ⊚%Ç- Ɔ A̧ Ɔ, wh hs bn d in Є A̧, @ nw wshs mr l i ⊚y b bn ps t ǂ °% ∓c.

≀ Ↄ- Ↄ Ⱥ Ↄ, is ths an ac % ur on f w @ a.

Ⱥ Ↄ- It is.

≀ Ð- Ↄ ≀ Ⓐ %₵, is h wh @ w q.

≀ Ⓐ%₵- ♓ i. Ð l @ t pd. ♓ is.

≀ Ð- ♓s h md stb pfc i ǂ pr °.

≀ Ⓐ%₵- ♓ hs.

≀ Ð- Ↄ wt fth r o b ds h xp t obt ths imp prv.

≀ Ⓐ%₵- Ↄf % ǂ p w.

≀ Ð ♓s h ǂ p w.

≀ Ⓐ%₵- ♓ hs n; ‖ hv i fr h.

≀ Ð- Ⱥdv @ g it. (Ð *n.*) ∓h p w is r. ≀ nc ǂ b is i psn % a ths ns qf, lt h wt unt ǂ Ⓣ Ⓐ cn b in % hs rqs @ hs a rt. (₵*l d @ rts t* ǂ Ⱥ.) Ⓣ Ⓐ.

Ⓣ Ⓐ- Ↄr ≀ Ð.

≀ Ð- ∓hr i wtho Ↄ Ⱥ Ↄ, wh hs bn dl in ϵ Ⱥ, @ nw whs m l i Ⓐy b bn ps t ǂ ° % ∓c.

Ⓣ Ⓐ- ‖ it an a % hs ow f w @ a.

≀ Ð- It i. ‖ h wh @ w q. ♓ i.

Ⓣ Ⓐ- Ð @ tr ppd.

≀ Ð - ♓ i.

Ⓣ Ⓐ - ♓s h m stbl pf i ⊣ prc °.

≀ Ð - ♓ hs.

Ⓣ Ⓐ - Ͽ w fth r o b d h xp t ob ths imp pr.

≀ Ð - Ͽf % ⊣ p w.

Ⓣ Ⓐ - ♓ h ⊣ p w.

≀ Ð - ♓ h nt; || h i f hm.

Ⓣ Ⓐ - ₵v i f ⊣ bn % ⊣ cf.

≀ Ð - (₵*s pw.*)

Ⓣ Ⓐ - ∓h p w i rt. ≀ nc Ͽr Ⱥ Ͽ is i psn % al ths ns qf, lt h en ths wf :: % Ŧcs, @ b rc i d @ an f.

Ⓣ Ⓐ - Ⓣhl ⊣ b is stdg i ⊣ Ⓣ, w wl sing ode —, on pg—.

≀ Ð - * (○*ps dr.*) Lt hm en ths w :: % Ŧcs, @ b rc i d @ an f.

Ⓣ Ⓐ - ***

Ȼ- (*Is cdc int* ⊣ :: @ *rc i frt* % ⊣ ≀ Ⓣ, *fc* ⊣ Ͼ.)

≀ Ð - Ͽr Ⱥ Ͽ, wn fs u end a :: % Ŧ @ Ⱥ Ⓐs, u wr rc on ⊣ pt % a sh ins prc ur n l b, ⊣ mr % wh ws thn xp t u.

|| am nw cmd t rc u on +| ngl % a s, ap t ur n r b, wh is t th u tt +| s % vr sh b a rl @ g fr ur prc thr lf.

ⓣⓛ- *

(ⓛ*usic.* ○*de.*)

≀ Þ or Çdtr- (∓*ks ct by r ar @ strs* Є *on* +| *n s %* +| *::. It is gd fm fr* +| ≀ Þ @ ⓛ*ar t wlk tghr, folwd by* +| ⓛs%c, Ɔ*rs ldg cs @* ≀ *twds in* +| *rear.*)

⌡ ⓣ- * ≀ ⓣ- * ⓣⓛ- * ⌡ ⓣ- **

Çhp- "∓hs h shwd m: @ bhl, +| L std upn a wl md b a plm-ln, wh a plml i hs hn."

≀ ⓣ **

Çhp- "Ąnd +| L sd unt m, Ąms, wt sest thu, @ || sd, Ą plm l.

ⓣⓛ- **

Çhp- ∓hn sd +| L, Ɔhl || wl st a plm l in +| mdst % m ppl Isl: || wl nt agn ps b thm an mr:"

≀ Þ- (*In* +| ≀ .) ***

⌡ ⓣ- * (℞*s.*) ⓣh cs hr.

≀ Ð- Ɔ Ѧ Ɔ, wh hs b d ini Ɛ Ѧ, @ nw whs m l i ⊚y b bn ps t +| ° % Ŧc.

⌡ ⊙- Ɔ Ѧ Ɔ, is ths an ac % ur ow f w @ a. It i. Ɔ ≀ Ð, is h wh @ wl q.

≀ Ð- Ӿ i. Ðl @ t ppd. Ӿ i.

⌡ ⊙- Ӿs h md stbl pf i +| pr °.

≀ Ð- Ӿ hs.

⌡ ⊙- Ɔ wt fr r o b ds h xp t obt ths imp prv.

≀ Ð- Ɔ f % +| pw.

⌡ ⊙- Ӿ h +| pw.

≀ Ð- Ӿ h nt; || hv i f h

⌡ ⊙- Ѧdv @ g i. (Ð *n.*) Ŧh p w is r. ≀ nc +| b is i psn % al ths ns qf, cd hm t +| ≀ ⊙ i +| ⊙, fr h ex.

≀ Ð- (*In* +| ⊙.) ***

≀ ⊙- * (℞*s.*) ⊙h cs hr.

≀ Ð- Ɔ Ѧ Ɔ, wh hs b d init Ɛ Ѧ @ nw wsh m l i ⊚y b bn ps t +| ° % Ŧc.

≀ ⊙- Ɔ Ѧ Ɔ, is ths an ac % ur ow f w @ a. It i. Ɔ ≀ Ð, is h wh @ wl q.

≀ ◗ - ⋊ is. ◗l @ tr pd. ⋊ i.

≀ ☉ - ⋊s h md stb pf i ǂ pr °.

≀ Э - ⋊ hs.

≀ ☉ - Э wt fh rt o b d h xp t obt ths imp prv.

≀ ◗ - Эf % ǂ pw.

≀ ☉ - ⋊ h ǂ pw.

≀ Э - ⋊ h nt; || h i f h.

≀ ☉ - Ѧdv @ g i. (◗ *n*.) ∓h pw is r. ≀ nc ǂ b is i psn % a ths ns qf, cdc h t ǂ ☉ ⊕ i ǂ Є, fr hs ex.

≀ ◗ - (|| *n* ǂ Є.) ***

☉ ⊕ - * ☉h cs h.

≀ ◗ - Э Ѧ Э, wh hs bn d init Є Ѧ @ nw whs mr l i ⊕y b bg ps t ǂ ° % ∓c.

☉ ⊕ - Э Ѧ Э, i ths an ac % ur o f w @ ac. It i. Э ≀ Э, is h wy @ w q.

≀ ◗ - ⋊ is. Dl @ t pd. ⋊ is.

☉ ⊕ - ⋊s h md stbl pf i ǂ prc °.

≀ ◗ - ⋊ h.

☉ ⊕ - Э wt fhr r o b ds h xp t ob ths imp prv.

≀ ◗- ⊃f % ⊣ pw.

⊙ ⊖- ♓s h ⊣ pw.

≀ ◗- ♓ hs n; I hv i f h.

⊙ ⊖- ⅍dv @ g i. (*Dn.*) Ŧh pw is r. ⊙hc cm u, @ wthr r u trv.

≀ ◗- Ŧm ⊣ ⊙, trg ⋲.

⊙ ⊖- ⊙y dd u lv ⊣ ⊙ @ tr ⋲.

≀ ◗- In sh % mr l i ⊖y.

⊙ ⊖- Snc ⊣ br is in psn % al ths ncs qf, @ i sh % mr l i ⊖y, rcdct h t ⊣ ≀ ⊙ i ⊣ ⊙, wh wl th hm hw t ap ⊣ ⋲ i d @ an f.

≀ ◗- (*℞cds Ⓒ by mch to ≀ sd % ⊣ ::, l fc, m ⋲; l f, m n; l f, m t w % ⅍; hlt, f ⊣ ≀ ⊙.*) ⊃r ≀ ⊙.

≀ ⊙- ⊃ ≀ ◗.

≀ ◗- It is ⊣ ○ % ⊣ ⊙ ⊖ tt u th ths b hw t ap ⊣ ⋲ in d @ an f.

≀ ⊙- Ⓒs ⊣ b t fc ⊣ ⋲.

≀ ◗- (*Caus b t f* ⋲.)

≀ ⊙- ⊃ ⅍ ⊃, adv o ur l f as ⋲ ⅍; (*Dn*) tk an adl s o u r f, (*Dn*) brg ⊣ h % ur l int ⊣ hol % ur r,

(*Dn*) thby fmg ╫ ngl % an ob, bd er f ╫ Ͼ. Ⓣ ⦹. Ͽ ≀ Ⓣ. ∓h b i in ○.

Ⓣ⦹- Ͽ Ⱥ Ͽ, bf u cn prc fh in Ŧ ⦹y, it wl b ncs fr u t tk a s o aprtng t ╫ ° % Ŧc, @ ||, ⦹s % ╫ ::, asu u thr is nthg thrn cntd wh wl cnfl w ur mrl, scl, o cvl dts o prvs, b th wt thy ma. Ⓣh ths asr-nc, r u wlg t tk ╫ o.

ͿȺͿ- || a.

Ⓣ⦹- ∓hn adv t ╫ sc Ⱥ % Ŧ ⦹y @ k on ur n r k, ur l fmg ╫ ngl % a sq; ur r h rs upn ╫)(Ͽ, ≀ @ Ꞓss, ur l in a vrt psn, ur ar fm a s.

Ꞓdtr or ≀ Ḍ- (*Ꝑlcs* Ꞓ)

≀ Ḍ- Ⓣ ⦹. Ͽ ≀ Ḍ. ∓h br is i d f.

Ⓣ ⦹- ***

Ͽn- (Ŧ*m eq lns drsng to* ╫ Ⱥ)

⦹s%c- (Ꞓ*rct* ╫ *ls as th ps insd @ fm rch at* ╫ Ͼ.)

Ⓣds- (*Wtho clms or escrt, ps insd* ╫ *ls @ tk thr sts und* ╫ *rch.*)

≀ ts- (*Ma fm rch fr* ⦹*ar* Ⓣ % Ⱥ.)

⊙⊙- (*Dcnds t ⩓.*) ⊙ ⩓ ⊙, if u r stl wl t t ⫳ o, sa I, prnc ur n i fl, (₵- I, ⩓ ⊙.) @ rp af m: Of m o f w @ a, in prs % ⩓ ⊙ ₵ @ ths wf :: % ꟻcs, erc t ⋊ @ ddc t ⫳ m % ⫳ ⋊ ≀s ⌡, d hb @ h, s @ sn p @ s, tt ‖ w k @ cl @ n rv an % ⫳ ss bl t ⫳ ° % ꟻc, wh ‖ h rc, am ab t r, or ma hrf b ins i, t an pr, unl i sh b t a wy b ꟻc, o wthn ⫳ bd % a js @ d cn :: % sh; @ nt unt h o thm unt b d trl, stc xm, o lf ⊙c inf, I sh hv fd h o thm js ent t r ⫳ s.

(2) ꟻm, I d p @ s tt I w an @ o al d §s @ r sms st t m f ⫳ b % a j @ d cns :: % ꟻcs, or hd m b a wy br % ths °, if wthn ⫳ ln % m ct @ ⫳ s @ ngl % m w.

(3) Fm, I d p @ s tt I w hlp, ai @ ast a pr @ dst ꟻcs, thy apg t m as sh, I fdg thm wy, @ cn d so wtho mtrl inj t ms.

(4) ₸m, I d p @ s tt I w n wr, ch n df a ₸c :: nr a b % ths ° t ⫲ v % anth, knly, nr sf i t b d b anth, if i m p t pr.

∓ al % wh || d s @ sn p @ s, wtho ny hst, mt rs or sc ev % md i m wte, bg ms un n l a p thn tt % hv m l b tn o, m h @ l tkn thc t ⫲ ∀ % Jhs, @ lf a pr t ⫲ vs % ⫲ a, sh I ev, kn o wf, vl ths m s o % ₸c. ≀ h m, ¢, @ mk m stf t k @ pf ⫲ s.

In tstm % ur snc, k ⫲ ⋊ ⦿ o wh ur h rs. (*Dn*) ⦿r ≀ ◗.

≀ ◗- ⦾ ⦿.

⦾⦿- ℞mv ⫲ ct. (*Dn*) ⦿ b, in ur prs stutn wt d u m ds.

⦿r ⦿- (*Prmptd by* ≀ ◗.) ⦿r l i ⦿y.

⦾⦿- Lt ⫲ b b br t l. (*Dn*) ⦿r ⩓ ⦿, on bn br t l in ths ° u bhl ⫲ ⊤ ¢ ∟s in ⦿y, as i ⫲ prc °, wh ths df: o pt % ⫲ c is ab ⫲ s; wh is t th u tt u h rc, @ r ntld t rc, m l i ⊙y, bt as o p i st hdn f ur vw, it i als t th u tt u r yt o mtl pt i ⊣| d rsp ꟻ ⊙y.

≀ Ð - (*To* Ҁ.) Bhl ⊣| ⊙ ⊙ aphg f ⊣| Ɛ, on ⊣| s, (*Tkn*) un ⊣| d, (*Gv*) @ § (*Gv*) % Ɛ Ѧ; o ⊣| s (*Tkn*) un ⊣| d (*Gv*) @ § (*Gv*) % ꟻc.

⊙⊙- ⊙y b, a ꟻc advs o hs r f, (Ѧ*d*) brng ⊣| h % hs l int ⊣| ho % h r, (*Dn*) thb fg ⊣| a % an o. Ths i ⊣| d (*Gs i*) @ al t ⊣| ps % u hs w tg ⊣| o; ths i ⊣| § (*Gs*) @ al t ⊣| p % ⊣| o. Ths d (*Gs*) @ § (*Gs*) r als t b gv as a sltn t ⊣| ⊙ ⊙ on ent o rt f a ꟻc ::.

Ð r Ð, bf rs f ⊣| Ѧ whr u hv tk ⊣| s o % ꟻc, I wl cl ur at t on % its ts. U hv sw tt u wl ans @ ob al d §s @ r sms st t u fm ⊣| b % a j @ d cnst :: % ꟻc, or hd u b a w b % ths °, if wth ⊣| l % ur ct @ ⊣| s @ ngl % ur w. Th lth % ur ct als t ur ablt t ob a sm, @ ⊣| s @ a % ur w, t ⊣| prpt % ans §s. Shd u rc a sm f ths o ny oth ::, hlth @ bsns prmtg, i wd b ur dt t ob i; hlh or b ṇt pmtg, i wd n b wthn ⊣| lh % ur ct. Shd u c a ◓c § gv at wt u dm an impr tm, or an imp plc, u r· nt bnd t ans i; it wd nt b wthn ⊣| s @ ngl % ur w. ◓y b, ur on gd jg-mt mst th u wn @ wr t ans ◓c §s.

I nw pr m r h i t % cntunc % fs @ bl l, @ wl inv u wh ⊣| pg, pw, r g @ w, bt as u r unins, h wh hs hthrt ans f u wl at ths t. Gv m ⊣| g % ∈ Δ. (*Gv.*) ∋ ≀ ◗.

≀ ◗- ◒ ◓. ◒ u b o o f. Ŧ.

◒ ◓- Ŧm w @ t w.

≀ ◗- F ⊣| g % ∈ Δ t ⊣| pg % Ŧc.

◒ ◓- ♇. (*Dn*) ◒ i tt.

≀ ◗- Th pg % Ŧc.

◒ ◓- ♓s i a nm. It hs. ◒l u g i t m.

≀ ☽- I dd n s r i, nth w || s i i.

⊙ ⊖- ♓ wl u ds % i.

≀ ☽- L or s i.

⊙ ⊖- ≀ i @ b. U b. ☽ u.

≀ ☽- (*Bgs—gvn.*)

⊙ ⊖- ⊙l u b o o f. ⊤. ⊤ w @ t w.

≀ ☽- F ⊣ pg % ⊤c t ⊣ r g % ⊣ s.

⊙ ⊖- ♇. (*Dn.*) ⊙t i tt.

≀ ☽- ⊤h r g % ⊤c.

⊙ ⊖- ♓s i a n. It h. ⊙ u g i t m.

≀ ☽- || dd n s r i, nth w I s i i.

⊙ ⊖- ♓w w u ds % i.

≀ ☽- L o h i. Lt i @ b. U b.

⊙ ⊖- ☽g u. (*Gv*) — is ⊣ n % ths g, @ shd alw b gv i ths cts mnr, b lt or hvg. ⊙n ltg, alws cm wh ⊣ l— (*Ads* Ͼ) ℞s, sl ⊣ ⌡ @ ≀ ⊙s, @ sfy thm tt u r i psn % ⊣ st, dg, §, pg, pw, rl g @ wd % ⊤c.

○fs- (*℞t t sts.* ⊙ ⊖- *To* ⊣ ⋲.)

☽n- (*Tk sts.*)

≀ ☽- (*Ͼds Ͼ drct t* ⌡ ⊙*s sta, on* ⊣ *st %* ⊤*c.*) ***

J ⊙- * (℞s) ⊙h cs h. A wy b ⊤c.
⋊w ma || k h t b sh.
⊙ cr §s @ ts. ⊙t r §s.
≀ ◗- ℞ ans, hrz @ prpds.
Ad a §. (≀ ◗ @ ⊙- ⊕*v dg.*)
⋊s tt an als.
It h; t ⊣ p % m hs wh t ⊣ o.
⋊v u a f §. || h. (≀ ◗ @ *b gv* §.)
⋊s tt an al.
It h; t ⊣ p % ⊣ o. ⊙t r tns.
≀ ◗- Crt fdl or bl gs whb o ⊙ ma k anth i ⊣ d as i ⊣ l.
J ⊙- Ad @ g m a t.
≀ ◗ @ C- (*Adv o* ⊣ *s %* ⊤*c @ gn g; cses* C*s t gv i t eh oth.*)
J ⊙- ⊙t i tt. ⊤h pg % ⊤c. ⋊s i a nm. It h. ⊙l u g i t m.
≀ ◗- I dd n s r i, n w I s i i.
J ⊙- ⋊w w u ds % i.
L or s i. S i @ b. U b. ⊙ u.
≀ ◗- (*Bgs—pw gvn.*) 3
J ⊙- ⊙l u b o o f. ⊤. ⊤ w @ t w.
≀ ◗- F ⊣ pg % ⊤c t ⊣ r g % ⊣ s

⌡ ⊙- ℟. (*Dn.*) ⊙t i tt.

≀ Ɔ- ₣h r g % ₣c.

⌡ ⊙- ♓s i a n. It hs. ⊙l u g i t m.

≀ ◗- || dd n s r i, nh w I s i i.

⌡ ⊙- ♓w w u ds % i.

≀ ◗- L o h i. L i @ b. U b.

⌡ ⊙- Ɔg u. (*Dn*) || am sfd.

≀ ◗- (*In* ⊙, Ꝕ *on st* % ₣*c.*)

≀ ⊙ * (℞) ⊙ c h. ₳ w b ₣c.

♓w m || k h t b sh. Ɔ cr §s @ tns.

⊙t r §s. ℞t ngs, hrzs @ pdlrs.

₳d a §. (≀ ◗ @ Ꝕ *gv dg.*)

♓s tt a al.

It h; t ⫞ p % m h wl tg ⫞ o.

♓v u a f §. || h. (≀ ◗ @ Ꝕ *g* §.)

♓s tt an als. It hs; t ⫞ p % ⫞ o.

⊙t r tns.

Ꝕr fdl or bl gs whb o ⊕ m k anth i ⫞ d a i ⫞ l. ₳d @ g m a t.

≀ ⦿ @ ₵- (∆*d o* ⊣ *st* % ⊤*c* @ *gv g; caus* ₵*s t g i t eh o.*) ⊙t i tt.

∓h pg % ⊤c. ⋈s i a n. I h.

⊙l u g i t m.

‖ dd n s r i, nh w I s i i.

⋈w w u ds % i. L o s i.

≀ ⊙- ≀ i @ b. U b. ⊖ u. (₵*v.*)

⊙l u b o o f. ⊤. F w @ t w.

⊤ ⊣ pg % ⊤c t ⊣ r g % ⊣ s.

₱. (*Dn*) ⊙t is tt.

∓h r g % ⊤c. ⋈s i a n. I h.

⊙ u g i t m.

‖ dd n s rc i, nh w i s i i.

⋈w wl u ds % i.

L o h i. L i @ b. U b.

⊖g u. (*Gv*) ‖ am sfd.

≀ ⦿- (₵*ds* ₵ ⊖, *on* ₽ *sd* % ⊣ ::. ⊙*n nr* ⊣ ∆—)

⊙ ⊙- * ⊖r ≀ ⦿.

≀ ⦿- ⊙ ⊙.

⊙ ⊙- ℞cdc ⊣ b t ⊣ ≀ ⊙ i ⊣ ⊙, wh w th h hw t wr hs a as ⊤c.

≀ Ↄ- (*Cndc* Ꞔ *t* ⫞ ⊙, @ *nr* ≀ ⊙.) Ↄr ≀ ⊙.

≀ ⊙- Ↄr ≀ Ↄ.

≀ Ↄ- It i ⫞ ○ % ⫞ ⊙ ⊙ tt u th ths b hw t wr h a as ⊦c.

≀ ⊙- (∓*cks up l c % a on* Ꞔ.) Ↄr ⩓ Ↄ, u hv alrdy bn inf tt at ⫞ bl % Ꝁ ≀ ∓ ⫞ df bds % wkm wr ds-tgshd b ⫞ mnr in wh thy wr thr as. ⊦cs wr thrs wh ⫞ l c tk up; thus wr urs unt fhr advcd.

≀ Ↄ- (Ꞔ*ds* Ꞔ *t* ⫞ ⊖.)

⊙⊙- ⊙y br, as u r nw cl as ⊦c, I prs u, mblmtcly, ⫞ w tls, wh r ⫞ ₿, ≀ @ ∟, @ r thu xpld:

∓h ₿ is an ins usd b op ⊙s t tr pndlrs, ⫞ ≀ t sq thr wk, @ ⫞ Lv t prv hztls; bt w, as ∓ @ ⩓ ⊙s, r tgt t us thm f m nbl @ gls prps. Th ₿ admns us t wk uprtly i or sv sts bfr ₵ @ m, sqg ou acns b ⫞ sq

% vrt, ev rmbg tt w r trvg upn ⊣ ⌊v % ∓m, t "tt undscvd cnt fm whs brn no trvl rtns."

‖ als prs u t prs jls, wh r ⊣ atn er, ⊣ ins tg, @ ⊣ fhl brs, wh tch us ths imp lsn. Th Ⱥt Єr rcs ⊣ sd fm ⊣ Instv ∓, @ ⊣ msts % Ŧ-Ⓛy r sfl ldgd in ⊣ rpst % ⊣ Ŧfl Ɔst. Ɔr ≀ Ð.

≀ Ð- Ⓣ Ⓛ.

ⓉⓁ- ℞cd ⊣ b t ⊣ pl whc h cm, inv h wh tt % wh h hs b dvs, @ rt h t a pl rpstg ⊣ Ⓛ Ç % Ꝁ ≀ ∓.

Ⓛs%c- (*Prcd t ⊣ Ⱥ, stg aprt.*)

≀ Ð- (*♅ls Ç bt thm @ tks hs pl.*)

Ç@Ⓛs%c- (*Sl; l f, mh t pr r; in-vs ⊣ br @ wn rdy gv alm.*)

ⓉⓁ- * Ɔ ⌡ Ⓣ.

⌡ Ⓣ- Ⓣ Ⓛ.

ⓉⓁ- Çl ⊣ cf f ℔ t rf, t rs ℔ at ⊣ sd % ⊣ g in ⊣ Є.

⌡ ⊙- *** ⊃n, (⊃*n gv § % fdlt.*) it is ⊣⊢ ○ % ⊣⊢ ⊙ ⊙ tt u b cld f ℔ t rf, to rs ℔ at ⊣⊢ sd % ⊣⊢ g in ⊣⊢ ⋲.

(*At refreshment.*)

—○—

SECOND SECTION

MIDDLE CHAMBER LECTURE

⊙s%c- (⊙*n* Ҁ*s r rdy.*) ***

⊙ ⊙- * (*Calls* ⊣| :: *t* ○.)

≀ Ɔ- (Ҁ*dcs* ⊣| Ҁ *insd % d @ bgs:*)

∓h scd sctn % ths ° hs rfrnc t ⊣| orgn % ⊣| instn, @ vws ⊙y und tw dnmntns—○prtv @ Spcltv.

Ɔy ○p ⊙y w ald t a ppr aplctn % ⊣| usfl rls % rchtctr, wnc a stcr wl derv fgr, str @ bty, @ wnc wl rsult a du prptn @ a js crspdc i al its pts. It frnshs us wh dwlgs @ cnvnt shltr fm ⊣| vcstds @ inclm % ssns; @ whl it dpls ⊣| efcts % hmn wsd, as wl in ⊣| chc as in ⊣| arngmt % ⊣| sndy mtrls % wh an edfc i cmpsd, it dmnsts tt a fnd % scnc @ inds i impltd i mn fr ⊣| bst, mst salutary @ bnfc prps

119–3

Ↄy Spc or Ŧ ⊙y w ln t sbdu +| psns, act upn +| sq, kp a tg % gd rpt, mntn scrcy @ prc chrty. It is s far intrwvn wh rlgn as t la us und oblgn t pa tt homg t Ↄ, wh at onc cnstus dty @ ou hpns. It lds +| cntm-pltv t vw, wh rvnc @ admrn, +| gl wks % crtn, @ insprs thm wh +| mst xltd ides % +| pfctn % thr Ↄv Çratr.

Th sc sctn % ths ° als rfs t +| org % +| ⌡ Sbth, as wl as to +| mnr in wh i ws kp b ou an bn.

In sx ds ₲ cr +| hv @ +| eth, @ rst on +| svth da. Ŧh sv, thrfr, ou anc bn cnsc as a da % rs fm thr ŧb, [thb njyg frqnt optnts t cntmplt +| gls wks % crn @ t ad thr g Çrtr.]

Ⱥt +| bldg % Ꝁ ʅ Ŧ thr wr egty ths Ŧcs mpld. Ŧhs wr al und +| imdt drc % ou anc op ₲ ⊙ ж Ⱥ. On +| ev % +| sx da thr wk ws in-spcd, @ al ths wh hd prvd thsl wth, b stc fdlty t thr dts, wr invsd wh crtn mst §s, gps @ ws, t enabl thm t gn adms int ⊣| ⊙ Ç % Ꝁ ≀ ∓. On ⊣| sm da @ hr Ꝁ ≀, acmpd b hs cnfdl ofcs, cnstg % hs Sc, ⊣| ≀ @ ȷ ⊕ds, rprd t ⊣| ⊙ Ç t mt thm. ℋs Sc h plcd nr hs prsn, ⊣| ≀ ⊕ at ⊣| inr @ ⊣| ȷ ⊕ at ⊣| otr dr, gvg thm stc instc t sfr nn t ent xcp sh as wr in psn % crt ⊙st §s, gs, @ ws prvsly estb; s tt wn ny dd ent, h, kng tt thy mst hv bn fthfl wkmn or th cld nt hv gnd adm, hd nthg t d bt ○d thr nms rcrdd as sh @ pa th hr ws, wh th rc in cn, wn @ oi, em % nrsh, rfs @ jy; @ af smly admsh thm % ⊣| rvnc du ⊣| gr @ sc nm % Ġ, sfrd thm t dprt i pc unt ⊣| tm shd arv fr cmc ⊣| flg wks wk. Ths, u wl prcv, ws al acmpl on ⊣| evg % ⊣| sx da, tt n unscy ℔ mt b pfm on ⊣| svth.

⊕, my b, r i psn % ⊣| sm msts §s, gs @ ws as wr ou anc bn, @ r nw ab t ndv t wk ou wa int a plc rpstg ⊣ ⊙ Ȼ % ꓘ ≀ ∓, @ shd w scd ǁ hv n dbt w wl b alk rc @ rwd.

THE PILLARS

In dng ths i wl b nsc fr us t mk an adv, emblty, thro a prch, up a flt % wng strs, cnstg % thr, fv @ sv sts, thro an otr @ an inr dr. In mkg ths adv w ncsl ps btw tw plrs, rpstg ths fams pls erc at ⊣ ntrc t ⊣ prch % ꓘ ≀ ∓, one on ⊣ r hd, ⊣ oth on ⊣ lf. Th nm % ⊣ o on ⊣ l hd ws ⊳, dntg str; ⊣ nm % ⊣ on o ⊣ rt, ⌡, dntg estblhmt, clctvl aldg t svrl prms % ȼ t ⊳, on % wh rds: "And thin hse @ thy kgdm shl b estb frev bfr th."

Thos tw plrs wr thrty @ fv cubts hi, @ ⊣ chptr tt ws on ⊣ tp % eh % thm ws fv cbts—in al frty cbts.

[∓h cmpstn ws % mltn or cst brs, ⊣ btr t wthstn inundtn or cnflgtn;

tt thy mt nt b rmvd b fld nr cnsmd b fir. Thy wr cst in ⊣| clay grs on ⊣| bnk % ⊣| rvr ⌡, btw Scth @ Zrd, whr Ꝁ ≀ ○d ths @ al ⊣| scrd vsls % ⊣| ∓ t b cst; th wr cst hlo fr ⊣| prps % cntg ⊣| rls @ rcds wh cmpsd ⊣| archvs % ou anc bn.]

Th chptrs wr ornmtd wh lvs % lly-wk, nt-wk, @ chns % pmgrnt. Th lly, fm its xtrm whtns, as wl as ⊣| rtrd situns i wh i grs, dnts pc; ⊣| nt-wk, fm ⊣| intm conctn % al its prts, un; @ ⊣| pmgt, fm ⊣| xubnc % its sd, plnt.

PEACE, UNITY AND PLENTY

(Ꝑc, tt hr on ⊣| brd pltfm % br lv, ⊣| hi, ⊣| lo, ⊣| rch, ⊣| pr, ma mt tghr wh on cmn prps, ⊣| prptuatn % eh oths frnsh @ eh os lv.

(Unt, bg lk tgr b a chn % scr frs.

(Ꝑlnty, tt tho it ma b gvn t sm t hv mr % ⊣| wlds gs thn oths, stl ⊣| mn tt has hs hlth, strgh @ ambtn hs indd hs plty.)

GLOBES

∓hs plrs r srmtd b t artf sphrl bds, on ╫ srfc % wh r rpsd ╫ cntrs, ses @ vrs pts % ╫ e, ╫ fc % ╫ hv, @ ╫ plt rv.

Çntmpg ths bds, w r inspd wh rv fr ₲ @ hs wks, @ r encrgd to stdy astrmy, geo, nvgn, @ ╫ rts dp upn t, b wh mnkd hs bn s mh bftd.

[Thr prncpl us, bsds srvg as mps to dstngh ╫ otwd prs % ╫ eth, @ ╫ stitun % ╫ fxd strs, is t ilst @ xpln ╫ phomna arsg fm ╫ anul rvltn % ╫ eth arn ╫ sn @ ╫ dirnl rotn % ╫ eth upn its ow axis. Th r invlbl ins fr imprvg ╫ mnd, gvg it ╫ ms dst ide % ny prblm or prpsn as wl as enblg i t slv ╫ sm.]

⊙e wl nw mk an adv, @ ascd ╫ t s⁺s. (*Ps btw ╫ plrs @ tk t stps.*)

∓h t sts ald t ╫ t prc jls: ╫ atv Є, ╫ inst ∓ @ ╫ fthfl ⊙, wh hv alrd bn xpl t u; th als ald t ⊣ t prn ofs % ⊣ ::, ⊣ ⓣ ⓛ in ⊣ ⅁, ⊣ ≀ ⓣ in ⊣ ⓣ, @ ⊣ ȷ ⓣ in ⊣ ≀.

ⓣe wl nw mk a fr advc @ asnd ⊣ f sts. (*Tks f sts.*)

Th f sts ald t ⊣ f ○s % arctr, @ ⊣ f hu sns.

ORDERS IN ARCHITECTURE

Ↄy ○ in Ą is mt a sys % al ⊣ mbrs, pprs @ ors % cls @ pilts: or, it is a rgl arng % ⊣ prjg pts % a bldg, wh, untd wh ths % a cl, fm a btfl, pfc @ cpl w.

Ɐm ⊣ fs fmatn % scty, ○ i Ą ma b trcd. ⓣn ⊣ rgr % sns oblgd mn t cntrv shltr fm ⊣ inclmc % ⊣ wthr, w ln tt thy fst plntd trs on end, @ thn ld oths acrs, t spt a cvrg. Th bnds wh cnctd thos trs at top @ btm r sd t hv gvn rs t ⊣ ida % ⊣ bas @ cptl % plrs; @, fm ths smp hnt, orgnl prcd ⊣ mr imprvd art % artctr.

Th f ○s r ths clsd: ⊣ ∓sc, Ↄrc, Ionc, Ꞔrnthn @ Ꞔmpst.

TUSCAN

(Th ∓scn is ⊣ mst smpl @ sld % ⊣ f ○s. It ws invtd i ∓scny, wnc it drvs its nm. Its clm is sv diamts hi; @ its cptl, bas, @ ntbltur hv bt fw mldgs. Th smplct % ⊣ cnstcn % ths clm rndrs it elgbl whr onmt wd b suprfls.

DORIC

(Th Ↄrc, wh is pln @ ntrl, is ⊣ mst anct, @ ws invtd b ⊣ ₲rks. Its clm is egt dimtrs hi, @ hs sldm ny onmts on bs o cptl, xcp mldgs; tho ⊣ frez is dstg by triglyphs @ metopes, @ triglyphs cmps ⊣ onmts % ⊣ frez. Th sld cmpsn % ths ○ gs i a prfnc in strcrs whr strgh @ a nbl smplct r dsrd. ∓h Ↄrc is ⊣ bst proprtnd % al ⊣ ○s. Th svrl prts % wh it is cmpsd r fndd on ⊣ natrl psn % sold bods.

IONIC

(∓h Ionc brs a knd % mn prprtn btw ⊣| mr sld @ ⊣| mr dlct ○s. Its clm is nne diamtrs hi; its captl is adrnd wh voluts, @ its crnic hs dntls. Thr r bth delcy @ ingnuty dsplyd in ths plr, ⊣| invntn % wh is atrbtd t ⊣| Ionians. ∓h fams tmpl % Diana, at ⋲phesus, ws % ths ○.

CORINTHIAN

(∓h Çrnthn, ⊣| rchst % ⊣| f ○s, is dmd a mstrpc % rt. Its clm is tn diamts hi, @ its cptl is adrnd wh to rws % lvs, @ egt voluts, wh sstn ⊣| abacus. ∓h frez i ornmtd wh curs dvics, ⊣| crnc wh dntls @ mdilins. Ths ○ is usd in ornt strctrs.

COMPOSITE

(Th cmps is cmpnd % ⊣| oth ○s @ ws cntrvd by ⊣| Ꞧmns. Its cptl hs ⊣| tw ro % lvs % ⊣| Çrnthn @ ⊣| vluts % ⊣| Ionc. Its clm hs qrtr-rds, as hv +| ∓s @ ◗rc ○s; it is tn dia hi, @ its cornc hs dntls, or smpl modlns. ∓hs plr is gnrl fnd i bldgs whr str, elgnc @ bty r dsplyd.)

∓h anct @ orgnl ○s % arctur, rvrd by ⊙s, r thr, +| Drc, Ionc, @ Çrthn, wh wr invd b +| ₲rks.

∓ thes +| ℞oms hv add tw, +| ∓scn, wh thy md plnr thn +| Drc, @ +| Çmpst, wh is mr ornmtl thn +| Çrnthn.

[∓h fst thr ○s aln, hwev, sho invtn @ prtcl chrctr, @ essntly dfr fm ech oth; +| tw othrs hv nthng bt wt is brwd, @ difr onl acdtly; +| ∓scn is +| Drc in its erlst stat, @ +| Çomps is +| Çrnth enrchd wh +| Ionc. ∓o +| ₲reks, thrfr, @ nt t +| ℞omns, w r ind fr wt i gt, judcs @ dstc i arctr.]

HUMAN SENSES

∓h f hmn snss r ⋊rng, Sng, ⊤lg, Smlng, @ ∓stg. ∓h fst thr % wh hv ev bn dmd prerqst t bng md a ⊙; fr b hrng w dstngh +| w, ≀ ; by seng w prcv +| §, (*Gv d* % ∓c.) @ by flg w rcv tt fndl or brthl grp (*Gv gp.*) whb on ⊙ ma kn anth i +| dk as in +| lt.

HEARING

[ӿrng is tt snc b wh w distg sds, @ r cpbl % enjyg al +| agbl chrms % musc. ⊙y it w r nbld t njy +| pls % socit, @ rcprcly to cmunct t eh oth ou thots @ intns, ou prps @ dsrs; @ thus ou rsn i rndrd cpbl % xrtng its utmst pwr @ nrgy. ∓h wis @ bnfct Ʌuth % Ɲtr intd b +| frmtn % ths sns tt w shd b socl crtrs, @ rcv +| grtst @ mst mprtnt prt % ou knl fm socl ntrcrs wh eh oth. ⊤r ths prps w r endwd wh hrng, tt, by a prpr xrtn % ou rtnl pwrs, ou hpins ma b cmplt. 3

SEEING

[Seng is tt sns b wh w dstgh objcs, @ i an instnt % tm, wth chng % plc or stutn, vw arms in btl ara, +| mst statl strcs, @ al ╪ agrb vrit dspld in ╪ lndscp % ntr. Ↄy th sns w find ou wa on ╪ pthls ocn, trvrs ╪ glb % eth, dtrm its figr @ dmnss, @ dlnat an regn o qrtr % it.

[Ↄy it w msr ╪ plnty orbs, @ mk nw dscvrs in ╪ sphr % ╪ fxd strs. Ŋa, mr, by i w prcv ╪ tmps @ dspns, ╪ psns @ afctns % ou flwcrtrs, whn th wsh mst t cncl thm; so tt, tho ╪ tng ma b tgt t li @ dsmbl, ╪ cntnc wl dspl ╪ hpcrcy t ╪ dscrng ey. In fin, ╪ ras % lt wh admnstr t ths sns, r ╪ mst astnshng prts % ╪ anmtd cratn, @ rndr ╪ ey a pculr obj % ad.

[Of al ╪ fclts, sht is ╪ nblst. Ŧh strctr % ╪ ey, @ its aprntcs, evnc ╪ admrbl cntrvncs % ntr fr pfmng al its vars xtrnl @ intnl motns; whl ╪ vrty dspld i ╪ eys % dfrt anmls, std t thr sval wys % lf, clrly dmnsts ths orgn t b ╪ mstr pc % ntr's wk.

FEELING

[∓lng i tt sns by wh w dstng ⊣| dfrnt qlts % bds, sh as heat @ cld, hrdns @ sftns, rfns @ smthns, figur, sldty, mtn @ xtnsn.

SMELLING

[Smlg is tt sns b wh w dstgn ods; ⊣| vrs knds % wh cnvy dfrt mprsns t ⊣| mnd. Ạnml @ vgtbl bds, @ indd mst oth bds, whl xpsd t ⊣| air, cntuly snd frth eflva % vst sublt, as wl in a stt % lf @ grth as in ⊣| stat % frmtn @ putriftn. ∓hs efllva, bng drwn int ⊣| nstrls alng wh ⊣| air, r ⊣| mns b wh al bds r dstngsd. ⋊nc it i evdt tt thr i a mnfst aprnc % dsgn in ⊣| grt Ҫrats hvg plntd ⊣| orgn % sml in ⊣| insd % tt cnl thro wh ⊣| air cntnly pss in rsprtn.

TASTING

[∓stng nbls us t mk a ppr dstcn in ⊣| chc % ou fd. ∓h orgn % ths sns grds ⊣| ntrnc % ⊣| alimty cnl, as tt % sml gds +| ntrc % +| cnl fr rsprtn. Ŧm +| situn % bth ths orgns, it i pln tt th wr intnd by ntr t distg whlsm fd fm tt wh is nauss. Ɛvrthg tt ntrs int +| stmc mst undrg +| scty % tstng, @ b it w r cpbl % dscrng +| chngs wh +| sm bdy undrg i +| dfrnt cmpsn % art, cokry, chmstry, phrmcy, @ s fth.

[Smlng @ ∓stg r inspbly cnctd, @ it is by +| unatrl knd % lf mn cmnl ld in socty tt thes sns r rndrd ls fit t prfm thr ntrl ofcs.

[∓h ppr us % thes f sns enbls us t fm jst @ acrt ntns % +| oprtns % ntr; @ whn w rflc on +| objcs wh wh ou sns r grtfd, w bcm cnscus % thm, @ r nabld t atnd t thm, til th bcm fmlr objc % thot.

[On +| mnd al ou knlg mst dpnd; wt thfr, cn b a mr ppr sbjc fr +| invstgtn % ⊙s.

[∓o sm up +| whl % ths trnscdt msr % ₵s bnty t mn, w shl add tt ⊙mry,

Imgntn, ∓st, ℞snng, ⍝rl ℘rcptn, @ al ⊣ actv pwrs % ⊣ sol, prsnt a vst @ bndls fld fr phlsopcl dsqstn, wh fr xcds humn inqry, @ r pculr msts, kn onl t ntr @ t ntrs ₲, t whm al r indtd fr cratn, prsvtn, @ evy blsg w njy.]

⍝ wl nw mk a stl fthr adv @ asn ⊣ sv stps. (⩚*dv.*)

ARTS AND SCIENCES

∓h svn lbrl rts @ scncs, r ₲ram, ℞hetc, Lgc, ⩚rth, ₲mt, ⍝sc, @ ⩚st.

GRAMMAR

(₲-mr is ⊣ scnc wh tchs us hw to xprs ou ids i crct lng, wh w aftrwds butfy @ adrn by mns % ℞htrc; whl Lgc instrcts us hw to thnk @ rsn wh prpty.

RHETORIC

(It is by ℞htc tt elgc % dctn is tgt. ∓o b an elqnt spkr, i fr fm bg ethr a cmn or an esy atnmnt; it is ⊣ rt

% bng prsuasv @ cmndng; +| art, nt onl % plsng +| fncy, bt % applg bth to +| undrstndg @ t +| hrt.

LOGIC

(∟ogc is tt scinc wh tchs us hw to fm clr @ dstnct ids, @ prvnts us bng misld by smltd or rsmblncs. ∓hs sc shd b cltvtd as +| fndtn or grndwk % ou inqrs; prtclrly in +| stdy % ths sblm prncpls wh clm ou attn as ⍝s.

ARITHMETIC

(Ⱥrth i +| scn % nmbrs, or tt brnch % mthmtcs wh cnsds +| prprts % nmbs in gnrl. ⊙e hv bt a vry imprfct ide % thngs wthot qntty, @ as imprfct an ide % qntty itslf wthot +| ad % Ⱥrth. Ⱥl +| wks % +| Ⱥlm r xprsd in nmbr, wght, @ msr; thrfr, to undrstnd thm rghtly, we oght to undrstd arthmtcl clcultns; @ +| grtr +| advncmnt we mk in +| mthmtcl scncs, +| mr cpabl w shl b % cnsdrng sch thngs as r +|

ordnry sbjcs % ou cncptn, @ b thrby ld t a bttr knwlg % ou grt Çratr, @ ⊣⊢ wks % Ӿs cratn.

GEOMETRY

Ģmt trts % ⊣⊢ prs @ prpts % mgtds in gnrl, whr lgth, brdth, @ thkns r cnsdrd—fm a pt to a ln, fm a ln to a sprfics, @ fm a suprfics to a sld.

A pt i tt wh hs pstn, bt nt mgntd, @ is ⊣⊢ bgnng % al gmtrcl mttr.

A ln hs lgth wht brdth.

A surfc is tt wh hs lgth @ brdth wthot thkns.

A sld i a mgntd wh hs lgth, brdth, @ thkns.

Ͽy ths scnc ⊣⊢ archtct is enbld to cnstrct hs plns @ xcut hs dsgns; ⊣⊢ gnrl, to arrng hs sldrs; ⊣⊢ engnr, to mk ou grnds fr ncmpmts; ⊣⊢ gogphr, to gv us ⊣⊢ dmnsns % ⊣⊢ wrld, @ al thngs thrn cntnd, t dlneat ⊣⊢ xtnt % ses, @ spcfy ⊣⊢ dvsns % mprs, kngds,

@ prvcs. Ↄy it, als, ⊣ astrnmr is enbld to mk hs obsrvtns, @ to fix ⊣ durtn % tms @ ssns, yrs @ ccls.

ORGAN

(*Ŧh Orgnst wl nw cmnc plng wh trmolo, as sft as psbl, grduly incrsg @ dmnshg untl ⊣ wd "war," thn pla ⊣ chrs % "Ŧh Str Spngld Ↄnr" wth fl orgn; thn vry sft untl ⊣ wds "plntv strn," thn ply fr lns % "Ӿm Swt Ӿm," wh trmlo; thn vry sft @ plntv untl ⊣ wd "unvrs," whn ⊣ ntir :: wl unt i sngng "Ↄe thou O Ꞡod," etc., tun "Old Ӿundrd."*)

MUSIC

(⊙usc is tt scnc wh afcts ⊣ pssns by snd. Ŧhr r fw wh hv nt flt its chms, @ aknldgd its xprssns t b intlgbl to ⊣ hrt. It is a lnguge % dltfl snstns, fr mr elqnt thn wds; it brths to ⊣ ear ⊣ clrst intmtns; it tchs @ gntl agtts ⊣ agrebl @ sblm pssns; it wrps us in mlncly, @ elvts u in jy; it dsslvs @ inflms; it mlts us in tndrns, @ xcts us to wr: (*Orgn-Str Spn Ͽ nr.*)

(∓h mrtl strns % ntnl airs hrd on ⊣| fld % btl hv thrld ⊣| sldr's hrt, csng hm to brn wh an emuls dsr to ld ⊣| prils advnc, @ anmtg hm to dds % hric vlor @ sblm dvtn; amdst ⊣| ror % cnon, ⊣| dn % msktry, @ ⊣| crnge % batl, h snks to ⊣| dst; rsng hmslf to tk on lng, lst lk % lf, h hrs in ⊣| dstnc tt plntv strn:

(*Home Sweet Home.*)

(Ạn ⊣| mlwng tds % old cthdrl airs vbrtng thro ails @ rchs hv stild ⊣| rufld spt, @ swpg aw ⊣| dscrdnt psns % mn, hv born thm alng its rsistls curnt, untl thr untd vocs hv jnd in sndg ald ⊣| chrs % ⊣| hvn-brn anthm,

"℘c on eth, gd wl twd mn."

(Ͽt it nv snds wh sh serphc hrmn, as whn mplyd i singg hms % gratud to ⊣| Ḉratr % ⊣| U.)

ⓣ ⓐ- ***

ⓗ rn- (*Sng*)

Be Thou, O God, exalted high,
And as Thy glory fills the sky
So let it be on earth displayed,
Till Thou art here, as there, obeyed.

ⓣ ⓐ- * (*Sts* ::.)

ASTRONOMY

(Astrm is tt scnc wh trts % ⊣ hvnl bds, thr motns, mgntuds, distncs, @ physcl cnstuns. ℋw elqnt % Dty is ⊣ clstl hmsphr, spngld wh ⊣ mst mgfcnt hrlds % hs infnt glry! ∓hy spk t ⊣ whl unvrs, fr thr i no ppl s barbs as t fl t undst thr lngug, nr ntn s dstnt tt thr vcs r nt hd am th.)

"The spacious firmament on high,
With all the blue ethereal sky,
And spangled heavens, a shining frame,
Their great Original proclaim.

"Th' unwearied sun from day to day
Does his Creator's praise display,
And publishes to every land
The work of an Almighty Hand.

"Soon as the evening shades prevail,
The moon takes up the wonderous tale,
And nightly, to the listening earth,
Repeats the story of her birth;

"While all the stars around her burn,
And all the planets in their turn
Confirm the tidings as they roll,
And spread the truth from pole to pole.

"What though in solemn silence all
Move 'round the dark terrestrial ball;
What though no voice nor minstrel sound
Among their radiant orbs be found;

"With saints and angels they rejoice,
And utter forth their glorious voice;
Forever singing as they shine,
'The hand that made us is Divine.'"— *Addison*

⊙y br, w r nw aprchg a plc rpsng ⊣⊢ otr dr to ⊣⊢ ⊙ ⚳ % ☧ ≀ ∓, wh w shl fnd prtl op, bt clsly tld by ⊣⊢ J ⊙, wh wl dmd % us ⊣⊢ pw % ∓c. Lt us adv @ mk a rg a.

≀ ⊅ - (*In* ⊣⊢ ≀ .) ***

J ⊙- * (℞*s.*) ⊙h c h.

≀ ⊅ - ∓w ∓cs, ndv t wk thr w int a plc rps ⊣⊢ ⊙ ⚳ % ☧ ≀ ∓.

⌡ ⊙- ⋊w d u xp t gn ad.

≀ ⋑- ⋑y ⫲ p % a Ŧc. ¢v i. ≀.
⊙t ds i dnt. ₱ln.

⌡ ⊙- ⋊w rpstd.

≀ ⋑- ⋑y a shf % c, sspdd nr a wfd, wh ths us tt whl w hv brd t et @ pr rng wt t d, w hv al tt ntr rqrs.

⌡ ⊙- ⋑y whm ws ths pw instd.

≀ ⋑- ⋑r ⌡, a ⌡g % Is, in a wr wh ⫲ ⋲phrs. Ŧh ⋲phrs hd lg bn a stbn @ rblus ppl, whm ⌡ hd strvn to subd by ml @ lnent msrs, bt wh efct. Ŧh, bng hghl incsd at ⌡ fr nt bng cld t ft @ shr i ⫲ rh spl % ⫲ Ⴀmnsh wr, gthrd tghr a mgt rm, crsd ⫲ ℞v ⌡, @ pprd t gv ⌡ btl; bt h, bng aprsd % thr aph, cld tgh ⫲ mn % Is, wnt fth, gv thm btl, @ pt thm t flt. Ŧo mk hs vctry mr cmpl, h stnd grds at ⫲ dft pss alng ⫲ bnk % ⫲ rvr, @ sd unt thm, if u c an strngrs ps ths wa, sa unt thm: "Ŋw sa ye, ≀." Ŧh ⋲phs, bg % a dif trb, cd nt fm t prnc ⫲ w, @ sd, "≀."

∓hs trflg dfct prvd thm enms @ cst thm thr lvs, @ thr fl tt da on ⫲ fld % btl, @ at ⫲ dfnrt pses alng ⫲ bk % ⫲ rv, frt @ t ths, aft wh Jpha rld qtl i Isr ntl ⫲ tm % hs dth, in al, sx yrs.

∓hs wd ws aftrwd usd t dstnsh a fd fm a fo, @ hs snc bn adptd as ⫲ ppr pw t b gvn bf entg an rgrl @ wl gnd :: % Ŧcs.

J ⓣ- || m sf; ps on.

≀ Ḋ- ⓐy br, w r nw aprhng a plc rpsg ⫲ inr dr t ⫲ ⓐ Ꞓ % Ꝁ ≀ ∓, wh w shl als fnd prtl op, bt cls tld b ⫲ ≀ ⓣ, wh wl dmd % us ⫲ rl g @ wd % Ŧc. Lt us advnc @ mk a rg al. (*In* ⫲ ⓣ.) ***

≀ ⓣ- (℞*is*) ⓣh cs h.

≀ Ḋ- ∓ Ŧcs, endvrg t wk thr wa int a plc rpsg ⫲ ⓐ Ꞓ % Ꝁ ≀ ∓.

⋊w d u xp t g ad. ↄy ⫲ r g @ w.

Ⱥd @ g ⫲ r g. (≀ Ḋ- *Ȼv r gp.*)

ⓣt s t. ∓h r g % Ŧc.

♓s i a nm. It h. ⊙l u gv i t m. || dd nt s rc i, nth wl I s i i. ♓w wl u ds % i. L or h i. L i @ b. U b. ⊙ u. (℞*l w gvn.)*

≀ ⊙- || m sfd; ps in.

≀ ⊙- (Ç*ndc* Ç *t* Ⱥ.) ⊙y br, w r nw i a pl rpsg ⊣⊢ ⊙ Ç % ₭ ≀ ₸.

MORAL ADVANTAGES OF GEOMETRY

⊙hld ⊣⊢ ltr ₲ sspd i ⊣⊢ ⊙. It is ⊣⊢ initl % ₲mty, ⊣⊢ bsis % ₸ ⊙y. ⊙y ₲mty w ma crsly trc nat thro hr vars wndgs t hr ms cncld rcses.

⊙y ₲mty w dscv ⊣⊢ pwr, wsdm, @ gdns % ⊣⊢ ₲t Ⱥrc % ⊣⊢ U, @ vw wh aw ⊣⊢ propns % ths vst sstm.

⊙y ₲mty w dsc hw ⊣⊢ plts mv in thr rspt orbts, dmstrt thr vrs rvltns, @ ac fr ⊣⊢ rtn % ⊣⊢ ssns @ ⊣⊢ vrit % scns wh eh ss dsplys t ⊣⊢ dscrg ey.

Ⱥbt us r nmbrls wlds, wh mv thro ⊣⊢ vst xpns, al fram b ⊣⊢ Dv Çr, @ al cndctd b ⊣⊢ unerg lws % ntr.

Ⳇ survy % ntr, @ ⊣ obsvtn % hr btfl prptns, fst dtrmnd mn t imit ⊣ dvn pln, @ std smtry @ ○. ∓hs gav ris t socts, @ brth t evy usfl rt. ∓h artc bgn to dsn; @ ⊣ plns wh h ld dn, imprvd b tm @ xprc, hv rsltd in wks wh hv bn ⊣ admtn % ev ag.

∓h lps % tm, ⊣ rthls hn % igrnc @ ⊣ dvstats % wr hv ld wst @ dstd mny vlbl mnumts % antqt, upn wh ⊣ utms xrtns % hu gnus hd bn mpl. ⋲v ⊣ ∓ % ≀, s spcs @ mgfc, @ cnstcd b s mny clbrtd rts, esc nt ⊣ unsprg rvgs % brbrs frc. Ŧ ⊙y, ntwstg, stl srvvs.

∓h atv er rcs ⊣ snd fm ⊣ inst tg, @ ⊣ ms % Ŧ ⊙y r sfly lgd i ⊣ rpst % ⊣ fthfl bst.

∓ls @ impltts % arctr, @ smblc mbs, mst xprsv, r slctd b ⊣ frtnt, t mprs upn ⊣ md ws @ sers trths; @ thus, thro a sucsn % ags, r trnsmtd unmprd ⊣ mst xclnt tnts % ou instn.

(If ev br admtd wthn ⊣ scrd wls % ths ⊙ Ç wl hd ⊣ lsns hr incled, @ rmbr tt as a Ŧ ⊙ h is als a bldr, nt % a mtrl edfc, bt % a ∓ mr glrs thn tt % ≀, a tm % hnr, % jst, % purt, % knlg, @ % trh, @ tt ths mblms % ⊣ opt ⊙'s rt indct ⊣ ℔s h i t pfm, ⊣ dngs h is t nctr, @ ⊣ prprtns h i t mk, in ⊣ uprerng % tt sprtl fabrc whrn h sol shl fd rst frev, @ fr mr.)

[⊙n lng yrs ag upn ⊣ Єstrn plns ws ths ou instutn st up, bsd up prcpls mr drbl thn ⊣ mtl wrgt int ⊣ stats % anc kgs. Δg af ag rld by, strm @ tmps hrld thr thndrs at its hd, wv af wv % brgt, insds snds crld abt its ft @ hepd thr slidg grns agst its sds; mn cm @ wnt in fltng gnrtns; ssns fld lk hrs thro ⊣ whrlng whel % tm; bt thro ⊣ tmps @ ⊣ strm, thr ⊣ atritn % ⊣ wvs @ snds % lf, thro gd rpt @ bd, it hs cntud t shd its bnfcnt inflc wdr @ wdr ov ⊣ eth.]

≀ ⋺- (*In* ⊣⊢ ∈.) ⊙⦿.

⊙⦿- (℞*s*) ⋺r ≀ ⋺.

≀ ⋺- ‖ hv ⊣⊢ pls % prstg ⋺r ⍋ ⋺, wh hs md an adv mblcy thro a prh, up a flt % wd sts, cnstg % th, fv @ s stps, thro an otr @ an inr dr, int a plc rpstg ⊣⊢ ⦿ Ϙ % Ꝁ ≀ ∓, @ nw awts ur plsr.

⊙⦿- ⦿y br, ‖ cngrtult u up ur arvl int a pl rpsng ⊣⊢ ⦿ Ϙ % Ꝁ ≀ ∓.
It ws thr o anc bn hd thr nms rcrd as fthfl wkm; i is hr u r ntltd t hv urs rcrd as sh. ⋺r ≀ ec.

≀ ec- ⊙ ⦿.

⊙⦿- ⦿k ⊣⊢ nsc rcd.

Sec- ∓h rcd i md.

⊙⦿- It ws thr als ou anc bn rcd thr wgs, cnstg % cn, wn @ ol, embl % nrshmt, rfs @ j. 3

[∓h wgs % a ⊤c bng cn, w @ o, ws t sgnfy tt ou anc bn, wh psd t ths °, wr entld t thr ws, nt onl fr ⊣⊢ necrs @ cmfrts % lf, bt mny % its suprflts;

@ ma ur indstrs hbts @ strc aplcn t bsns procr fr u a plnt % ǂ crn % nrshmt, ǂ wn % rfsmt @ ǂ oi % j.]

Ⓣ⌓- Ŧh lt ₲, t wh ur atn hs bn drcd on ur psg hthr, hs a stl hghr @ fr mr sgfct mng. *** (Ⓣ*shfl @ evbd shd b on ǂ lvl.*) It is ǂ initl % ǂ gt @ scd nm % ₲, bf whm al, fm ǂ Ɛ Ⱥ i ǂ Ω- Ɛ Ȼ t ǂ Ⓣ ⌓ in ǂ Ɛ, shd hmbl, rvntl @ dvtly bw.

Ⱥl- (Ⓓ*w*)

Ⓣ⌓- * (*Sts* ǂ ::.) ⌓y br, thr is als a lctr cnctd wh ths °, cnstng % a sers % q @ as, wh wl nw b psd btw ǂ ≀ Ⓓ @ mys. ₱a str atn, fr, wr u at an tm undrgng an exmn, hs ans wd b urs, @ it wl b ncs fr u t bc prfc in thm bf u cn b rsd t ǂ sbl ° % ⌓ ⌓.

└Ç

Ⓣ⌓- Ͽr ≀ Ͽ. ≀ Ͽ- Ⓣ⌓.

℞ u a ⊤c. I m; tr m.

Ͽ wt wl u b tr. Ͽ ⊣⊢ ≀.

Ⓣh b ⊣⊢ ≀.

Ͽcs i is an emb % mrlt @ on % ⊣⊢ wk tls % ⊤c.

Ⓣt is a ≀.

Ⱥn ang % nty °s, or ⊣⊢ fo pt % a crc.

Ⓣt mks u a ⊤c. ⌓ o.

Ⓣhr wr u md a ⊤c.

Ⓣthn ⊣⊢ bd % a js @ dl cnst :: % ⊤cs, asmb in a plc rpsntng ⊣⊢ ⌓ Ç % Ꝁ ≀ ∓, frshd wh ⊣⊢ ⋊ Ͽ, ≀ @ Çs, tghr wh a chtr o dspsn fm sm ₵ Ͽ % cmp jrs emp it t wk.

⋊w ma I kn u t b a ⊤c.

Ͽy crt §s @ tkns. Ⓣt r §s.

℞t ngls, hrzs @ pdlrs. Ⱥdvc a §.

Çdt- (₵v §) ⋊s tt an alsn. 147–3

It h, t ⊣⊢ psn % m hns whl tkg ⊣⊢ o.

⋊v u a fth §. I hv. (₵*vs* §.)

⋊s tt an al. It hs, t ⫞ p % ⫞ o.

⊙t r tkns.

Ϙrt frn or brl gps whb on ⊙ ma kn anth i ⫞ dk as i ⫞ lt.

Ѧdvc @ gv m a tk. (₵*vs ps gp.*)

⊙t is tt. ⊤h pg % ⊤c.

⋊s it a nm. It hs.

⊙l u gv it t m.

‖ dd nt s rc i, nth wl I s i i.

⋊w wl u dsp % i. L or sl i.

≀ i @ bg. U bg. ⊙gn u.

(⊙*gns—pw gvn.*) ⊙l u b o o fm.

⊤. ⊤m wt @ t wt.

⊤m ⫞ pg % ⊤c t ⫞ rl g % ⫞ s.

Ꝑ. (₵*vn*) ⊙t is tt. ⊤h rl g % ⊤c.

⋊s it a n. It h. ⊙l u gv i t m.

‖ dd n s rc i, nth w I s i i.

⋊w wl u dsp % it. L or h i.

L i @ bg. U bg. ⊙g u.

(⊙*gns; rl w i gv.*)

⊙hr wr u ppd t b md a ⊤c.

In a rm adjng ⊣| bd % a js @ dl cns :: % ŦFcs.

⋊w wr u ppd.

Dvs % al mt sbs, nh n nr cld, bf nr shd, rt k @ br br, hw @ a ct twc ar m rt ar, cl as ϵ Å; i wch cdn I ws cd t a dr % ⊣| :: @ csd t gv th dst ks, wh wr ans by th wthn.

⊙h ws a ct twc arn ur r a.

∓o th m tt as Ŧc I wd b und a dbl ti t ⊣| Ŧty.

∓ wt dd ⊣| thr ks ald.

∓ thr prc jls.

⊙t ws sd t u fm wthn.

⊙h cs hr. Ur ans.

Å wth br, wh hs bn dl ini ϵ Å, @ nw whs mr lt i ⊕y by bg pssd t ⊣| ° % Ŧc.

⊙t wr u thn askd.

If it ws an ac % m ow f wl @ ac; if || ws wth @ wl ql, d @ tr ppd; if || hd md stbl prfc in ⊣| prc °;

al % wh bg ans i +| aftv, I ws as b wt fth r o b || xpd t ob ths im prv.

Ur an. Ↄf % +| pw.)(d u +| pw.

|| hd nt; m cdct hd @ gv i fr m.

⊙t wr u thn tld.

Snc || ws i psn % al ths ncs qlfcs, I shd wt unt +| ⊙ ⊙ cld b inf % m rqs @ hs ans rtd.

⊙t ws hs ans wn rtd.

Lt hm ent ths wfl :: % ⊤Fcs, @ b rc i d @ anc fm.

)(w wr u rc.

On +| ng % a sq, apld t m n r b, wh ws t th m tt +| sq % vrt shd b a rl @ gd fr m prctc thro lf.

)(w wr u thn dspsd %.

Ꝑdctd twc rg ard +| :: @ t +| ʝ ⊙ in +| ≀, whr +| sm qs wr ask @ ans rtd as at +| d.

)(w dd +| ʝ ⊙ dsp % u.

Ↄrc m t b cdcd t +| ≀ ⊙ in +| ⊙, whr +| sm qs wr skd @ ans rtd as bfr.)(w dd +| ≀ ⊙ dsp % u.

⦿rc m t b cdctd t ⊣| ⓣ ⓛ in ⊣| Є, whr ⊣| sm qs wr skd @ ans rtd as bfr; wh als dmnd whc || cm @ wthr trvlg.

Ur ans. ₸m ⊣| ⓣ, tvlg Є.

ⓣy dd u lv ⊣| ⓣ @ trv Є.

In srh % mr lt i ⓛy.

⋊w dd ⊣| ⓣ ⓛ ds % u.

○d m rcd t ⊣| ≀ ⓣ in ⊣| ⓣ, wh tgt m hw t aph ⊣| Є in du @ an f.

ⓣt ws tt d @ anc fm.

Ⱥdv on m r f, brg ⊣| hl % m l int ⊣| hol % m r, thb fmg ⊣| ngl % a ob, bd erc, fcg ⊣| Є.

ⓣt dd ⊣| ⓣ ⓛ thn d wth u.

Md m a ₸c. ⋊w. In d fm.

ⓣⓛ- ⓣt ws tt d fm.

Ꝁnlg o m n r k, m l fmg ⊣| ng % a s; m r h rst up ⊣| ⋊ ϑ, ≀ @ Ǫs, ⊣| l in a vrtl psn, m ar fg a sq, i wh d f || tk ⊣| s o % ₸c.

⋊v:u ⊣| o. || hv. Ꞧp it.

||, Ⱥ Ↄ, % m ow f w @ ac, i pr % Ⱥ Ģ @ ths w :: % Ŧs, er t ӿ @ dc t +| mr % +| ӿ ≀s ⌡, d hb @ h sl @ s p @ s tt I w k @ cn, @ nv r an % +| ss bl t +| ° % Ŧc, wh || hv rc, am ab t r, or ma hrf b ins i, t an pr, nls i sh b t a wy b Ŧc, or wthn +| bd % a j @ d cns :: % sh; @ nt unt hm o thm ntl b d tr, stc x, or l ⊙c in, || sh hv fd h o thm jsl ent t rc +| sm.

(2) Ŧm, || d p @ sw tt I wl an @ ob al d §s @ r sms st t m fm +| bd. % a j @ d cns :: % Ŧs, o hn m b a wy b % ths °, if wth +| l % m ct @ +| sq @ ng % m w.

(3) Fm, I d p @ s tt I wl hl, ai @ ast al p @ ds Ŧs, thy apl t m as sh, || fdg thm wy, @ cn d s wtho mtrl inj t ms.

(4) Ŧm, || d p @ s tt || wl n wr, ch nr df a Ŧc :: nr a b % ths ° t

⊣| v % anthg, knl, nr sf i t b dn b anth, if i m pw t prv.

T al % wh I d sl @ snc p @ s, wtht an hst, mtl rsv or sc ev % mn i m wtev, bdg ms un n ls a p thn tt % hv m l b t o, m h @ l tk thc t ⊣| V̇ % Jhs, @ lf a pr t ⊣| vlts % ⊣| ai, shd I e, kn or wlf, vl ths m s o % ⊤c. ≀ hl m ₲, @ mk m stfs t kp @ pfm ⊣| sm.

A̤ft ⊣| o, wt wr u ask.

⊙t || mst dsrd.

Ur ans. ⊙r lt i ⊙y. Dd u rc it.

|| dd, by ○ % ⊣| ⊙ ⊙.

○n bg bt t l, wt dd u bh.

∓h th gt lts in ⊙y as in ⊣| prc °, wth ths dfrnc, on pt % ⊣| cs ws ab ⊣| sq, wh ws t th m tt I hd rc, @ ws ntld t rc, mr lt i ⊙y; bt as on pt ws stl hdn fm m vw, it ws als t th m tt || ws yt on mtrl pt in ⊣| dk rsptg ⊤ ⊙y.

⊙t dd u nx bhld.

∓h ⊙ ⊚ aph fm ⫲ €, on ⫲ st, un ⫲ dg @ § % ∓c, wh prs hs r h i tk % cntnc % fdsh @ br lv, @ invs m wh ⫲ pg, pw, r g @ w, ○d me t rs, sl ⫲ ⌡ @ ≀ ⊙s, @ sfy thm tt ‖ ws i psn % ⫲ s, dg, §, pg, pw, rl g @ w % ∓c.

♓w wr u thn dspd %.

℞cdtd t ⫲ ≀ ⊙ in ⫲ ⊙, wh tgt m hw t wr m ap as ∓c.

♓w shd a ∓c wr hs a.

⊙th ⫲ 1 cr tkd up.

⊙th wt wr u thn prstd.

∓h wkg ts % ∓c, wh r ⫲ ℘, ≀ @ L, @ r ths xpld: ∓h ℘ is an ins usd by opt ⊚s t tr ppndls, ⫲ ≀ t sq thr wk, @ ⫲ L to prv hztls: bt w, as ∓ @ ⅄ ⊚s, r tgt t us thm fr mr nbl @ gls prps. ∓h plm admns us t wlk uprtly i ou svrl sta bfr ₲ @ mn, sqrg ou acns by ⫲ sq % vrt, evr rmbrng tt w r trvlng on ⫲ Lv % tm to tt undscvd cntry fm whs brne no trvlr rtns.

⊙th wt wr u thn prsntd.

∓hr prcs jls, ╫ atntv ear, ╫ nstctv tng, @ ╫ fthfl brst; thy tch us ths imprt lsn: ∓h atntv ear rc ╫ snd fm ╫ nstv tng, @ ╫ msts % ∓ ⊙y, r sfly ldgd i ╫ rpstry % ╫ fthfl brst.

♓w wr u thn dsp %.

℞cndctd t ╫ plc whnc I cm, invstd wh tt % wh I hd bn dvstd, @ rtnd t a plc rpsntg ╫ ⊙ Ҁ % Ꝁ ≀ ∓m.

— SYMBOLISM —

[If ╫ obj % ╫ f ° is t smboliz ╫ strgls % a cdt grpng i dkns fr intlcl lt; tt % ╫ sc ° rpsts ╫ sm cdt ꞗg amd al ╫ dfclts tt encmbr ╫ yong bgnr i ╫ atnmt % lrng @ scnc. ∓h ⊖ ⅄ is t emrg fm dkns t lt; ╫ ∓c is t cm ot % igrnc int knwlg. ∓hs °, thfr, by ftng embls, i intdd t typfy ths strgls % ╫ ardnt md fr ╫ atnmt % trh, mrl @ intlcl trh, @ abv al tt Dvn trh, ╫ cmprhsn % wh surpsth hu unsdg, @ t wh, stndg i ⊣⊢ ⊙dl Ç aft hs ibs asct % ⊣⊢ wndg strs, h cn onl aprxmt by ⊣⊢ recpn % an impfc yt glrs rwd in ⊣⊢ rvltn % tt "hiroglhc lt wh nn bt cftmn ev sw."]

⊙⊙- ∓h, my br, cnclds ⊣⊢ scnd ° % ⊙y, wh ⊣⊢ xcptn % ⊣⊢ charg.

CHARGE.

⊙r, bng advcd t ⊣⊢ scd ° % ⊤ ⊙y, I cngrlt u on ur prfrmt. ∓h intrnl, @ nt ⊣⊢ xtnl, qlfs % a mn r wt ⊙y rgrds. Ⱥs u incrs i knlg, u wl impv in socl intrcrs.

It is unscry t rcptult ⊣⊢ dts wh as a ⊤c u r bnd t dschrg, or t enlg on ⊣⊢ ncsity % a strc adhrnc t thm, as ur ow xprnc mst hv estblhd thr vlu. Ou lws @ rgltns u r strnsly t sprt, @ b alws rdy t asst i sng thm dly xctd. U r nt t palat, or agrvt, ⊣⊢ offns % ur bn; bt in ⊣⊢ dcsn % evr trsps ags ou rls, u r t jdg wh cndr, admsh wh fdshp, @ rphnd wh jstc.

[Ͽ jst @ fr nt; nvr spk il % an mn.
"Ꭿvd sspcn! Lk ⊣⊢ fbld upas, it blts al hlthy lf @ mks a dsrt rnd it.

["Ŋthg s fr, nthg s pur cn lv, bt by suspcn ma b mrrd @ blstd; n pth s strght bt t suspn's ey lks trtrs @ bnt fm its tru nd."

[∓h std % ⊣⊢ lbrl rts, tt vlbl brch % educn wh tnds s efctuly to plsh @ adrn ⊣⊢ md, is ernstly rcmndd t ur cnsdrtn, espcly ⊣⊢ scinc % Ģmty, wh is estblhd as ⊣⊢ bsis % ou rt.

[Ģmty, or ⊙y, orgnly snonms trms, bng % a dvn @ morl ntr, i enrhd wh ⊣⊢ ms usfl knlg; whl i prvs ⊣⊢ wndfl prptis % ntr, it dmnsrts ⊣⊢ mr imprt trhs % mrlty.]

Ur pst bhvr @ rgl dprtmt hv mrtd ⊣⊢ hnr wh w hv nw cnfrd; @ in ur nw chrctr i is expctd tt u wl cnfm t ⊣⊢ prcpls % ⊣⊢ ○ by stdly prsvrg i ⊣⊢ prctc % ev cmndbl vrtu. Sh is ⊣⊢ ntr % ur engmt as a ∓c, @ t thes dts u r bnd b ⊣⊢ ms scrd tis.

∓hs, m br, cnclds ⊣| scnd ° % ⊙y. U wl stp t ⊣| ⊙ % ⊣| ∆, slt @ rtr.

∓h Scty wl ntfy u whn t prst ursl fr ⊣| thd °. (*Or*)

(*Fr clsg scnd @ rsmg thd, c Index.*)

(*Clsg thd, c Index.*)

CHARGE

[⊙y br, u hv nw bn psd t ⊣| ° % ∓c, @, rjcng wh u in ur advcmt, I chrg u tt ⊣| intrnl, @ nt ⊣| xtrnl, qlfcns % a mn r wt ⊙y rgds.

[Ou lws @ rgulns u r strnsly t sprt, @ b alws rdy t ast i seng thm du ex. U r nt t palit o agrvt ⊣| ofncs % ur bn, bt in ⊣| decsn % ev trsps agst ou rls, u r t jdg wh imprtlt, admnsh wh frshp, @ rphnd wh jstc.

[Ɲvr spk il % an mn unls u kn tt wt u sa i tru. ∓o sa wt u d nt kn t b tr is as rphnsbl as t sa wt u k t b nt tr. ⊙r in mnd tt ⊣| trth cn nv ovtk a li, onc strtd. ⊙ny a far fam hs bn trnshd b a crls o mal wd.

[“⊙h stls m prs, stls trsh; ts smthg, nthg; tws mn, ts hs, @ hs bn slav t thsnds; bt h tt filchs frm m my gd nm, rbs m % tt wh nt enrchs hm, @ mks m pr indd.”]

[Ur gd rptatn @ chrc hv meretd ⊣⊢ hon w hv cnfrd, @ it is expc tt u wl cnfm t ⊣⊢ prnc % ⊣⊢ ○, by stdl prsvg in ⊣⊢ prtc % ev vrtu. Sh is ⊣⊢ ntr % ur engmt as a ⊤c, @ t thes dts u r bnd b ⊣⊢ mst sacd tis. (*Or*)

(Upn ⊣⊢ vry nm % ths ° is basd ⊣⊢ chg wh nw ⊣⊢ instrcv tngu cnvys t ⊣⊢ atnv er, wh ⊣⊢ hp tt it ma b lgd whn ⊣⊢ fthfl brst, “⊤c,” ⊣⊢ crf % flwkmn.

(In ⊣⊢ prvdc % ₲, wh ⊣⊢ brth % lf eh % us bcm a mbr % ⊣⊢ hu fmly. In maturt w stnd fcg ⊣⊢ neds @ rspsblts % lf. Ⱥs ⊤cs, w r espc pontd to or du t ou nbrs.

(₲d nv brt us int bng t lv i ⊣⊢ naro grov % a slfsh indvlsm, bt as bn, on % anth, i mutl depndc @ suprt. Ŋthg ds

+| ⋊ ⅁, +| rul @ gd % ou fth @ prtc, mr strnusl th; nthg ds ⊙y nr infixbly dmd.

(Ŋo hshld cn fshn +| hm whr dissn @ slfshns knll +| dth % unit @ pc. Ŋo comunt cn prtc chacrt whr pety strif i brn % mschvs tngs. Ŋo cty cn bcm a plc % prsps grth whs ctzns cr ltl @ do ls fr its advcmt. Ŋo stat cn derv +| bnft % its on rsrcs whs ppl oby bt +| on lw % indvdul incltn @ grd.

(Ŋo gvmt cn std fim whs adhrnts r blnd t +| unaltrabl lw, "In unin is strgh, in hrmn is pc." Ⱥltho bt on mn amg mny, u cnnt escp o shirk ur shr in ths grt rspnsblt.

(Ur prsnl cntct wh oths ma b cicm-scbd by +| lmt % +| crcl wthn wh ur da lf is lvd; bt ur inflnc, psng thro @ fm thos whm tt crcl ma srrnd, wl rh fthr thn u shl cncv.

(⊙y bds u do ur bst in tt wh lis nrst t u; t c in ur nghbr wt u dsr ur nbr shd c in u; t rmb tt thr i n term so oftn usd wthn ou mdst, n wds mr freightd wh ⫞ stgh % mns vry bst chrctcs, no clm s glstng wh ⫞ tis % hnst afctn, a ou psw % grtg, "⊙ br.")

—○—

⊕ ⊙- * Ͽr ⌡ Ͽ.

⌡ Ͽ- (℞*s*, §.) ⊕ ⊙.

⊕ ⊙- Ꜹsrtn if an Ꞓdts r in wtg. If s, thr nms @ fr wt °.

⌡ Ͽ- (*Obts crd wh nm % Ꞓ fm* ⫲ ∓ @ *rprts.*) ⊕ ⊙.

⊕ ⊙- Ͽr ⌡ Ͽ.

⌡ Ͽ- Ͽr Ꜹ Ͽ is i wtng fr ⫲ th °.

⊕ ⊙- Ͽrn, Ͽr Ꜹ Ͽ is i wtg fr ⫲ thd ° % ⊙y. ♓ hvg md stbl pfc in ⫲ prc °, if thr is n objcn, I shl cnfr ⫲ ° upn hm. (℘*ses*) ∓hr bng n obj, I wl prcd. * Ͽr ≀ @ ⌡ ⊙s % c.

≀ ⊙ % c- (Ͽ*th rs.*) ⊕ ⊙.

⊕ ⊙- ♓w shd a br b ppd fr ⫲ thd ° % ⊙y.

≀ ⊙ % c- Ͽy bg dvs % al mtlc sbts, nthr nk nr clth, bf nr sh, bth ks @ bs br, h-w @ a c-t thr ts ar hs bd, clth as ∓c.

Ⓣ (⊥)- ℞pr to ⱶ prptn-rm, whr Ͽr Ѧ Ͽ is i wtg. Ⓣhn ths ppd, cs hm t mk ⱶ usl al at ⱶ inr dr.

(⊥)s%c- (℞*pr t* ⱶ Ѧ, *slt, l fc, mh t prp-rm @ ppr* Ç, *slpr on l ft, etc. In* ⱶ *mntm* ⱶ :: *prcds wh rglr busns, or cls t rfsmt.*)

Ͽr Ѧ Ͽ- (*In prp-rm.*) ***

≀ Ḋ- (℞*is.*) Ⓣ (⊥).

Ⓣ (⊥)- Ͽr ≀ Ḋ.

≀ Ḋ- ∓hr i an al at ⱶ inr dr.

Ⓣ (⊥)- Ѧtn t ⱶ al @ asrtn ⱶ cs.

≀ Ḋ- ***.

≀ (⊥)%c- *

≀ Ḋ- (*Opns dr.*) Ⓣh cms hr.

≀ (⊥)%c- Ͽr Ѧ Ͽ, wh h bn dl intd Ͼ Ѧ, psd t ⱶ ° % ∓c, @ nw whs ftr l in (⊥)y b bng rsd t ⱶ sb ° % (⊥) (⊥).

≀ Ḋ- Ͽr Ѧ Ͽ, is ths an ac % ur on fr wl @ ac.

Ͽr Ѧ Ͽ- It is.

≀ Ḋ- Ͽr ≀ (⊥)%c, is h wh @ wl q.

≀ (⊥)%c- Ӿ is. Dl @ tr ppd. Ӿ is.

≀ ☽- ⋊s h md stbl pfc i ⊣ prc °.

≀ ⊙%c- ⋊ hs.

≀ ☽- ⊙ wt fth rt o bn ds h xpc t obtn ths imp prv.

≀ ⊙ %c- ⊙nf % ⊣ p-w.

≀ ☽- ⋊s h ⊣ pw.

≀ ⊙ %c- ⋊ hs nt; I hv i fr hm.

≀ ☽- ⩓dvr @ gv i. (*Dn.*) ∓h p-w is rt. Snc ⊣ br is i psn % al ths nc qlfs, lt hm wa ntl ⊣ ⊙ ⊙ cn b infd % hs rqs @ hs ans rtd. (*Ͼls dr @ rtns t ⊣ ⩓.*) ⊙ ⊙.

⊙ ⊙- ⊙r ≀ ☽.

≀ ☽- ∓hr i wtht ⊙r ⩓ ⊙, wh hs bn dl init Ͼ ⩓, psd t ⊣ ° % ∓c, @ nw wshs fr l i ⊙y b bg rsd t ⊣ sb ° % ⊙ ⊙.

⊙ ⊙- Is i an ac % hs ow f wl @ ac.

≀ ☽- It is.

⊙ ⊙- Is h wh @ wl ql.

≀ ☽- ⋊ is. Dl @ tl ppd. ⋊ is.

⊙ ⊙- ⋊s h md stbl pfc i ⊣ prc °

≀ ☽- ⋊ hs.

ⓣ ⓛ- ⊢ wt fth rt or bn ds h xpc t obt ths imp prv.

≀ ⊳- ⊢nf % ⊣ p-w.

ⓣ ⓛ- ♓s h ⊣ p-w.

≀ ⊳- ♓ hs nt; I hv it fr hm.

ⓣ ⓛ- ♆v i fr ⊣ bn % ⊣ cft.

≀ ⊳- (*♆vs p-w audbly.*)

ⓣ ⓛ- ∓h p-w i rt. Snc ⊣ br is in psn % al ths nsc qlf, lt hm en ths wfl :: % ⓛ ⓛs, @ b rc i d @ anc fm.

○rg or ⓣ ⓛ- ⓣhl ⊣ br is in ⊣ ⓣ, w wl sng ode —, on pg —.

≀ ⊳- * (*Ops dr.*) Lt hm ent ths wfl :: % ⓛ ⓛs, @ b rc i du @ anc fm.

ⓣ ⓛ- ***

₵dt- (*Is cndc int* ⊣ :: @ *rc nr* ⊣ *dr; thn t frt* % ⊣ ≀ ⓣ, *fcg* ⊣ ⊕.)

≀ ⊳- ⊢r ⩐ ⊢, wn fst u ntrd a :: % ∓ @ ⩐ ⓛs u wr rc on ⊣ pt % a sh ins pr ur n lf br; on ur scnd entc u wr rc on ⊣ ngl % a sq, apld t ur nk rt b, ⊣ mrls % wh wr thn xpld t u. I am nw cmd t rc u o ⊣ xtrm pts % ⊣⊢ cps, xtdg fm ur n rt t ur n l bs, (*Plcs cps.*) wh i t th u tt as wthn ⊣⊢ brst r cntnd ⊣⊢ mst vtl prts % mn, s btwn ⊣⊢ xtrm pts % ⊣⊢ cps r cntd ⊣⊢ ms vlbl tnts % ⊤ ⊙y, wh r fdshp, mrlt, @ brly lv.

(*Music. Ode.*)

⊙ ⊙- *

≀ ⊃ or Ϛdctr- (*Tks Ϛ by r ar @ strts ⊖ on ⊣⊢ ℞ sd % ⊣⊢ ::. It is gd fm fr ⊣⊢ ≀ ⊃ @ ⊙ar t wlk tghr, fold by ⊣⊢ ⊙s % c. ⊃rs ldg Ϛs @ Stwds in ⊣⊢ rer.*)

⌡ ⊙- *

Ϛhp- ℞mbr nw thy Ϛrtr i ⊣⊢ ds % thy yth, whl ⊣⊢ ev ds cm nt,

≀ ⊙- *

Ϛhp- nr ⊣⊢ yrs dr ngh, wn thou shlt sa, || hv no plsr in thm; whl ⊣⊢ sn, or ⊣⊢ lt, or ⊣⊢ mn, or ⊣⊢ strs, b nt drknd, nr ⊣⊢ clds rtn aft ⊣⊢ rain.

⊙ ⊙- *

Ꞓhp- In ⊣| da wn ⊣| kprs % ⊣| hs shl trmbl, @ ⊣| strg mn shl bw thsl,

⌡ (⊤)- **

Ꞓhp- and ⊣| grnds shl ces, bcs th r fw, @ thos tt lk ot % ⊣⊦ wdws b dkd, @ ⊣| dr shl b sht in ⊣| sts,

≀ (⊤)- **

Ꞓhp- wn ⊣| sd % ⊣| grdg is lw, @ h shl rs up at ⊣| vc % ⊣| brd, @ al ⊣| dghtrs % musc shl b brt lw;

(⊤) (⊥)- **

Ꞓhp- als wn thy shl b afrd % tt wh is hi, @ frs shl b in ⊣| wa,

⌡ (⊤)- ***

Ꞓhp- and ⊣| almd tr shl flrsh, @ ⊣| grshpr shl b a brdn, @ dsr shl fl;

≀ (⊤)- ***

Ꞓhp- bcs mn goth t hs lg hm, @ ⊣| mrnrs go abt ⊣| strts: or evr ⊣| slvr crd b loosed, or ⊣| gldn bwl b brkn, or ⊣| ptchr b brkn at ⊣| fntn, or ⊣| whl bkn at ⊣| cstn;

(⊤) (⊥)- ***

Ꞓhp- ∓hn shl ╫ dst rtn t ╫ eth as it ws; @ ╫ sprt shl rtn unt ȼ wh gv i.

≀ Ð- (*In* ╫ ≀ .) ***

⌋ ⊙- * (℞*s.*) ⊙h cs h.

≀ Ð- Ɔr Ⱥ Ɔ, wh hs bn dl init Ͼ Ⱥ, psd t ╫ ° % ∓c, @ nw whs fr lt i ⊙y by bg rs t ╫ sb ° % ⊙ ⊙.

⌋ ⊙- Ɔr Ⱥ Ɔ, is ths an ac % ur ow fr wl @ ac.

Ɔr Ⱥ Ɔ- It is.

⌋ ⊙- Ɔr ≀ Ð, is h wh @ wl q.

≀ Ð- ♓ i. Ð1 @ tr ppd. ♓ is.

⌋ ⊙- ♓s h md stbl pfc i ╫ prc °.

≀ Ð- ♓ hs.

⌋ ⊙- Ɔ wt fthr rt o bn ds h xpc t ob ths imp prv.

≀ Ð- Ɔnf % ╫ pw.

⌋ ⊙- ♓s h ╫ pw.

≀ Ð- ♓ hs nt; ‖ hv i fr hm.

⌋ ⊙- Ⱥdvc @ gv i. (*Dn.*) ∓h pw i rt. Snc ╫ br is in psn % al ths ncs qlf, cdc hm t ╫ ≀ ⊙ i ╫ ⊙, fr hs ex.

≀ ☽- (*In* ⫲ ⊙.) ***

≀ ⊙- * (℞*s.*) ⊙h cs h.

≀ ☽- ☽r ⩓ ☽, wh hs bn dl init ⊖ ⩓, psd t ⫲ ° % ⫪c, @ nw wsh fr lt i ⊕y b bg rs t ⫲ sb ° % ⊕ ⊕.

≀ ⊙- ☽r ⩓ ☽, is ths an ac % ur ow f wl @ ac.

☽r ⩓ ☽- It is.

≀ ⊙- ☽r ≀ ☽, is h wh @ wl q.

≀ ☽- ♓ is. ☽l @ tr ppd. ♓ i.

≀ ⊙- ♓s h md stbl prf i ⫲ prc °.

≀ ☽- ♓ hs.

≀ ⊙- ☽ wt fth rt o bn ds h xpc t ob ths imp prv.

≀ ☽- ☽nf % ⫲ pw.

≀ ⊙- ♓s h ⫲ pw.

≀ ☽- ♓ hs nt; ‖ hv i fr hm.

≀ ⊙- ⩓dvc @ gv it. (*Dn.*) Th pw is rt. Snc ⫲ br is in psn % al ths ncs qlf, cdc hm t ⫲ ⊙ ⊕ i ⫲ ⊖, fr hs ex.

≀ ☽- (*In* ⫲ ⊖.) ***

⊙⊕- * ⊙h cs h.

≀ ⦘- ⦘r Å ⦘, wh hs bn dl init ∈ Å, psd t ⫲ ° % ⊤c, @ nw whs fr lt i ⊙y b bng rs t ⫲ sb ° % ⊙ ⊙.

⊙ ⊙- ⦘r Å ⦘, is ths an aċ % ur ow f wl @ ac.

⦘r Å ⦘- It is.

⊙ ⊙- ⦘r ≀ ⦘, is h wh @ wl q.

≀ ⦘- ⋊ is. ⦘l @ tr pd. ⋊ i.

⊙ ⊙- ⋊ h md stb prf i ⫲ prc °.

≀ ⦘- ⋊ hs.

⊙ ⊙- ⦘ wt fth. rt o bn ds h xpc t ob ths imp prv.

≀ ⦘- ⦘nf % ⫲ pw.

⊙ ⊙- ⋊s h ⫲ pw.

≀ ⦘- ⋊ hs nt; ‖ hv i fr h.

⊙ ⊙- Ådvc @ gv i. (*Gvn.*) ∓h pw is r. ⊙nc cm u, @ wthr r u trv.

≀ ⦘- ⊤r ⫲ ⊙, trv ∈.

⊙ ⊙- ⊙h dd u lv ⫲ ⊙ @ trv ∈.

≀ ⦘- In sh % fr lt i ⊙y.

⊙ ⊙- Snc ⫲ br is in psn % al ths ncsr qlf, @ i sh % fr lt i ⊙y, rcdc hi t ⫲ ≀ ⊙ i ⫲ ⊙, wh wl th hm hw t aph ⊣⊢ Є i d @ an fm.

≀ Ɔ̣ - (*Rcdcs Ç b mchg t ≀ sd % ⊣⊢ ::, l fc, mch Є, l f, m Ŋ, l fc, m t ⊤⃝ % Ѧ, m hlf wa t ⊣⊢ ⊤⃝, hlt, fc ⊣⊢ ⊤⃝.*) Ɔr ≀ ⊤⃝.

≀ ⊤⃝ - Ɔr ≀ Ɔ̣.

≀ Ɔ̣ - It is ⊣⊢ ○ % ⊣⊢ ⊤⃝ ⊥⃝ tt u th ths br hw t ap ⊣⊢ Є i d @ an f.

≀ ⊤⃝ - Çs ⊣⊢ br t fc ⊣⊢ Є.

≀ Ɔ̣ - (*Caus br t fc* Є.)

≀ ⊤⃝ - Ɔr Ѧ Ɔ, adv on ur l f as Є Ѧ; (*Dn.*) advc on ur r ft as Ŧc; (*Dn.*) tk an adnl st on ur l f, (*Dn.*) brg ⊣⊢ hl % ur r t ⊣⊢ hl % ur l, (*Dn.*) thb fmg ⊣⊢ ngl % a sq, bd er, fc ⊣⊢ Є. ⊤⃝ ⊥⃝.

⊤⃝ ⊥⃝ - Ɔr ≀ ⊤⃝.

≀ ⊤⃝ - ∓h br is in ○.

⊤⃝ ⊥⃝ - Ɔr Ѧ Ɔ, bfr u cn prc fth in Ŧ ⊥⃝y, it wl b ncsr fr u to tk a sl o aprtg t ⊣⊢ ° % ⊥⃝ ⊥⃝, @ ||, ⊥⃝st % ⊣⊢ ::, asur u tt thr is nthg thrn cntnd wh wl cnflc wh ur mrl, socl o cvl dts o prv, b th wt th ma. ⊙th ths asrnc, r u wlg t tk ǂ o.

⊙r △ ⊙- || m.

⊙ ⊙- ǂhn adv t ǂ scd △ % ǂ ⊙y @ kn on bh nk ks, bh hs rstg upn ǂ ⟳ ⊙, ℇ @ ₵.

₵dr or ℇ ⊙- (*Plc* ₵.)

ℇ ⊙- ⊙ ⊙. ⊙r ℇ ⊙. ǂh br i i d f.

⊙ ⊙- ***

⊙n- (*Fm eql lns drssg to* ǂ △.)

⊙s%c- (*Crct* ǂ *lns as th pas insd @ fm arch at* ǂ ⊙.)

⊙ds- (*Wtht colms o escrt, ps insd* ǂ *lns @ tk thr stns und* ǂ *arch.*)

ℇ tds- (*Ma fm arh fr* ⊙*ar w %* △.)

⊙ ⊙- (*Dcnds t ach in* ǂ ⊙.) ⊙r △ ⊙, if u r stl wlg t tk ǂ o, sa I, (*Dn.*) prnc ur nm in fl, (*Dn.*) @ rp af m: Of m o f w @ a, in prs % △ ₵ @ ths wfl :: % ⊙ ⊙s, er t ⟳ @ ddc t ǂ mr % ǂ ⟳ ℇs ℌ, d hb @ h sl @ s p @ s tt || wl k @ ccl, @ nv rvl, an % ǂ ss bl t ǂ ° % ⊙ ⊙,

wh || hv rc, am ab t r, o ma hrf b nstd i, t an psn, unl i shl b t a wh br ⊙ ⊙, o wthn ⊣| bd % a j @ dl cns :: % sh; @ nt un h o thm unt b d tr, st xmntn o lf ⊙c inf || sh hv fd h o th jstl entld t rc ⊣| s.

(2) Ŧm, || d p @ s tt || wl supt ⊣| cn % ⊣| ₵ :: % ⊣| St % Ŋ Y, als al ls, rls @ eds % ⊣| sm, or % an oh ₵ :: fm whs js || ma hrftr ha; tgh wh ⊣| b-ls, rs @ rgs % ths or an oth :: % wh || ma bc a mb, so fr as ⊣| sm sh cm t m knl.

(3) Ŧm, I d p @ s tt || w ans @ o al d §s @ rg sm st t m fm ⊣| bd % a j @ d cns :: % ⊙ ⊙s, or hnd m b a wy br % ths °, if wthn ⊣| lh % m ct.

(4) Fm, || d p @ s tt I wl hl, ad @ ast al pr @ ds ⊙ ⊙s, thr ws @ ors, th aplg t m as sh, || fdg thm why, @ cn d s wht mtl inj t ms o f.

(5) Ŧm, I d p @ s tt I wl kp +| ss % a wh ⊙ ⊙, wn cm t m as sh, as scur @ invlt i m b as th wr i hs bf cmc.

(6) Ŧm, || d p @ s tt I wl nt gv +| ₲ ♓ § % Ð % ⊙ ⊙, xc fr +| bf % +| Ȼf whl at w, or +| inst % a b, nls || am in rl ds, @ shd I c tt § gv, or hr +| ws acmp +| sm, || wl hst t +| rlf % +| on s gv it.

(7) Fm, || d p @ s tt I wl n gv +| s fr +| ⊙st w i an oth mn thn tt in wch I rc it, wch wl b on +| f ps % fsh @ at l b.

(8) Ŧm, I d p @ s tt I wl n wr, ch nr df a ⊙ ⊙ ::, nr a b % ths °, t +| vl % anthg, knl, nr sf i t b d b anthr, if in m pw t prv.

(9) Ŧm, I d p @ s tt I w n vl +| chs % a ⊙ ⊙s wf, wd, mh, str o dr, n sf it t b d b anh, if i m p t pvt.

(10) Ŧm, || d p @ s tt I w n b pr at +| initg, ps o rs % an ol m i

dot, a y mn un ag, an irlgs lbt, an aths, a psn % unsd m, a eunc or a w, kng thm t b sh.

(11) Fm, || d p @ s tt I w n b p at +| int, psg, o rs % a Ç clndsly, nr hld ⊙c intrcs wh a clnds ⊙, or wh on wh hs bn sspd or xpld, kn h t b sh, ntl dl rstd.

T al % wh I sl @ sn p @ s, wtho ny hst, mtl rs or sc ev % m i m wtev, bdg ms un n ls a p thn tt % hv m b sv i twn, m bs tkn thc @ b t as, @ +| ashs th% sc t +| f win % h, tt thr mt rmn nthr trak, tr nr rmb am mn or ⊙s % s v @ prj a wh as || shd b sh I ev, kn o wlfy, v ths m s o % ⊙ ⊙. ≀ h m ¢, @ mk m stf t kp @ p +| sm.

In tstm % ur snc, k +| ⊙ ⊙ upn wh ur hs rs. (*Dn.*) ⊙r ≀ ⊙.

≀ ⊙- ⊙ ⊙.

⊙⊙- ℞mv +| c-t. ⊙e nw hld +| br b a strgr ti. (*Dn.*) ⊙r Æ ⊙, i ur prs sitn wt d u ms dsr.

Ͽr Ѧ Ͽ- (*Ꝑrmtd.*) ⊤r l i ⊙y.

⊙ ⊙- Lt ¦¦ br b brt t l. (*Dn.*) ⊙y br, on bn bt t l in ths ° u bhl ⊣⊢ th gt lts i ⊙y, as in ⊣⊢ prc °, wh ths dfc: bh pts % ⊣⊢ cs r ab ⊣⊢ s, wh i t th u tt u hv rcd, @ r ntld t rcv, al ⊣⊢ lt tt cn b cnfd upn or cmcd t u i a ⊙ ⊙ ::.

≀ Ͽ- (*Ѧdrsg* ⊣⊢ Ͼ.) Ͽh ⊣⊢ ⊙ ⊙ aphg fm ⊣⊢ Є, on ⊣⊢ st, (∓*kn*) und ⊣⊢ dg (¢*v*) @ § (¢*v*) % Є Ѧ; on ⊣⊢ st (*Tn*) und ⊣⊢ dg (¢*v*) @ § (¢*v.*) % ⊤c; on ⊣⊢ st, (*Tn*) und ⊣⊢ dg (¢*v*) @ § (¢*v*) % ⊙ ⊙.

⊙ ⊙- ⊙y br, a ⊙ ⊙ advs on hs l f, (*Ѧdv*) brg ⊣⊢ h % hs r to ⊣⊢ hl % hs l, (*Dn*) thb fm ⊣⊢ ngl % a s. ∓hs i ⊣⊢ dg, (¢*s it.*) @ al t ⊣⊢ psn % ur hs whl tk ⊣⊢ o; ths i ⊣⊢ §, (¢*n.*) @ al t ⊣⊢ p % ⊣⊢ o. ∓hs dg (¢*n*) @ § (¢*v*) r alw t b gvn as a sltn t ⊣⊢ ⊙ ⊙ on ntg o rtr fm a ⊙ ⊙ ::.

On ntg ths or an oth :: i ths jrsdc, adv t ⊣| Δ̸ @ obs ⊣| psn % ⊣| cs. Shd bh ps b bnh ⊣| sq, i wl b a sur indn tt ⊣| :: is o on ⊣| f °, whn u wl slt ⊣| ⊙ ⊙ wh ⊣| dg (₵*s it.*) @ § (₵*s it.*) % ⊙ Δ̸. Shd o p b a ⊣| s, it wl b an eql sr ind tt ⊣| :: is o o ⊣| snd °, whn u w slt ⊣| ⊙ ⊙ wh ⊣| dg (₵*n*) @ § (₵*v*) % Ŧc. Shd bh ps b abv ⊣| sq i wl als b an eqly sr ndcn tt ⊣| :: i o on ⊣| th °, whn u wl sl ⊣| ⊙ ⊙ wh ⊣| dg (₵*v*) @ § (₵*n*) % ⊙ ⊙.

|| nw prst m r h i tk % cntnunc % fsh @ bl lv, @ w inv u wh ⊣| pg, @ pw; bt as u r uninsd, h wh hs hthrt ans fr u wl at ths tm. ₵v m ⊣| r g % Ŧc. (*Dn.*) ⊙r ≀ ⊙. ⊙ ⊙.

⊙l u b o o fm. Ŧ.

Ŧm wt @ t wt. 3

Ŧ ⊣| r g % Ŧc t ⊣| pg % ⊙ ⊙.

₱. (*Dn*) ⊙t i tt. Ŧh pg % ⊙ ⊙.

♓s i a nm. It hs. ⊙l u gv i t m.

≀ ⊙ - || dd nt s rc i, nth w I s i i.

⊙ ⊚- ♓w wl u dsp % i.

≀ Ɔ- L or sl i. Sl i @ bg. U bg.

⊙ ⊚- Ɔg u. (₵*n.*) – is ⫲ n % ths g. U shd alw rmbr i, fr shd u b prst at ⫲ o % a ::, ths pw w b dmd % u b o % ⫲ Ɔs, @ shd u b unbl t gv it, it wd cs cnfsn in ⫲ cft. ℞s, slt ⫲ ⌡ @ ≀ ⊙s, @ sf thm tt u r a dl obld ⊚ ⊚, in psn % ⫲ st, dg, §, pg, @ pw. Ofs rsm ur stns. (℞*tn t* Є.)

⊙dns- (⅄*s* ⫲ ⊙ ⊚ *pses, rsm thr stns, flwd b* ⊚s%c.)

Ɔrn- (∓*k thr sts.*)

≀ Ɔ- (Ç*dcts* ⫲ Ç *drct t* ⌡ ⊙*s sta, on* ⫲ *stp %* ⊚ ⊚.) ***

⌡ ⊙- * (℞*s*) ⊙h cs h.

≀ Ɔ- ⅄ dl obgtd ⊚ ⊚.

⌡ ⊙- ♓w m I k hm t b sch.

Ɔ crt §s @ a tkn. ⊙t r §s.

℞t ngls, hrzls @ prpls. ⅄dv a §.

(≀ Ɔ @ Ç ₵*v dg.*) ♓s tt an alsn.

It hs, t ⫲ psn % m hs whl tk ⫲ o.

♓v u a fth §.

|| hv. (≀ ☽ @ *br gv* §.) ♓s tt an al.
It hs, t ⫲ pn % ⫲ o. ⊙t is a tkn.
Ⱥ crt frnd or brl g whb on ⊙ ma k anth i ⫲ dk as i ⫲ lt.
Ⱥdv @ gv m a tkn.
(≀ ☽ @ Ꞓ *advc on* ⫲ *stp %* ⊙ ⊙ @ *gv pg; caus* Ꞓ*dts t gv i t eh oth.*)
⊙t i tt. ∓h pg % ⊙ ⊙. ♓s i a n.
It hs. ⊙l u gv i t m.
|| dd nt s rc i, nth w I s i i.
♓w wl u dsp % i. L or sl i.
Sl i @ bg. U bg.
☽g u. (₲*vn*) || am stfd.
≀ ☽ - (*In* ⊙, *cdt o stp %* ⊙ ⊙.) ***
≀ ⊙ - * (℞*s.*) ⊙h cs h.
Ⱥ dl obgd ⊙ ⊙.
♓w m I k hm t b sh.
☽ crt §s @ a tkn. ⊙t r §s.
℞t angs, hrzls @ prpls. Ⱥdvc a §.
(₲*v dg.*) ♓s tt an alsn.
It hs, t ⫲ psn % m hs wl tk ⫲ o.
♓v u a fth §.
|| hv. (≀ ☽ @ Ꞓ *gv* §.)

)(s tt an als.

It hs, t ǂ pn % ǂ o.

⌽t is a tkn.

Ⱥ crt frnd or brl g whb on ⍜ m k anth i ǂ dk as i ǂ lt.

Ⱥdv @ gv m a tkn.

(*Ⱥdv on ǂ stp % ⍜ ⍜ @ gv pg, cses Ȼdts t gv i t eh oth.*)

⌽t i tt. ∓h pg % ⍜ ⍜.

)(s i a nm. It hs. ⌽l u gv i t m.

|| dd nt s rc i, nth w I s i i.

)(w wl u dsp % i. L or sl i.

Sl i @ bg. U bg.

Ͽg u. (₲*n.*) I m stfd.

≀ Ͽ- (*Ȼndcts ǂ Ȼ Є, on Ŋ sd % ǂ ::. ⌽hn nr ǂ Ⱥ—*)

⌽ ⍜- * Ͽr ≀ Ͽ.

≀ Ͽ- ⌽ ⍜.

⌽ ⍜- ℞c ǂ br t ǂ ≀ ⌽ in ǂ ⌽, wh wl th hm hw t wr hs a as ⍜ ⍜.

≀ Ͽ- (*Ȼdcs ǂ Ȼ bf ǂ ⌽ @ upn stp.*) Ͽr ≀ ⌽.

≀ ⌽- Ͽr ≀ Ͽ.

≀ Э- It is ╫ ○ % ╫ Ⓣ Ⓞ tt u th ths br hw t wr hs ap as Ⓞ Ⓞ.

≀ Ⓣ- (*Ⱥrngs Çs ap.*) Эr Ⱥ Э, u hv alrdy bn infd tt at ╫ bld % Ꝁ ≀ ∓ ╫ dfrt bnds % wkmn wr dstgshd b ╫ mnr i wh th wr thr aps. Ⓞ·Ⓞs wr thrs thus; thus wr urs.

≀ Э- (Ç*dcs* ╫ Ç *t* ╫ Ⓒ)

ⓉⓄ- Ⓞ br, as u r nw clth as Ⓞ Ⓞ, I prs u, mblmtcly, ╫ wkg tls, wh r al ╫ tls % Ⓞy, espcl ╫ ∓rl, an inst usd b optv Ⓞs t spd ╫ cmt wh uni ╫ svrl prts % a bld int on cmn ms; bt we, as ∓ @ Ⱥ Ⓞs, r tght to us i fr ╫ mr nbl @ glrs prps % sprdng ╫ cmnt % brthly lv @ afctn—tt cmnt wh unts us int on sacd bnd o soci % frds @ brs, amg whm n cntntn shd evr xst, sve tt nbl cntntn, or rthr emultn, % wh bs cn wk @ bs agre.

ⓉⓄ- Эr ≀ Э.

≀ Э- Ⓣ Ⓞ.

⊙ ⊙- ℞cdc ⊣ br to ⊣ plc whc h cm, invst hm wh tt % wh h hs bn dvst, @ i du tm rtn hm to ⊣ :: fr fthr instn.

⊙s%c- (*℘rcd t ⊣ Δ, stdng aprt.*)

≀ ⊙- (*℘lc Ç btw thm @ tks hs pl.*)

⊙s%c @ ⊙r Δ ⊙- (*Slt, l fc, mh to pr-rm. ∓h br is rinvstd whl—*)

(∓h :: *ma prcd t bsns, or cl fm* ℔ *to rfsmt. ∓h ⊙st or* ≀ ⊙, *shd appt asstnts fr wk % scd sctn.*)

—○—

SECOND SECTION

Ⓐs%c- (*Ⓥhn Ꝗs r rdy.*) ***

ⓋⒶ- * (*Ꝗls* ⫲ :: *t* ○. *Lts of.*)

≀ Ɒ- (*Ꝗdcs* ⫲ Ꝗ *insd %* ⫲ *dr.*) Ⓐ

br, in ur fthr prgrs in ths °, it wl b ncsy f u t rpst ou an oprtv ₲ Ⓐ ⋊ ⩞, ⫲ wds sn, wh fr hs intgt @ fdlt bcm emintly dstgshd, @ whs nm is hld in hh vnrtn b ⫲ crf. It i fr tt rsn u r nvsd wh ths j, as ⫲ aprpt mblm or bg % hs ofc.

U wl thrf prcv tt u r nt yt fly invs wh al ⫲ ss % a Ⓐ Ⓐ, nr d I k tt u ev w b; fr, lk h, it wl b nsy fr u t gv u sfcty prf % ur fdlt t ⫲ trst alrd rpsd i u. In dng ths ur pth m b bst wh dngs @ dfclts, @ ev ur l itsl ma b thtnd. 183–3

U wl thfr smn t ur ad al ur frtd, tt trly dstngd Ⓐc crdnl vrtu, t nabl u t ndr ⫲ trls wh r bf u. ⋊mn l, my br, is a cnst scn % trls, @ w wk.

frl mrtls r tgt t plc ou dpndc upn ⊣ Sp Ⱥr % ⊣ U aln fr supt, prtcn @ dlvrnc.

At ur ini int ⊙y u wr tgt tt bf ntrg upn ny gt or impt undtkg u ougt alw t nvk ⊣ ad % Ͽ. ∓hn u hd a fthl fd t pra fr u; nw u ms pry fr usl.

U wl thf sf urs t b ag hw, rpr t ⊣ sa Ⱥ % ∓ ⊙y @ thr k @ pra, eth orl o mntly, as u chs. ⊙n u shl hv cncld ur dvo, sa am audbly, rs @ prc in ⊣ fthr crms % ⊣ °.

≀ Ͽ- (*Ꝑlcs hw, @ cndcs Ꞔ t ⊣ Ⱥ: lts trnd on: aft am, tks Ꞔ b ⊣ r rm, @ prcds drc t* ⌡ ⊙ *st i ⊣* ≀, *whr –a stps Ꞔ by plcg r h on hs l sh.*)

–Ⱥ- ₲ ⊙ ⋊ Ⱥ, I am gl t mt u al; ths i an oprtnt I hv sgt. U prsd tt wn ⊣ ∓ shd b cmpl to gv us ⊣ s w % ⊙ ⊙, to nabl us t ob mst's wgs whl trv i frn lnds. Ͽhl, ⊣ ∓ i ab cmpltd, @ I dmd ⊣ s w % ⊙ ⊙.

≀ ☽- ∓hs i nthr tm nr pl t gv +| s w % (⊥) (⊥). (⊤)t unt +| ∓ is cmpltd @ ddctd, thn, if fnd why, u wl rcv it; othws u cnnt.

-A̧- Çnnt! ∓lk nt t m % tm nr plc; gv m +| sc wd % (⊥) (⊥).

≀ ☽- || wl nt.

-A̧- (⊤)l nt! Ģv m +| s w % (⊥) (⊥) ths inst, or I wl t ur l.

≀ ☽- || shl nt.

-A̧- ∓hn d.

≀ ☽- (Ç*ndcs* Ç *t* (⊤).)

-○- (*L hn on r shld.*) Ģ (⊥))-(A̧, || dmd +| s w % (⊥) (⊥).

≀ ☽- || cnnt gv it.

-○- Çnnt! Ģv m +| s w % (⊥) (⊥).

≀ ☽- || wl nt.

-○- (⊤)l nt! Ģv m +| s w % (⊥) (⊥) ths inst, or I wl tk ur lf.

≀ ☽- || shl nt.

-○- ∓h d.

≀ ☽- (Ç*nd* Ç *t* +| (⊣).)

–⊙- (Ↄ *th hns.*) ₵ ⊙ ⋊ Ѧ, I dmd ⫲ sc wd % ⊙ ⊙.

≀ Ↄ- || cnnt gv it.

–⊙- Çnnt; || hrd ur cvlg wh –a @ –o; frm thm u hv escpd, fm m u cnnt. ₵v m ⫲ s w % ⊙ ⊙.

≀ Ↄ- || wl nt.

–⊙- ⊚l nt; I hld in m hd an inst % d. ₵v m. ⫲ s w % ⊙ ⊙ ths ins, or I wl tk ur lf.

≀ Ↄ- ⊙y l u ma tk; m intg nv.

–⊙- ∓hn d.

–Ѧ- Ѧls, wt hv w dn.

–○- Sln ou ₵ ⊙ ⋊ Ѧ, @ nt obtd ⫲ s w % ⊙ ⊙.

–⊙- Dnt cvl abt ⫲ s w % ⊙⊙. Lt us br ⫲ b in ⫲ rbsh, @ mt at lw tw fr cnsltn.

–Ѧ@○-Ѧgrd.

(∓*hy tk up* ⫲ Ↄ @ *crry it* ⊚ % Ѧ.)

–⊙- Ↄ pnctl at lw tw.

–Ѧ@○- Ѧgrd.

(*Lts td dn @ lo t is strk.*)

-⊙- Is tt u, -a. -Ⱥ- It is.

-M- Is tt u, -o. -○- It is.

-⊙- Ⱥst m t cr ǂ b a wstrly crs t ǂ br % a hl, whr I hv a gr prpd, @ br it.

-Ⱥ@○- Ⱥgrd.

(*Ᵽlc* Ɔ *btwn* ǂ Ⱥ @ ⓣ; *hd t* ⓣ.)

-⊙- || nw prps tt w plnt ths sp % ac at ǂ hd % ǂ gr, to mrk ǂ spt shd futr occsn rqr us t fnd it.

-Ⱥ@○- Ⱥgrd.

-⊙- Ŋw lt us mk ou esc fr ǂ rlm. (Ɽ*fns tk thr sts, lts trnd up, cnfsn.*)

(○*fs chng ttls.*)

Ɽ ʅ - * Ɔr ϰ, Ɽ % ∓.

ϰ Ɽ % ∓- ⊙ Ɛ Ɽ ʅ.

Ɽ ʅ - ⓣht is ǂ cse % ǂ cnfsn, @ wh r nt ǂ cft prsng thr Ϸ as usul.

ϰ Ɽ % ∓- ∓hr r no dsgns upn ǂ trsbrd whby ǂ cft cn prsu thr Ϸ, @ ɸ ⊙ ϰ Ⱥ, is mssg.

Ɽ ʅ - ɸ ⊙ ϰ Ⱥ mssg. ϰ hs evr bn pnctl in ǂ prfmc % evy dut. I fr sm acdt hs bfaln hm. Çse strc srh t b md in @ abt ⊣ svrl aprtmts % ⊣ ∓, @ c if h cn b fnd.

⋈ Ꞧ % ∓- Çfm, asmbl. (∓*w Çfn, wrng thr aps as* ⊙ ⊙, *mh nth, fc* ⊣ ⊙ @ *gv* § % *fdlt.*) ⊙k strc srh in @ abt ⊣ svrl aptmts % ⊣ ∓m, @ c if ₲ ⊙ ⋈ Ⱥ cn b fnd.

(*Çrfmn mh ard on nth sd %* ⊣ ::, *mkng inqry, wh is ansd by bn or* ⊣ *flwg cfm.*)

1st Çfm- ⋈v u sn ou ₲ ⊙ ⋈ Ⱥ.

Ⱥ ⊃r or 2 Çfm- ꞑt snc h tw ystr.

2d Çfm- ⋈v u sn ou ₲ ⊙ ⋈ Ⱥ.

Ⱥ ⊃r or 3d Çf- ꞑt snc h tw ystr.

3d Çfm- ⋈v u sn ou ₲ ⊙ ⋈ Ⱥ.

Ⱥ ⊃r or 4th Çfm- ꞑt sc h tw ystr.

4th Çfm- ⋈v u sn ou ₲ ⊙ ⋈ Ⱥ.

Ⱥ ⊃r or 1st Çfm- ꞑt snc h tw ys.

1st Çfm- (*In* ⊣ ⊙.) ⊃r ⋈ Ꞧ % ∓.

⋈ Ꞧ % ∓- Çfm.

1st Çfm- Strc srh hs bn md in @ ab ⊣ svrl aprtmts % ⊣ ∓, @ ou

₵ ⊙ ϰ Ⱥ cnnt b fnd; h hs nt bn sn snc h tw ystr. (Ꞓ*fm rtr.*)

ϰ Ꞧ % ∓- ⊙ ⋲ Ꞧ ≀.

Ꞧ ≀ - Ͽr ϰ Ꞧ % ∓.

ϰ Ꞧ % ∓- Strc srh hs bn md in @ abt ǂ svrl aprtmts % ǂ ∓, @ ₵ ⊙ ϰ Ⱥ cnnt b fnd; he hs nt bn sn snc h twl yst.

1st Ꞓfm- ***

₵rd- Ͽr ϰ Ꞧ % ∓, thr is an alm.

ϰ Ꞧ % ∓- ⊙ ⋲ Ꞧ ≀.

Ꞧ ≀ - Ͽr ϰ Ꞧ % ∓.

ϰ Ꞧ % ∓- ∓hr is an alm.

Ꞧ ≀ - Ⱥtn t ǂ alm @ asrt ǂ cs.

ϰ Ꞧ % ∓- Ⱥtn t ǂ al @ asrt ǂ cs.

₵rd- * (*Ops dr.*) ⊛h cs h.

1st Ꞓ- ∓w Ŧcs skg audc wh Ꞧ ≀.
⊛e hv an imprt cmctn.

₵rd- (Ꞓ*ls dr-*) Ͽr ϰ Ꞧ % ∓, twl Ŧcs skng audc wh Ꞧ ≀, @ sa th hv an imprt cmctn.

ϰ Ꞧ % ∓- ⊙ ⋲ Ꞧ ≀.

Ꞧ ≀ - Ͽr ϰ Ꞧ % ∓.

♓ Ꝁ % ∓- ∓w ⊤cs skg adc, @ sa thy hv an impt cmctn.

Ꝁ ≀ - Ꜷdmt thm.

♓ Ꝁ % ∓- (∓*o grd.*) Ꜷdmt thm.

∓w ⊤cs- (Ͼ*ntr, sx on eh sd %* ⫞ ::, *mrh t* ⫞ Ͼ, *fc in, mrh twds* Ꜷ, *frmng smi-crcl in frt %* Ͼ, *knl on r k, @ gv d-g %* ⊤c.)

1st Ȼfm- ⊙ Ͼ Ꝁ ≀ .

Ꝁ ≀ - Ȼfm.

1st Ȼfm- ⊙e twl, wh thr oths, ent int a cnsprc t xtrt fm ou ₲ ⊙ ♓ Ꜷ, ⫞ sc wd % ⊙ ⊙ or tk hs lf. ℞flctg on ⫞ nrmt % ⫞ crm, w hv rcntd, @ appr bf u, clthd in wt glvs @ aps, tkns % inoc, @ hmbly crav ur prdn. ⊙e fr, hwvr, tt ⫞ oths hv bn s bse as t crry thr mdrs dsgn int xectn.

Ꝁ ≀ - ℞s, rpr t ur ℔. Ur prdn wl dpnd upn ur futr cndc.

∓w ⊤cs- (Ȼ*ontr-mch @ eh sx ps ot ovr xctly sam rt as thy entd.*)

Ꝁ ≀ - ⊃r ♓ Ꝁ % ∓.

ж ·K· % ∓- ⊙ ∊ ·K· ≀.

·K· ≀- Çse ⫞ sev rls % wkm t b cld, @ c wh, if an, r msg.

ж ·K· % ∓- Ͽr Sec.

≀ ec- Ͽr ж ·K· % ∓.

ж ·K· % ∓- Çl ⫞ svrl rls % wkm, @ c wh, if an, r msg.

≀ ec- (*Çs t ant-rm.*) Çfm, asmbl fr rll-cll. (*Çls rll.*)

Amos, Caleb, Ezra, –Δ

Joshua, Hezekiah, Nathan, –○

Samuel, Isaiah, Aholiab, –⊙

Gideon, Haggai, Daniel.

≀ ec. Ͽr ж ·K· % ∓.

ж ·K· % ∓- Ͽr Sec.

≀ ec- ∓h sev rls % wkm hv bn cl, @ thr r msg –a, –o @ –m, brs @ mn % ∓y.

ж ·K· % ∓- ⊙ ∊ ·K· ≀.

·K· ≀- Ͽr ж ·K· % ∓.

ж ·K· % ∓- ∓h svrl rls % wkmn hv bn cld, @ thr r msg –a, –o @ –m, brs @ mn % ∓y.

₭ ≀ - ⊃r ⋊ ₭ % ∓, twl ⊤cs apd bf m ths mng, clthd i wt gls @ aps, tns % inoc, @ cnfsd tt th, wh t oths, hd entrd int a cnsprc t xtrt fm ₲ ⊙ ⋊ ⩓ ⫲ sc wd % ⊙ ⊙ or tk hs lf. ꝶfg on ⫲ enrmt % ⫲ cr, thy hd rcntd, @ hmbly crvd m prdn. ∓h frd, hwev, tt ⫲ oths hd bn so bs as t crry thr mrds dsgn int xctn. Slct fm ⫲ dfr bnds % wkm thos twl ⊤cs, dvd thm int prts % thr, @ snd thm ⋲, ⊙, Ꞃ @ ≀ in sh % ⫲ absnts.

⋊ ₭ % ∓- Ꞔfm, asmbl.

∓w ⊤cs- (*⩓smbl, sx on eh sd, mch int* ⫲ ::, @ *fm sm ccl wst %* ⩓, *fcng* ⫲ ⊙, *gvg § % fdlty.*)

⋊ ₭ % ∓- U wh aprd bfr ₭ ≀ ths mng @ cnfsd, dvd int prts % thr, @ trv ⋲, ⊙, Ꞃ @ ≀ in srch % ⫲ absts, @ rtn nt wtht tdngs.

1s Ꝑrt- Lt us prsu a wsl crs. (⊤c ⊙.)

2d Ꝑr- Lt us prsu a esl crs. (⊤c ⋲.)

3d Ꝑ- Lt us g nth. (⊤c Ꞃ.)

4th Ꝑrt- Ꭺn we sth. (₸c ≀ .)

(*Ꭺl mch i ⊣ drcts mntnd @ 2d, 3rd @ 4th prts tk sts.*)

1st Ꞔfm- (*Ꞃr otr dr.*) Ꞔmpns hr is a se-frg mn. Lt us inqr % hm.

2d @ 3d Ꞔfm- Ꭺgrd.

1st Ꞔfm- Sr, hv u sn an strngs ps ths wa.

≀ fm- ‖ dd, thr ystr.

1st Ꞔfm- ʘl u dscrb thm.

≀ fm- ₸m thr gnrl aprc I spsd thm t b mn % ∓y; fm a strg fmly rsmb, brs, @ fm thr bng clhd i wt glvs @ aps mst hv bn wkm fm ⊣ ∓m. ∓h wr ndvrg t obt psg t ϵ thopa, bt Ꝁ ≀ hvg isud an edc frbdg an prs t lv ⊣ rlm wtht hs ps, @, nt hvg it, thy fld t obtn psg, @ rtnd int ⊣ cnty.

1st Ꞔfm- ∓hs r tdngs.

2d Ꞔf- ∓hs is imprtnt 3

3d Ꞔ- Lt us g up @ rprt.

1st @ 2d Ꞔfm- Ꭺgrd. (*ʘch t* ϵ.)

(*Ꞔfm alws go up t* ϵ *on nrth sd %* ::, *alws dwn on sth sd.*)

1st Ꞔfm- ∓dgs, ⊙ ⋵ ꝁ≀ .

ꝁ≀ - ⊕t tdgs.

1st Ꞔfm- ⊕e wh trvl a wstl crs on arvg at ⫞ cty % Jpa, fl in wh a sfrng mn, % whm w inqd if h hd sn an strgs ps tt wa. ⋊ rpld tt h hd, thr ⫞ da bfr, wh fm thr gnrl aprnc h spsd t b mn % ∓y; fm a strg fmly rsmblc, brs, @ fm thr bng clthd i wt gls @ aps, mst hv bn wkm fm ⫞ ∓m. ∓h wr ndvg t obt psg t ⋵ thopa, bt ꝁ≀ hvg issd an edc frbdng an prsn t lv ⫞ rlm wtht hs ps, @, nt hvg it, thy fld t obtn psg, @ rtnd int ⫞ cntr.

ꝁ≀ - ∓hs, n dbt, wr ⫞ rfs; bt ths is nt stsfcty. ∓rvl as bf, wh ⫞ pstv asrnc tt if u d nt sccd in brng ⫞ rfs to jstc u wl b dmd ⫞ mrdrs % ꝕ ⊙ ⋊ ⩓, @ sfr acdgly.

1st Ꞔfm- Lt us agn prsu a wsl crs.

2d @ 3d Ꞔfm- ⩓grd. (*⩓l trvl* ⊕.)

1st Ꞔfm- Ꞔmpns, I am wry, @ wl st dn to rst @ rfs msl.

2d Çfm- (*Çntnu mchg.*) Çm alg. ⊙e hv an imprtnt dt t prfm.

1st Çfm- Ӿl, cmpns. On atmtng to rs I acdtl cgt hld % ths sp % ac, wh so easl gv wa as t xct m sspcn. (*2d @ 3d Çfm rtn.*)

2d Çfm- ∓h ert sms t hv bn rcntl dstrbd.

3d Çfm- It prsts ⊣ aprnc % a gr.

–Ѧ- ○, tt m t hd bn c a, m t t ot @ br i ⊣ sd % ⊣ c at lw w mk, wh ⊣ t ebs @ fs twc i tf hs, er I hd bn acs t ⊣ md % ou ₲ ⊙ Ӿ Ѧ.

3d Çfm- ∓t's ⊣ vc % –a.

–○- ○, tt m l b hd bn t o, m h @ l tkn thc t ⊣ ⩛ % Jhspht, @ lf a pr t ⊣ vlts % ⊣ ar, er I hd bn acs t ⊣ m % ou ₲ ⊙ Ӿ Ѧ.

2d Çfm- ∓t's ⊣ vc % –o.

–⊙- ○, tt m bd h bn sv i tw, m bls tn thc @ bn to shs, @ ⊣ shs thr% scd t ⊣ fr ws % hv, tt thr mt rmn nthr trk, trc, nr rmbrc, amg mn or ⊙s, % so vl @ prj a wrh as I, wh hv sln ou ₲ ⊙ ⋊ Ⱥ.

1st Ꞔfm- ∓t's ⊣ vc % –m. Lt us rsh in, sz, bnd @ tk thm bfr ·Ꝁ ≀.

2d @ 3d Ꞔfm- Ⱥgrd.

(℞*fs r tkn up nth sd* % ⊣ :: *t* ⊣ ⋲.)

1st Ꞔfm- ∓dgs, ⊙ ⋲ ·Ꝁ ≀.

·Ꝁ ≀ - ⊙t tdngs.

1st Ꞔfm- ⊙e trv as drc, @ on arvg at ⊣ br % a hl I, bng wery, st dn t rst @ rfsh mslf. On atmptg to rs I acdtl cght hld % a spg % ac, wh so esly gv wa as to xcit m sspcn. I thupn hld m cmpns, @ whl cnvrsg on ⊣ sngulrty % ⊣ ocrnc w dstcly hrd vcs issung fm ⊣ clfts % ⊣ ajct rcks, ⊣ fst % wh w rcgnd a tt % –a, xclmg: ○, tt m th hd bn ct ac, m tg tn ot @ br i ⊣ snd % ⊣ c at l wt mk, whr ⊣ td ebs @ fls twc i twf hrs, er I hd bn accs t ⊣ mdr % ou ₲ ⊙ ⋊ Ⱥ; ⊣ scnd as tt % –o, xclm: ○, tt m l br hd bn tn op, my hr @ lg tkn thnc t

⊣ V̇ % Jhspht, @ lf a pr t ⊣ vlts % ⊣ ar, er I hd bn accs t ⊣ mr % ou ₲ ⊙ ♓ Ą; @ ⊣ thd as tt % –m, xclmg: O, tt my bd hd bn sv i twn, m bls tkn thnc @ brd t ashs, @ ⊣ ashs th% sctd t ⊣ fr wns % hv, tt thr mt rmn nth trk, trc, nr rmbrc, amg mn o ⊙s, % so vl @ prj a wrh as I, wh hv sln ou ₲ ⊙ ♓ Ą. ⊚e thrupn rshd in, sezd, bnd, @ hv thm bfr u.

ℛ ≀ - –Ą, u std chgd wth bg accs t ⊣ mr % ₲ ⊙ ♓ Ą. ⊚t sa u t ⊣ chrg, gl or nt g.

–Ą- ₲.

ℛ ≀ - –O, u std chgd wth bg accs t ⊣ mr % ₲ ⊙ ♓ Ą. ⊚t sa u t ⊣ chrg, gl or nt g.

–O- ₲.

ℛ ≀ - –⊙, u stnd chrgd wh ⊣ mr % ₲ ⊙ ♓ Ą. ⊚t sa u t ⊣ chrg, gl or nt g.

–⊙- ₲.

ꝁ ≀ - Vl @ imps wrhs, rflc on ⊣ enrm % ur crm @ ⊣ ambl chrc % hm u hv sln. Lk up @ rcv ur sntc, wh is tt u b tkn wtht ⊣ wls % ⊣ cty @ svrly xcutd, agrbly t ⊣ imprcts fm ur ow mths. ⊝gn, *

(℞*fs tkn dn s sd % :: @ arn* ⊣ *Ѧ. ₵fm rtn t* ⊖ *on nth sd % ::.)*

1st ₵fm- ⊙ ⊖ ꝁ ≀.

ꝁ ≀ - ₵fm.

1st ₵- ∓h rfs hv bn xct ag t u cmd.

ꝁ ≀ - ∓is wl. ɲw g fth i sh % ⊣ bd % ₲ ⊙ ⋊ Ѧ, @ if fd mk dlgt srh on @ abt it fr anthg whby it ma be clrly idntfd.

1st ₵fm- Lt us rpr t ⊣ br % ⊣ hl whr I st dn t rst @ rfs msl.

2d @ 3d ₵fm- Ѧgrd. (℘*rcd* ⊙.)

1st ₵f- ∓hs sms t b ⊣ spt.

2d ₵- Ys, hr is ⊣ sp % ac.

3d ₵f- It prsts ⊣ aprc % a gr.

1st ₵fm- Lt us rmv ⊣ er. (*Dn*) ⋊r is a bd, bt i s mgl @ pt a cndtn tt it i imps t prsu ⊣ srch. Lt us std asd untl ⊣ eflva pss of (₲*v d* % ⊙ ⊙; *trn hd t lf.*) Ɲw lt us rsum ⊣ srch. (*Dn.*) ⋊r is a jl.

2d Ꞓfm- Lt us rmv i @ g up @ rpt.

1st @ 3d Ꞓfm- Ⱥgrd.

(Ꞓ*fm tk jl up nth sd %* ⊣ :: *t* ⊣ ⊖.)

1st Ꞓfm- ∓dgs, ⊙ ⊖ Ʀ ≀.

Ʀ ≀ - ⊙t tdgs.

1st Ꞓfm- ⊙e wnt fth as drc, @ on arvg at ⊣ br % ⊣ hl whr I st dn to rst @ rfsh msl, dscvd ⊣ aprc % a gr; on rmvg ⊣ eth, a bdy, bt in s mgld @ ptrd a cndtn tt w fd ou hns invlt in ths psn (₲*vs d* % ⊙ ⊙.) t grd ou nstls fm ⊣ eflva arsg thrfm. Ⱥft ⊣ eflva hd psd of w md dlgt srch on @ ab ⊣ bd, bt fnd nthg sv ths jl.

Ʀ ≀ - Ᵽrst ⊣ jl.

1st Ꞓfm- (*Ᵽrsts jl.*)

Ʀ ≀ - (*Sotto voce.*) ∓hr cn b n dbt as t ⊣ dth % ₲ ⊙ ⋊ Ⱥ, as ths is ⊣ jwl wh h wr. ⊖r ⋊ Ʀ % ∓.

ϰ K % ∓- ⊙ ⋲ K ≀.

K ≀- ∓hr cn b no lngr a dbt as t ⫲ dth % ₲ ⊙ ϰ Δ, or as t ⫲ idnty % ⫲ bd, as ths is ⫲ jwl wh h wor. Δls, I fr ⫲ ⊙st's wd is lst, fr u wl rmbr tt it ws agrd btwn uslf, msl @ ₲ ⊙ ϰ Δ, tt ⫲ sc wd % ⊙ ⊙, shd nt b gvn unls w thr wr prst @ agrd. On % ou nmb is n mr. ‖ prps tt u asmbl ⫲ crft, rpr wh m t ⫲ gr, fr ⫲ prps % rsng ⫲ bd @ brng i up to ⫲ ∓m fr mr dcnt intrmt. I als prps tt ⫲ fs § gvn on arvg at ⫲ gr @ ⫲ fs wd spkn aft ⫲ bd shl hv bn rsd, shl b rspctvly ⫲ g hl § % dst % ⊙ ⊙ @ ⫲ wd a sbst fr tt wh i ls, unls ⫲ wsd % fu gns shl ds @ bg t l ⫲ t wd.

ϰ K % ∓- Δgrd- ⊖r ⊙rshl.

⊙sl- ⊖r ϰ K % ∓.

ϰ K % ∓- Δsb ⫲ crf.

⊙sl- Ꞔrfmn, asmbl on ⫲ nth sd % ⫲ hl, tw by tw, fcg ⫲ ⋲.

(*∓h cft asbl, ⊙sl at ⊣ hd,* ⊙s%c, *Ꝁ ≀ wh ⋊ Ꝁ % ∓ on hs l, flwd by ₵fm in tws, Stwds @ ₵hp| in ⊣ rer.*

(*₱rcsn pss th ts ard. ∓h ⊙rshl, at ⊣ ⋲ dvds it int sngl fil whl—*)

Solemn strikes the funeral chime,
Notes of our departing time.
As we journey here below,
Through a pilgrimage of woe.

Here another guest we bring—
Seraphs of celestial wing,
To our funeral altar come,
Waft a friend and Brother home.

Lord of all! below—above—
Fill our hearts with truth and love;
As dissolves our earthly tie,
Take us to Thy Lodge on high.

(*On arvg at ⊣ gr ⊣* ⊙s%c *fm rch fr* Ꝁ ≀, ⊣ ⊙*shl tks hs plc at sth % ⊣* ⅁, ⋊ Ꝁ % ∓ *at its ft:* ⊣ ₵*hpln at* Δ; *bn gv § % fdlty @ rmn in* ○.)

Ꝁ ≀ - (*₲vs § % dst, onl onc.*) ○ a, b c, ws d e f g h i j.

Ꝁ ≀ - ⊃r ⋊ Ꝁ % ∓.

⋊ Ꝁ % ∓- ⊙ ∈ Ꝁ ≀.

Ꝁ ≀ - ∈ndv t rs ⊣ bd b ⊣ g % ∈ ⩜.

⋊ Ꝁ % ∓- (∈*ndv, bt fls.*) Owg to ⊣ hgh stt % ptrfcn, ⊣ bd cnnt b s rsd; ⊣ sk sls fm ⊣ fls.

Ꝁ ≀ - ∈ndv t rs ⊣ bd b ⊣ g % ∓c.

⋊ Ꝁ % ∓- ∓r ⊣ rsn bf asnd, ⊣ bd cnnt b s rsd; ⊣ fls clvs fm ⊣ bn.

Ꝁ ≀ - ⊃r ⋊ Ꝁ % ∓, in ou prsnt emrgncy, wt shl w d.

⋊ Ꝁ % ∓- ℘ry.

Ꝁ ≀ - (℞*mvs hs ht.*) ⊃n, lt us pr.

(⩜*l k on l k.*)

Ꞓhp- ∓ho, ○ ₲, knst ou dn-stng @ ou uprsg, @ undst ou thts afar of. Shld @ dfn us fm ⊣ evl intnts % ou enms, @ suprt us und ⊣ trls @ aflcs w r dstnd t ndur, whl trvlg thro ths val % ters. ⊙n tt is bn % wom is % fw das, @ fl % trbl. ⋊ cmth frth as a flwr, @ is ct dn; h fleh als as a shdo, @ cntnuth nt. Seng hs das r dtrmnd, ⫞ nmbr % hs mnths is wh ∓h; ∓ho hst apntd hs bnds tt h cnnt ps; trn fm hm tt h ma rst tl h shl hv acmplhd hs da.

Ⱡr thr is hop % a tr if it b ct dn tt i wl sprt agn, @ tt ⫞ tndr brch th% wl nt cs. ⊖t mn dith @ wsth aw: yea, mn gvth up ⫞ ghst @ whr is h. ⱯS ⫞ wtrs fl fm ⫞ se, @ ⫞ ffd dcth @ drith up, so mn lth dn @ rseth nt tl ⫞ hvns b n mr. Yt ○ L, hv cmpsn o ⫞ chldrn % th cre; admnstr thm cfrt in tm % trbl @ sv thm wh an evlstg slvn. Ɐmn. ≀ m it b.

[Yt, O L, ou trs is i ∓he. ⊙e kn tt ⫞ br wh hs bn fthfl unt dth wl rs agn, @ t hm wl b gvn ⫞ sc % tt hdn @ mystrs pwr wh brgs ot % dh @ sdn dstrcn ⫞ blsd asrnc tt whn ou ethly hs % ths tbnl shl b dslvd, w hv a bldg % ₲, a hs nt md wh hns, etnl i ⫞ hvs.

[Ⱥn whn ths mrtl shl hv pt on immrtlt, thn shl hv bn brt t ps ⊣⊢ sayg tt is wrtn, Dth is swlod up in vctry. ○ dth, whr is thy stng, O grv, whr is th vctry. ⊙e bsch ∓h, O ₲, tt ⊣⊢ tru lt % ∓th, ⋊op @ Lv ma cntu to ilumn ⊣⊢ lf % ev uprt ⊙ @ fthfl br untl ⊣⊢ dwn % tt nw-brn da % ⊣⊢ sol, whn t hm tt ovcmth shl b gvn a wt stn, @ upn tt stn a nw nm, wh no mn knth svg h tt rcth it. Ⱥmn. (*Or.*)

(O ₲, ⊣⊢ ⊙vlsg, wh hst md dh t b ⊣⊢ gong fm dkns int lt, ⊣⊢ stp fm dngr t sfty, ⊣⊢ trng % ⊣⊢ lef % myst to ⊣⊢ pgs % knlg, ⊣⊢ gt fm lf tmprl unt ⊣⊢ lf etrnl, th us t blv in its misn % frndlns, rth thn ⊣⊢ acstn % its enmty. ⊙t ev ma b ⊣⊢ mnr % its apch, gv us ⊣⊢ wl t prclm ⊣⊢ cred % soros trst, ₲ knth bst.

(⊙a w lk byd its vl % morng untl w th its wgs % dlvrc.

(∓thr, ∓h knst ⊣⊢ btl % lf, ⊣⊢ cnflct wh evl, ⊣⊢ strgl fr ⊣⊢ msty. ∓hn ow nat i t pty, t encrg @ t rscu.

(ⓦhn w dspnd, chr us; whn w stmbl, gd us; whn w jrny, g bfr us; wn w std jst otsd ∓hy dr, bd u ntr i @ b wlc hm. So shl ou hrts @ lps b attd fm ⊣⊢ dscds % erths jngls int ⊣⊢ wndrs hrmns % hvns sngs % adrn @ w shl b ∓hn @ ∓h wlt b ous thru ⊣⊢ glrs % ⊣⊢ etrnl ags, bcs ∓h rt ou ₲d fr evlsg @ or ₲d wh ev shl b, wld wtht nd. Ѧmn.) (*Or.*)

[In lf, chr u wn w dpd, gid us wn w stmbl, rs us whn w fl, g bfr us as w jrny, @, whn w wt jst otsd ∓h dr, bd us entr in @ b wlc ⋊om. ∓hr w shl b ∓hi @ ∓ho wlt b ous thro ⊣⊢ glrs % ⊣⊢ etr ags, bcs ∓ho art ou ₲, fm evlstg, @ ou ₲d wh ev shl b, wld wtht nd. Ѧmn. (*Or.*)

(∓ho, O ₲, knst ou dwnsitg @ ou uprsg, @ unstdt ou thts afr of, shld

@ dfd us fm ⊣| evl int % or enms, whl trvg thrgh ths vl % trs.

(Ąs ⊣| sed wh w so mst di i ordr tt a nw lf ma b its ow, a rchr frutg @ a mr glors hrvs ⊣| rslt, so mst w di unt ou snfl ntr i ordr tt w ma rs t a nwns % lf, a lf % fth, % hp, % nblst @ trust lv fr ou flw mn.

(₲rnt, w besch ∓h, tt in s fr as ⊣| lssn % ⊣| rsrcn % ⊣| bdy @ ⊣| imrtlty % ⊣| sol (wh ths prs momt i intnd t typf) is xmplfi i acrdc wh ∓hy ho wl @ prps, to bls it t ou wtng hrts to-nt.

(Ąn ∓hine, ○ rightus ∓thr, b al ⊣| gl fr ev @ ev. Ąmn.)

⊖n- ≀ mt it b.

Ꝃ ≀ - ⊖n, ris. (*Dn.*) ⊖r Ӿ Ꝃ % ∓, asst m t rs ⊣| bd % ₲ ⦶ Ӿ Ą b ⊣| strg gp % ⦶ ⦶ or ln's pw.

(*∓h ⦶ shl stps bck as* Ꝃ ≀ pss *ard t ft %* ⊣| ⊖, *@* Ӿ Ꝃ *%* ∓ *stps t* ⊣| *nth sd. Ąs* Ꝃ ≀ *tks gp,* Ӿ Ꝃ *%* ∓ *tks* ₵ *l h in hs l @ wh* ⊣| *rt assts*

⊣| ⍜shl t rs ⊣| ⊳, plcg Ꝗdts h on ꝁ ≀ bk. ⏀ gvn on ⊣| f p % fls.)

⏀⍜- ⍜y br, ⊣| wds u hv jst rcd r ⋊brw wds, @ sgfy, ⏀, ∓h ⊳, @ alds t a prtclr ti i ur o, whrn u swr tt u wd nt gv ⊣| sb fr ⊣| ⍜s w i an oth mnr thn tt in wh u rcd it, wh wd b on ⊣| f ps % fls @ at l b.

∓h f ps % fls r: Ŧ t f, k t k, b t b, h t b, @ m t e, @ thy tch us ths imp ls:

Ŧ t f, tt w sh b ev rd t g o f, @ ev b-f, on a wh ⍜ ⍜s ernd, shd hs ncsts rqr it @ w b n bt prvdd;

ꝁ t k, tt w shd ev rmb ou bn in ou dvs t D;

⊳ t b, tt ⊣| ss % a wr ⍜ ⍜, wn cmc t us as sh, shd b as scr @ invlt i ou b as th wr i hs bf cmc;

⋊ t b, tt w sh b e rd t st fr a h t sp a flg br, @ ast h o a lf oc;

⍜ t e, tt w sh b ev rdy t whs ws cns in ⊣| e % an erng br, @ wr hm % aprhg dg.

⊙y br, I wl nw instc u as t ⊣ mnr % ar at ⊣ r g % ⊙ ⊙; bt as u r uninstrctd, h wh hs hthrto ansd fr u wl at ths tm. ₲v m ⊣ pg % ⊙ ⊙. (₲*vn*) ⊖r ≀ ⊖. (*Rsp.*) ⊙l u b o o f.

₸m. ₸m wt @ t w.

₸ ⊣ pg % ⊙ ⊙ t ⊣ r g % ⊣ s.

₰s. (₲*vn.*) ⊙t i tt.

₸ r g % ⊙ ⊙ or ∟ ₰.

⋊s i a n. It hs. ⊙l u gv i t m.

≀ ⊖- ₰ urs i a p p t r i @ I w.

⊙⊙- ⊙k ⊣ df, m b. ⋊rtf u ans hv bn, I dd n s r i, nh wl I so imp i; nw i is, ₰ urs i a p p t r i @ I w. ⊙t i tt p p.

≀ ⊖- O ⊣ f ps % fls.

⊙⊙- ⊙t r ⊣ f ps % fls.

≀ ⊖- ₸ t f, k t k, b t b, h t b, @ m t e.

⊙⊙- (*Advs on ⊣ f ps, as thy r nmd by ≀ ⊖, @ gvs wd.*)

(₲*r hl § ma b xpld at ths tm or i ⊣ hstrcl lctr.*)

⊙⊙- ⊙y br, ╫ ☿ ⋊ § % ☽ % ⊙ ⊙, is gn in ths mnr—(☿*s g h* §.)—Ꞔpy, m brs. ℞g ╫ hs tw h, ╫ rms fmg a s, @ lwrg by t mts t ╫ s, @ alds t a ptclr ti in ur o, whrn u swr tt u wd nt gv ╫ ☿ ⋊ § % ☽ % ⊙ ⊙, xcp fr ╫ bf % ╫ cf whl at wk or ╫ inst % a b, nls u wr in r ds. Shd it b in a pl wh ╫ § cd n b sn, ╫ ws "○ p, q r, s t u v w x y z," r t b subs, bt ╫ § @ wds r nv t b gvn tgh.

Shd u s tt § or hr ths wrds, u wl hstn t ╫ rlf % ╫ on s gvg thm, fr u ma rst asrd tt th cm fm on wh hs trv ╫ sm rd @ rcd ╫ sm lt i ⊙y tt u h.

☽r ≀ ☽, cndct ╫ br t ╫ Ꞓ, wh h wl rc fthr instns. 3

—○—

THIRD SECTION

HISTORICAL LECTURE

⊙ ⍝- Scrd hst infms us tt it ws dtrmnd in +| cncls % infnt wsd tt a ∓ shd b fndd at ȷ, wh shd b ercd t ₲, @ ddc t ϰ ϰ nm.

∓h hi hnr @ dstgd prv % prfg ths sc srvc ws dnd to Dv, Ꝃ % ||, bcs, a +| Scps inf us, h hd md grt wrs @ shd bld abndty.

⊙e als lrn fm +| sm sc src tt +| ₲ % || hd prms ☽ tt ot % h lns ϰ wd ras u sd t srv ϰm. ∓hs dvn @ mmrbl prms ws afws ffld i +| prsn % ≀, @ i hs splnd @ unxmpld cr % prspt.

Ⱥf ☽ hd bn gthd t hs fths, @ +| lst hns pd t hs mry, ≀ wldd +| sptr % ||, pc rnd wthn hr brds, @ +| chldn % || lkd fwd wh pclr ssfn fr +| dspla % tt wsdm wh ws dstnd t astnh @ amz +| wld.

In ⊣ snd mth % ⊣ fth yr % hs rn, ≀ cmncd ⊣ erctn % ths edfc, ⊣ crs wkmnsp % wh ws clcltd t xct ⊣ wndr @ admrtn % al scdng ags.

It ws lctd o ⌓t ⌓rh, nr ⊣ plc whr Ⱥbr ws abt t ofr u hs sn Isc, @ whr Đ mt @ apsd ⊣ dstryg angl, wh ws vsbl ovr ⊣ thrshng-flr % Ornn, ⊣ Jbust.

Ⱥbt th tm, Ꝁ ≀ rcd a cngty ltr f Ӿ, Ꝁ % ∓y, ofrng hm evy astc i hs pwr, @ mnfstg a st dsr t prtcpt i ⊣ hi hnrs thn clstrg ard ⊣ ∓h % ||.

∓hus ws ⊣ bldg prgsg, wh ⊣ astc % Ӿ, Ꝁ % ∓, @ un ⊣ imdt sprvsn % o an op ₲ ⌓ Ӿ Ⱥ, @ ws wl-ni cmpltd, whn svrl % ⊣ Çrt, i an atpt t xtrt fm ₲ ⌓ Ӿ Ⱥ, ⊣ sc w % ⌓ ⌓, bcm hs assns. ∓hus fr a shrt prid ws ⊣ bld impdd i its prgs.

U, my br, hv ths ev rpsntd ou anc op ₲ ⌓ Ӿ Ⱥ, whs cstm it ws ev da at hi twl, whl ⊣ crf wr at rfs, t ent

+| ∓m @ dr hs dsns upn +| trs-bd, af wh h rprd t +| Unf ≀ ≀ t ofr up hs prs t +| evr lvg @ tru Ġd. Af pfmg ths pius dvos, on +| da % hs dh, he atmtd t ps ot at +| sth gt, whr h ws acstd b – a, wh thrc dmd +| sc wd % ⊙ ⊙, @ on hs thd rfsl stc hm wh a tw-fr-nch gg acrs +| th; h thn atmtd t ps ot at +| ws gt, whr h ws acs by – o, wh als thc dmd +| sc wd % ⊙ ⊙, @ on hs thd rfsl stc hm wth +| ngl % a sq on +| rt br; h thn atmtd t ps ot at +| est gt whr h ws acs b – m, wh also thrc dmd +| sc wd % ⊙ ⊙, @ on hs thd rfsl stc hm wth a s-ml on +| fr-h, wh fld h lfls at hs ft.

Th rfs thn brd +| bd in +| rbs, @ agrd t mt at lw twl fr cnsltn. Thy acrdly mt, @ crrd +| b a wstl crs t +| br % a hl, whr th hd a gr prprd, @ brd it, pltg a sp % ac at +| hd % +| gr to mrk +| spt shd futr occsn rqr thm t fnd it, @ thn endvd t mk thr escp fm +| rlm.

It ws als ⫲ cstm % ≀ Ꝃ % Is ev mrng t ent ⫲ Tm fr ⫲ prps % inspg ⫲ wk @ c if i ws bng cmpltd in al its prts agrbl t ⫲ plns wh h hd rcd fm Dv, hs fthr. On arvg at ⫲ ∓ on ths ocs, h fnd ⫲ cft in cnfsn. ♓e rprd to ⫲ hl % audc, whr h mt ♓ Ꝃ % ∓, % whm h enqrd ⫲ cse, @ ws infmd tt thr wr no dsns on ⫲ trs-bd @ tt ₲ ⊙ ♓ Ⱥ ws msg. ♓e thn ○d strc srch t b md in @ ab ⫲ svl apts % ⫲ ∓m t c if h cld b fd. Stc srh ws acdl md, bt wthot tdgs; h hd nt bn sn snc h twl ⫲ da bfr.

Ⱥbt ths tm twl ⊤cs aprd bf Ꝃ ≀, clthd in wht gls @ aps, tkns % inocs, @ cnfsd tt thy wh thr oths hd entrd int a cnsprcy t xtrt fm ₲ ⊙ ♓ Ⱥ ⫲ sc wd % ⊙ ⊙ or tk hs lf. ℞lctg on ⫲ enrmty % ⫲ crm, th hd rcntd, @ hmbl crvd hs prdn. ∓hy frd, hwevr, tt ⫲ oths hd bn so bs as to cry thr mrds dsgns int xctn.

⋊ ○d thm t rpr t thr ℔, at ⊣ sm tm infmg thm tt thr prdn wld dpnd upn thr futr cndc.

⋊e thn ○d ⊣ sv rls % wkm t b cld t c wh, if an, wr msg. ∓h rls wr accrdly cld, @ thr wr mssng, – a, – o @ – m, brs @ mn % ∓. ⋊e thn rqstd ⋊ Ꝁ % ∓ t slct fm ⊣ dfn bns % wkm ⊣ twl ∓cs wh hd aprd bfr hm, dvd thm int prts % thr @ snd thm ⊖, ⊙, Ω @ ≀ in srh % ⊣ absnts.

∓hs wh prsd a wsl cr, on arvg at ⊣ cty % ⌡ pa, fl in wh a se-fr mn, % whm th inqd if h hd sn an strngs ps tt wa. ⋊e rpld tt h hd, thr ⊣ da bfr, wh, frm thr gnrl aprnc, h spsd t b mn % ∓y, fm a strg fml rsmblc, brs, @ fm thr bng clthd in wt gls @ aps mst hv bn wkm fr ⊣ ∓m. ∓h wr ndvg t obtn psg t ⊖thp, bt Ꝁ ≀ hvg isud an edc frbdg an psn t lv ⊣ rlm wtht hs ps, @ nt hvg it, th fld to obt psg @ rtd int ⊣ cnty.

⊕h ths infmn th rtd t ꝁ≀, wh sd tt thse, n dbt, wr +| rfns, bt tt i ws nt stfctry, @ ord thm t agn trvl, wh +| pstv asrc tt if th dd nt sccd i brngg +| rfns t jstc th wd b dmd +| mrds % ₲ ⊙ ϰ ⅄ @ sfr ac.

∓h trvld as drctd, @ on arvg at +| brw % a hl, on % +| cmpns, bg wry, st dn t rst @ rfs hmslf. On atmtg t rs, h acdly cgt hl % a spg % ac, wh so esl gav wa as t xct hs ssps. ϰe thrpn hld hs cmps, @ whl cnvsg upn +| snglrty % +| ocrc th dstcly hrd vcs issug fm +| clfs % +| ajc rks, +| fs % wh th rcgnzd as tt % – a, xclmg: "○, tt m th hd bn c ac, m tg tn ot @ br in +| snd % +| c at lw wt mk, whr +| td eb @ fls twc i twf hrs, er I hd bn acsr t +| mr % ou ₲ ⊙ ϰ ⅄;" +| scd as tt % – o, xclmg: "○, tt m l bs hd bn tn op, m hr @ ln tkn thnc t +| V % Jhsopht, @ lf a pr t +| vltrs % +| ar, er I hd bn accsr t +| mr %

ou Ģ ⊙ ⋊ Ѧ; " @ ǂ thrd as tt % – m, xclmng: "○, tt m bd hd bn sv i twn, m bls tkn thnc @ brd t ash, @ ǂ ah th% sctd t ǂ fr wnds % hv, tt thr mt rmn nthr trk, trc, nr rmbc, amg mn or ⊙s, % s vl @ prj a wrch as I, wh hv sln ou Ģ ⊙ ⋊ Ѧ." ∓h thrpn rshd in, szd, bd @ tk thm bfr Ꝁ≀, wh, aft du cnfs fm ea, ○d thm to b tkn wtht ǂ wls % ǂ cty @ svly xcd, agbly t ǂ imprcts % thr ow mths. ∓h rfs wr xcd agbl t hs cmd. ⊤m ths xclmts hv arsn ǂ pnlts % ǂ Obs wh u hv tkn in ⊙y.

Ꝁ≀ thn ○d ǂ ⊤cs t g fth in srh % ǂ bd % Ģ ⊙ ⋊ Ѧ, @ if fnd, t mk dlgnt srch on @ abt it fr anth whby it mht b clrly idntfd.

∓h wnt frh as drc, @ on arvg at ǂ br % ǂ hl whr ǂ wry cmpa st dn t rs @ rfsh hmsl, dscvd ǂ aprc % a gr, @ on rmvg ǂ eth, a bd, bt in sh a mngld @ ptrd cdtn tt th fnd thr hns invltry in ths psn (*D-g* % ⊙ ⊙.) t grd thr nstls fm +| eflv arsg thrfm. Ꭺft +| eflv hd psd off thy md dlgnt srch on @ abt +| bd, bt fnd nthg sv a jl, wh th agrd t rmv, @ g up @ rpt.

Ꝁ≀, on bhldg +| jwl, sd thr cd no lngr b an dt as t +| dh % ¢ ⊙ ⋊ Ꭺ, or as t +| idnty % +| bd, as tt ws +| jwl wh h wr. Ꭺls, h frd +| ⊙st's wd ws lst, fr it ws agrd btwn hmslf, ⋊ Ꝁ % ∓ @ ⋊ Ꭺ tt +| sc wd % ⊙ ⊙ shd nt b gvn nls th thr wr prs @ agrd.

On % thr nmbr ws n mr. ⋊ prpsd t ⋊ Ꝁ % ∓ t asmbl +| crf @ rpr wh hm t +| gr fr +| prps % rsg +| bd @ brg i up t +| ∓ fr mr dcnt intr.

⋊e als prpsd tt +| fs § gvn on arv at +| gr @ +| fs wd spkn aft +| bd shd hv bn rsd shd b, rsptvly, +| g h § % dst % ⊙ ⊙ @ +| wd a sbst fr tt wh ws ls, nls +| wsd % ftr gnrts shd dsc @ brg t lt +| tr wd. ∓hs § i +|

₲ ♓ § % ☽ % ⊙ ⊙, @ ⊣| wd aludd t ws tt gvn t u on ⊣| f ps % fis @ a l b.

∓h g h § % d % ⊙ ⊙ i gv i ths mnr—(₲*s it.*) Ȼp, m br. ℞ u h t h, ur as fg a s, @ lr thm b t mts t ⊣| sd, @ alds t a prtc t in u o, whrn u s tt u w n g ⊣| ₲ ♓ § % ☽ % ⊙ ⊙, xc f ⊣| b % ⊣| cf wh at w or ⊣| ins % br, nls u w in r d. Shd it b i a p wh ⊣| § c n b s, ⊣| ws "○ p, q r, s t u v w x y z," a t b sbs. Sh u c tt § o h ths ws, u w hstn t ⊣| rl % ⊣| on s gv thm, fr u ma rs asrd tt th cm f on wh hs tv ⊣| sm r @ rc ⊣| sm l i ⊙y tt u h.

∓hs wr ⊣| rmns % ₲ ⊙ ♓ Ⱥ rsd fm thr hmbl rstg-plc, cnvd t ⊣| ∓m, @ thnc t ⊣| plc % brl, wh ws as nr ⊣| unfsd ≀ ≀ as ⊣| Jsh lws alwd, @ ovr hs grv ws erctd a mnumt % ⊣| fi-nst mrbl, on wh wr dlntd a bkn clm @ a vrgn wpng; in hr r h a sp % ac, in hr l an urn, bfr hr an opn bk, @ ∓im bhd unfldg @ cntg ⊣ rglts % hr hai. ∓h brkn col dnts tt on % ⊣ prcpl suprts % ∓ ⊙y hs fln; ⊣ vrgn wpg, ⊣ untml dh % $ ⊙ ⋈ Δ; ⊣ sp % ac, tt wh ld t ⊣ tmly rcvry % hs rmns; ⊣ urn tt hs ashs r sfl dpstd; ⊣ op bk, tt hs mry is on prptl rcd amg ⊙s; ∓m dnts tt alth $ ⊙ ⋈ Δ is n mr @ ⊣ sc wd % ⊙ ⊙ is lst, yt tm, ptnc @ prsv, wh acmplh al thgs, ma yt dscv, @ brg t lt ⊣ tr wd.

∓hr wr tw rmkbl evts atndg ⊣ erc % ths edfc. Scrd hsty nfms us tt thr ws nt hrd ⊣ snd % ax, hmr o an mtl tl i ⊣ bldg; @ Jsphs nfms us tt, alth a ltl m thn sv ys wr mpld i its ercn, it dd nt rn xcp i ⊣ nt-ssn @ whl ⊣ crf wr fm ꝥ t rfmt. ∓hs w rgd as a stkg mnfstat % ⊣ suprtndg cr % ☽ Prvdc.

It is sd t hv bn sptd by ften hndd @ ffty-thr clms, @ to thsd nn hnd @ sx plsts, al hwn fm ⊣ fns mbl.

∓hr wr mpld in its ercn thr ɕ ⊙s, thr thsn thr hnd ⊙s, or Ovs % ⫲ wk, egty thsn ⊤cs, or hewrs i ⫲ mntns @ qrs, @ svty thsn ⋲ Ⱥs, or brs % brds. Ⱥl ths wr cld @ argd i sch mnr, by ⫲ wsdm % Ҡ ≀, tt nthr env, dscd, nr cnfs ntrprtd o dstb ⫲ pc @ gd-flsp wch prvld amg ⫲ wkm.

—O—

[∓hs hv I rhsd t u ⫞ lgnd % ⫞ dh % ♓ Ⱥ, a hstry vnrtd as a rmnscnc % das lng psd @ rgrdd by ⊙s wh pclr rvrc, nt s mh fr ⫞ hsty itsl, as fr ⫞ slm @ sblm doctrn it is intnd t imprs o ou mds—⫞ rsurctn % ⫞ bdy @ ⫞ imrtlty % ⫞ sl.

϶t in ordr tt u ma flly cmprhnd @ aprct ⫞ intmt cnctn % ⫞ whl ⊙c sys, by ⫞ rltv dpndc % its svr prts, I prps bfly t rvw ⫞ tchgs % ⫞ tw prcdg °s bfr ntrng upn ⫞ fld % trth prsntd i ⫞ sb ° % ⊙ ⊙.

[Ur admsn amng ⊤ ⊙s in a stte % bldns @ dstutn ws mblcl % ⫞ entrc % al mn upn ths thr mrtl stt % xistc, whn, wk @ hlpls, th r ncsrly dpndt upn oths fr prtcn @ lf. 221–3

[Ⱥs ⫞ nblst emtns % ⫞ hrt r cld fth by hlpls infncy, so is ⫞ ° % ϵ Ⱥ intndd to incult ⊣ strkg lssn % ntrl eqlt @ mutl dpndc. It tght u, in ⊣ actv prncpls % unvrsl bnfnc @ chrty, t sk ⊣ solc % ur ow dstrs by xtndg cmfrt @ cnsltn t ur flo-crtrs in ⊣ hr % thr aflctn. It enbld u t fre ⊣ mnd fm ⊣ domn % prd @ prjdc; t lk byd ⊣ nro lmts % hmn instns, @ t vw in evy sn % Δdm a br % ⊣ dst. Δbv al @ byd al, it tgt u t bnd wh hmlt @ rsgntn bfr ⊣ ₲ Δ % ⊣ U, t ddct t ⋊m ur hrt ths purfd fm ev mlgnt psn, @ prpr ur md fr ⊣ rcptn % trh @ wsdm.

[₱rcdg onwd, stl gidd b ⊣ prcpls % brl lv, rlf @ trth, u wr psd t ⊣ ° % ∓c, whr u wr enbld t cntmplt ⊣ intlctl fclts; t trc thm fm thr orgn thr ⊣ pths % hvn-bn scnc, evn t ⊣ thrn % ₲ ⋊ms. ∓h scts % ntr @ ⊣ prncls % mrl trh wr ths unvld bf u. U lrnd ⊣ jst estmt % tho wndrs fclts whrw ₲ hs ndwd ⊣ crts fmd af ⋊s on img,

@ u flt ⊣⊢ du ♓ hs impsd upn u % cltvg th dvn atrbts wh unrmtg cr @ atntn, tt u ma thb b nbld t glrfy ♓ @ rndr urs a cntbtr t ⊣⊢ hpns % mkd.

[∓o ⊣⊢ mn whs mnd hs ths bn mld t vrt @ scic, Ŋtr prsts on grt @ usfl lsn mr, ⊣⊢ knlg % hmsl. Sh lds u b cntmpltn t ⊣⊢ clsg hrs % ur xistc; @ wn, b mns % tt cntmpltn, sh hs cndctd u tho ⊣⊢ vars wndgs % ths mrtl lf, sh fnly instcs u hw t di. Sh lds u t rflc upn ur invtbl dstny, @ prmts ⊣⊢ inwd mntr t sa tt dh hs n stng eql t ⊣⊢ stn % flshd, @ tt ⊣⊢ crtny % dh at an tm is btr thn ⊣⊢ psblty % dshnr.

[Of ths grt prncpl ⊧ ⊙y afrds a gls xmpl in ⊣⊢ unshkn fdlt @ nbl dh % ou ₲ ⊙ ♓ Ꭿ, whm u hv ths evg rpsd, @ I trs i wl b a strkng lsn t us al, shd w ev b plc i a smlr stat % tril.

[Ꭿn nw, m br, lt us smblz ⊣⊢ dh % ou ₲ ⊙ ♓ Ꭿ, @ aply hs prprtn fr @ rdns in fcng dh, t ousls.

[∓h lgnd infms us tt aftr h hd drn hs dsgn upn +| ttsl-brd, h ws bst b thr rfns ech i trn mr pwrfl @ dtrmd thn +| oth, wh ovrc hm @ fnl tk h l.

[∓hs it is wh mn. Strng in yth @ cnfdt i hs strgh, h strts fth t xect +| dsgs wh h hs drn upn +| gr trs-bd % hs lf; bt at +| vr outst h mts hs fs nmy, hs – a, in hs ow evl psns—in envy, hat, licnts @ dbuchy—dfcg +| butfl mirr % hs sol b thr bnfl inflnc. ⊖t thes ma b ovcm; @, stl strg i fth @ hp, h prss frwd on lf's jrny t mt hs scnd @ stl strngr enmy, hs – o, fitly rpsntd by srro @ msftn, by disea or pvrty, b +| cldns % fls frds or +| hs-tlty % opn enms.

[⊍ry @ fnt fm +| cnflc, stl strglg fr +| rt, upwd lkng wh ey % fth, tho thes enms b sbdud, h mts in +| evng % hs das, hs thrd @ trbl enm, hs – m. ∓o hm ths enmy is ⊃h—D, fm whm thr cn b n escp—⊃h, bfr whm al mst yld, whthr thy b ⊣⊢ yng, ⊣⊢ btfi, or ⊣⊢ gftd—lk – m a rlntls enm, instng upn hvg hs vctm.

[∓o ⊣⊢ crls @ thtls ⊣⊢ lsn wd end hr; bt ⊣⊢ uprgt @ tru ⊙ ma prsu i fthr, @ apl i t ⊣⊢ etrnl slvn % hs sol, so btfly tpifd b ⊣⊢ evrgn sp % ac, wh tchs us, tt alth ou fral bds mst, sonr or ltr, mldr i ⊣⊢ bsm % ou mthr er, yt thro ⊣⊢ mrts % ⊣⊢ dvn prms cntnd in ⊣⊢ ♁rt Lt in ⊙y, w ma cnfdntly hp tt ou sols wl blm i imrtl gren.

[℞mbr, thn, tt as ⊣⊢ bd % ou ♁ ⊙ ⋊ ⚠ ws brd i ⊣⊢ rbs % ⊣⊢ ∓, so shl urs b brd in eths frdly bsm; as h ws rsd, so lkws mst u b rsd—nt, indd, by ⊣⊢ brthly grp % an erhly mstr, bt at ⊣⊢ awfl cmd % ⋊m wh rls hvn @ ⊣⊢ er, @ in ans t whs sumns @ wd grvs wl b opn, ses gv up thr dd, @ al ⊣⊢ prfn @ initatd wl stnd bfr ⋊s jgmnt-st i ⊣⊢ ♁rd Ori % ⊣⊢ Unvrs to rndr unt ⋊m thr drd accnt. 3

[Lt, thn, m br, trh @ jstc, rlgn @ piety, b ur cnstnt am @ end. Lt ⫲ ∓m, wh u hv, in prt, ths evg rsd, b btfd, @ adrnd wth chrt's chocs jls, @ s acptbl t ⫲ Ⱥl-≀ ⊖y, tt wn, at ⫲ cls % a vrtus lf, u r sumnd hnc b ⫲ Omnifc ⊙d, u ma b admtd t tt glrs @ clstl ∓m, tt hs nt md wh hs, whs archtc is ⫲ ₲ ⊙ % ⫲ U, whs thrn is ⫲ etrnl hvns.]

⊙y br, ths brgs us to ⫲ snd cls % mblms, wch cntn mny vl @ ins lsns.

— THREE PILLARS —

∓h thre pllrs wr xplnd in a prcdg °, @ thr rpsntd ⊙sd, St, @ ⊙t. ∓h r hr mr fly xpld. ∓hy rpsnt ou thr anc ₲ ⊙s: ≀ Ꝁ % Is, ⋊ Ꝁ % ∓ @ ⋊ Ⱥ: ⫲ plr ⊙s, ≀ Ꝁ % Is, by whs ws ⫲ ∓m ws erc wch hs s hnrd @ xl-td hs nm; ⫲ plr Strg, ⋊ Ꝁ % ∓y, wh strnghd Ꝁ ≀ i hs grt @ imprt un-tkg; @ ⫲ plr ⊙t, ⋊ Ⱥ, ⫲ wds sn, % ⫲ trb % Ŋpthli, by whs cunng wk-mnshp ⫲ tm ws s btfd @ adnd.

⊖ Δs hld thr mtgs on +| gr flr % ·Ƙ ≀ ∓, sv cnstg a ::, on ⍜ ⍜ @ sx ⊖ Δs; ∓cs hld thr mtgs in +| ⍜ Ç % Ƙ ≀ ∓, fv cnstg a ::, tw ⍜ ⍜s @ thr ∓cs, @ ⍜ ⍜s hld thr mtgs i +| unfs ≀ ≀ % ·Ƙ ≀ ∓, thr cnstg a ::.

— THE THREE STEPS —

∓h thr Stps usly delintd upn +| ⊤sts crpt, r mblmtcl % +| thr prncpl stgs % hmn lf, Yth, ⍜nhd @ Δg.

In Yth, as ⊖ Δs, we shd ocpy ou mnds in +| atanmnt % usfl knlg; in ⍜nhd, as ·∓cs, we shd apl ou knlg t +| dschg % ou dts t ₲, ou nbr, @ ou-sls; so tt in ag, as ⍜ ⍜s, w ma enjy +| hpy rflctn cnsqt on a wl spt lf, @ di i +| hp % a glrs imrtlt.

— POT OF INCENSE —

∓h Ꝑt % Incns i an mblm % a pur hrt, alws an acptbl ofrng t De, @ as ths glws wh het, so shd ou hts cntnly glo wh grtud t ou bnfcnt Çr fr +| mnfld blsgs @ cmfrts w njy.

∓h ⊙hv i an mblm % ndstry, tchg +| prctc % tt vrtu t al mn. ⩚s w cm int +| wld ratnl @ intlgt bgs, so shd w ev b indstrs, nvr cntnt t b idl, whl ou felo crtrs r in wnt, if it is in ou pwr t relv thm.

⊙hn w tk a srvy % ntr, w vw mn in hs infcy, mr hlpls thn +| bru crtn. ӿe lis lngshg fr das, mths @ yrs, totly incpbl % prvdng sustnc fr hmsl, % gurdng agst +| atck % +| wld bsts % +| fld, or shltrg hmsl frm +| inclmcs % +| wethr. It mt hv plsd +| grt Ȼr % hv @ eth t mk mn indpndt % al oth bngs, bt as dpndnc is on % +| stngs bnds % socit, mn wr md dpndt on on anthr fr prtcn @ secrty, whrby thy enjy btr oprtnts t fm +| tis % lv @ frshp. ∓hus ws mn fmd fr socl @ actv lf, +| nblst wk % Ꞡ; @ h tt wl so demn hmsl as nt t endvr t ad t +| cmn stk % knlg @ undstg, ma b dmd a usls mbr % scty, unwthy % ou prtcn as ⊙s.

— BOOK OF CONSTITUTIONS —

∓h ↄk % Çns grdd b ⊣ ∓s Sd rmds us tt w shd ev b wchfl @ grdd in ou thts, wds @ actns, prtcly whn i ⊣ prsnc % ⊣ enms % ⊙y, ev rmbrg thos trly ⊙c vrts, silnc @ crcmspcn.

— SWORD AND NAKED HEART —

∓h sd ℘ntg t a Ŋ ӿrt ilustrts tt jstc wl sonr or ltr ovrtk us; @ altho ou thts, wds, @ acns ma b hdn fm ⊣ eys % mn, yt tt

— ALL-SEEING EYE —

Ⱥl-≀g ⓒ whm ⊣ ≀, ⊙ @ ≀ trs ob @ undr whs wtchfl cr evn cmts prfm thr stupndus rvlutns, srchs ⊣ nrmst rcsses % ⊣ hmn hart, @ wl rwrd us acdg t ou mrts.

— ANCHOR AND ARK —

∓h Ⱥnchr @ ⊣ Ⱥrk r mblms % a wl-grndd hop, @ a wl-spt lf. ∓hy r mblcl % tt dvn Ⱥrk, wh brs us ovr ths tmpsts c % trbls, @ ⊣ Ⱥnchr wh shl sfly moor us in ⊣ pcfl hrbr wh ⊣ wkd ces frm trblg, @ ⊣ wry r at rst.

— FORTY-SEVENTH PROBLEM —

∓h ⊤rty-svh Ᵽrblm % ⊙ucld tchs ⊙s t b gnl lvrs % ⊣⊢ rts @ scncs, [@ ws ⊣⊢ rslt % ⊣⊢ ℔s % ou anc br. Ᵽyth-gs. Amg hs mst ntwthy achvmts ws ths prblm, tt ⊣⊢ sqr ercd upn ⊣⊢ hy-potus % a rt-ang trngl is eql t ⊣⊢ sm % ⊣⊢ sq upn ⊣⊢ to othr sds.]

— HOUR GLASS —

∓h ⋊r-⊕ls i an mblm % hmn lf. ⊙hld, hw swftly ⊣⊢ snd rns, @ hw rpdly ou lvs r drwg t a cls. ⊙e cnt wtht astmt bhld ⊣⊢ ltl prtcls wch r cntd i ths mchn; hw th ps aw almt imprcbly, @ yt, t or srps, i ⊣⊢ shrt spc % a hr th r al xhstd. ∓hus wsts mn. ∓da, h pts fth ⊣⊢ tndr lvs % hp; tmw, blsms, @ brs h blng hnrs thk upn hm; ⊣⊢ nx da cms a frst wh nps ⊣⊢ sht; @ whn h thks hs grtns i stl asprg, h fls, lk atm lvs, t nrch or mth eth.

— THE SCYTHE —

∓h Scth i an mblm % tm, wh cts ⫞ brtl thrd % lf, @ lnchs us int etr. ϑhld, wt hvc ⫞ scth % tm mks amg ⫞ hmn rac. If b chnc w shd scp ⫞ nmrs ils incdt t chdhd @ yth, @ wth hlth @ vgr arv t ⫞ yrs % mnhd; yt, wthl, w mst sn b ct dn by ⫞ al-dvrg scth % tm @ b gthd int ⫞ ln whr or fths hv gn bf us.

— — —

‖ wl nw cl ur atntn t ⫞ thd @ lst cls % mblms, wch r as sc as an prtn % ⫞ ° u hv rc, @ I trs u wl ev rtn thm as sh. *** ∓h r ⫞ ≀ ⊙, ≀ , Ҫ @ ≀ % Ⱥ.

∓h ≀ ⊙ is mblcl % tt wth wch ₲ ⊙ ⋊ Ⱥ ws sln; ⫞ ≀ , % tt wh ws usd in op hs gr, rmndg us tt er lng a smlr ins ma b usd t op ou grs; @ ⫞ Ҫ % tt wch inclsd hs rmns.

∓hs, m br, r strkg mbls @ t a rflc mnd afrd sbjcs fr srs cntmpltn; bt wn w rflc on ⫳ ≀ % Ʌ fnd blm at ⫳ hd % ⫳ gr, w r rmnd tt w hv an imrtl prt wthn us wh wl srvi ⫳ grv. @ wh wl nv, nv, nv d. * (*Sts* ::.)

---o---

Ͽr, ur zel fr +| instutn % ⊙y, +| prgs u hv md i +| msty, @ ur cnfmty t ou rgltns, hv pntd u ot as a ppr obj % ou fvr @ estm. 233–3

U r nw bnd b dt, hon, @ grtud t b fthf t ur trs, t suprt +| dig % ur chcr on ev ocsn, @ t enfrc, by prcpt @ xmpl, obdnc t +| tents % +| Ŧrt.

In +| chctr % a ⊙ ⊙, u r authrzd t crct +| errs @ irglrts % ur uninfmd bn, @ t grd thm agst a brh % fdlt. Ŧo prsv +| rputn % +| Ŧrt unsld mst b ur cnst cr, @ fr ths prps it i ur prv-nc t rcmd t ur infrs, obdnc @ sbmsn; t ur eqls, crtsy @ afblty; t ur suprs, kdns @ cnsdrtn. Unvsl bnvlc u r al-ws t inclct, @, b +| rglrt % ur on bhvr, afrd +| bst xmpl fr +| cdc % oths ls infmd. Ŧh anc lnmks % +| Ŧrt, ntrstd t ur cr, u r crfly t prsv, @ nvr sfr thm t b infrgd, o cntnc a dviatn fm +| estbl usgs @ cstms % +| Ŧrt.

Ur vrtu, hon, @ rputn r cncrd in suprtg wh digt +| chrc u n br. Lt no mtv, thfr, mk u swrv fm ur du, vilt ur vws, o btr ur trs, bt b tru @ fthfl, @ imiat +| xmpl % tt clbrtd art-st whm u hv ths evg rpsntd. ∓hus u wl rndr ursl wthy % +| hon wh w hv cnfrd, @ mrt +| cnfdc w rps i u.(*Or*)

(⊙y b, eh % ou thr °s hs its rsptv parmnt dty. ∓t % Ɛ Ą is ur du to ₲; tt % +| Ŧc is ur du t ur nbr; @ tt % ths, +| ⊙ ⊙ °, is ur du to ursl. ∓hr is no straind rvrsl % ○ in ths, nr ds ⊙y dfr wh ntr or rvltn in hr sqnc % tchng. ₲ cms fst alws, fr in ⋊m w lv @ mv @ hv ou beng. Ou nbr cms scd bcs ₲ ⋊msl hs s ord in thos tn grtr Çmndmts wrtn wh ⋊s on fngr % Dvty. ⊕e ousls, cm lst bcs wtht du t ₲ w shd lck +| strgh to prfm, @ wtht du to ou nbs w shd lck ⊣| ₵ld ℞l, wh aln shws us ⊣| dmnd % a du t ousls.

(Ur mnhd ds nt dpnd upn ur posn, bt upn ur chcr i lf. ∓h estblsmt as wl as ⊣| acklmt % tru mnhd is in ur on hds. ∓o mny thk tt rputatn ensurs it; do nt wat fr tt. Sek ⊣| tru dfntn % a mn @ thn xmplfy it. Do nt hv tw chctrs, on fr ur flos @ anthr fr prvcy. Ͽ a tru mn i ur on hom as wl as ot in lf. Scrn t debs usl bcs ⊣| dr % pblcty is lckd. Lt evn ur on solitd kp cmpny wh ⊣| gntlmn wthn it. Spk ⊣| sm lngug to mn tt u d t ur mthr. Lk upn wmn as u wd hv othr mn lk upn ur sstrs. ℞snt ⊣| uncln spch as a chlng agst ur clm t gd brdg. Dmd rspcfl trtmt fm ur nbr, bt fst cmnd ur on slf-rspct. Lt nthg b mr intolrbl i ur sgt thn ⊣| ltng dwn % ursl t a lwr lvl. Ͽid mn cm up t u, bt rfus t dscnd a sngl stp t thm.

⊳ nt msr ur imprtc by ur ttls or ur mny, bt by ⊣ txtr % ur chrctr @ ⊣ clnlins % ur spch. ⊙k oths t kn alws tt a gntlmn stds bfr thm. ∓h tchgs % ths °, thn, is tt it is ur du t mk ⊣ mst @ ⊣ bst % ursl. It is ur du as a mn amg mn; as a sn, or hsbnd, or fthr: as a ctzn % ths grt ℞pblc; as a dl ob ⊙ ⊙; as ⊣ mst glrs climx % al crtd thgs; fr ⊣ tr mn is ⊣ humn img % ⊣ ⊙s ₲.)

(*Or*)

[∓hus hv w ndvrd prtily t xpl t u ⊣ fms @ crmns % ur initn, psg @ rs. || ma wl sa prtl, fr ⊣ intlgt mn sn bcms cnvncd tt thr i nt an obsrvc in ∓ ⊙y wch hs nt a dp sgfnc. Sk dl-gntly @ u wl fnd ⊣ ilstrns % its sm-blc tchgs alm infnt. ∓h anct lnmks, as prstd t ur vw in ⊣ cmns % ths °, evn wh a flst xpsn % thr lwfly accptd mng, cn b bt ⊣ mrst otlin % ⊣ vrd shps % strgh @ buty wh eh sccdg ag hs frmd in acrdc wh its ow pculr cst % thgt, @ wh imgntn cn awkn int cntls frms % grcfl lf. I trs u wl cnstly srch fr a depr mning bnth ⊣ instcn alrd gvn. Ŧhs u wl rliz hw ⊣ fndrs % ⊣ vars anc mysts, amd unvsl idltr, b adptng ⊣ unty % ⊣ sstm evn i ⊣ infnity % its elmts, pprd thr mnds t rcv ⊣ rvltns % its dvn authr; hw, in rcvg ⊣ bnfc adptn % al its prts t ⊣ wnts % evry crtr, fndg i xtrnl natr a vsbl mblm % ev grt mrl trh, @ a typ % eh mysts emtn % ⊣ sol, ⊣ cnclsn brk upn thm irrsistbl tt ⊣ authr % ths hrmns cratn mst b infntly gd @ jst @ wis, @ tt ⋊ is ⊣ onl ₲. It wl nt, thfr, b amis t drc ur atn t a sngl xmpl, nt as an ancly rcvd xpln % ⊣ obj % ⊣ °, bt as on amg ⊣ mass % ilstrtns wh ou symbls wl sggst. Ur rpsntn % o ₲ ⌓ ⋊ Ѧ i a tp % ⊣ uprt mn in hs prgrs thro lf. Ȼndwd lk

⊣| wd's sn t crry ou ⊣| dsgns % ⊣| ₲ Ą % ⊣| U, h ntrs at ⊣| sth gt upn ⊣| suny prod % yh. ӾR h mets wth alrmts, wch, lk ⊣| robr, wd trn hm fm ⊣| pth % dty; bt, def t ⊣| sirn tns, sstnd b ⊣| unerng dctats % ⊣| montr wthn, h mvs on t ⊣| wst gt, o mdl prid % lf. ӾR h i agn assld b msftn, dis @ trls, tmptg hm t btra hs trs; bt, wh intgty t dply rtd t b shkn b ⊣| vcstds % ft, h trds ⊣| wa % lf un-fltrgly @ arvs in old ag at ⊣| est gt, tt opng thro wh h lks ot upn a brhtr @ a btr wld. ӾR h mts ⊣| inoxrabl enmy t whm al mst yld. Ąt ⊣| fatl blo % Dh h snks t ⊣| dst @ i brd in ⊣| rbs % hs ethl ntr, bt nt frevr; fr b ⊣| Spg % Ąc w r rmndd tt thr is a sprtl prt wthn us wh wl srvv ⊣| grv @ wh wl nv, nv di; @ as ⊣| rmns % ou lamntd ₲ ⊙ wr rsd fm thr hmbl rstg-plc @ cnvd t ⊣| ∓m, @ thnc to ⊣| plc % burl, wh ws as nr to ⊣| unfs

≀ ≀ as ⊣ Jsh lw wd alw; s ma w, whn cld fm ou gvs by ⊣ al-pwrfl vc % ⊣ ≀ ȼ ⊙ % ⊣ U, b cndcd t ⊣ ♓ % ♓, thr t rst scurly in ⊣ prtcng lv % ou ♓vnl ⊤thr thro ⊣ bndls ags % a nvr-ndg hpns.

In cnclsn, m br, lt m sa t u, @ nt onl t u, bt t ev br prsnt, lt us cltvt asidusly ⊣ rspctbl chctr % ou prfsn. ϿY ⊣ sq lt us lrn mrlty, by ⊣ lvl, eqlt, @ by ⊣ plm, rctud % lf @ cndc. Lt us imit ⊣ xmpl % tt clbrtd artst wh, whn asltd b ⊣ rblus cftmn, mn-tnd hs intgrt evn in dh, @ seld hs prncpls wh hs bld. Lt us emult hs unfgd pity t ȼ @ hs unswvg fdlt t hs trst; @ as ⊣ evgrn sprg % aca dsgntd hs tmpry rstg-plc, s ma vrtu, by hr ev-blmg lvlns, dsgnt us as ⊤ @ Ⱥ ⊙s. ⊙th ⊣ trwl lt us sprd lbrly ⊣ cmt % brl-lv @ afcn; crcmscbd b ⊣ cmps, lt us pndr wl al ou wds @ actns. Lt al ⊣ enrgs % ou sols @ ⊣ prfctn %

ou mnds b mpld in atnng +| aprbtn % +| Ġ ⊙ on hgh, so tt whn w cm t di, wh jy w ma hal +| smns % +| Ġr ⊙rdn abv t rpr fm ou ℔ hr on eth t etrnl rfsmt in +| prdis % Ġ. ∓hr, b bnft % a §, a wd, an unblmshd lf @ a frm rlic upn Dv ℘rvdc, ma w gan +| fvr % a spdy ntrc t +| Ġ :: on hi, whr +| Ġ Ѧ % +| U frev prsds, @ whr, std at ♓s r hn, ♓ ma b plsd t prnc us uprt mn @ ⊙s, ftly pprd, as lvng stns, fr tt sprtl bldg, tt hs nt md wh hns, etrnl in +| hvns.

[∓nly, m br, cngrtltg u mst sncrly, lt m enjn upn u tt ur hnr @ rputn r cncrd in suprtg wth dgty +| ⊙c chctr u nw br. Lt n motv mk u swrv fm ur duts, vilt ur vws, or btra ur trs; bt b tru @ fth, @ imit +| xmpl % +| clbrtd artst whm u hv ths evg rp-sntd, @ thus rndr ursl wthy % +| hnr w hv cnfrd @ mrit +| trus tt w hv rpsd i u.]

(⊥)y br, ths cnclds ⫲ thd ° % (⊥)y. U wl stp t ⫲ Sec's dsk @ sgn ⫲ by-lws, thby cnsmtng ur mbshp wh ⫲ ::.

(*Çlsg, See Index.*)

LECTURE

(⊤)(⊥)- (⊢)r ≀ (⊢). (⊤) (⊥). ℞ u a (⊥) (⊥). || am.

(⊤)t indcd u t bcm a (⊥) (⊥).

∓t I mgt obt ⫲ (⊥)st wd, trav in frgn cntrs, wk @ rcv (⊥)st wgs, @ b thby btr enbld to spt msl @ fml @ cntrbt t ⫲ rlf % dstrsd wthy (⊥) (⊥)s, thr ws @ ors

(⊤)t mks u a (⊥) (⊥). (⊥)y o.

(⊤)hr wr u md a (⊥) (⊥).

(⊤)thn ⫲ bdy % a jst @ dly cstd :: % (⊥) (⊥)s, asmb i a pl rpst ⫲ unfs ≀ ≀ % Ƙ ≀ ∓m, fur wh ⫲ ⋊ (⊢), ≀ @ Çs, tghr wh a Çhtr o Dspntn fm sm Ç (⊢)d % cmp jrs mpr it t wk.

⋊w m I kn u t b a (⊥) (⊥). 3

(⊢)y crt §s @ tkns. (⊤)t r §s.

℞t ngls, hrzls @ pdlrs.
Ⱥdvc a §. (≀ ☽ @ ₵ *gv dg.*)
♓s tt an alsn.
It hs, t ╫ ps % m hs wl tk ╫ o.
♓v u a fth §. ‖ hv. (₲*vs* §.)
♓s tt an al. It h, t ╫ p % ╫ o.
⊙t r tkns.
₵rt frn or br gps, whb on ⊙ ma kn anth i ╫ dk as i ╫ lt.
Ⱥdvc @ gv m a tk. (≀ ☽ - ₲*v ps gp.*
⊙t is tt. ∓h pg % ⊙ ⊙.
♓s it a nm. It hs. ⊙l u gv i t m.
‖ dd nt s rc i, nth wl I s i i.
♓w w u ds % i. L or s i. ≀ i @ b.
U bg. ☽g u. (≀ ☽ *bg.*)
⊙l u b o o fm. ∓. ∓m wt @ t w·
∓ ╫ pg % ⊙ ⊙ t ╫ rl g % ╫ s.
☧. (₲*vn.*) ⊙t i tt.
∓h r g % ⊙ ⊙, or l pw.
♓s i a nm. It hs. ⊙l u gv i t m
☧ usl i a pr psn t r i @ I w.
⊙t is tt pr ps. On ╫ f ps % fs.
⊙t r ╫ f ps % fs.

∓ t f, k t k, b t b, h t b, @ m t e. (*⊙d gvn on f ps % fs.*)

⊙hr wr u ppd t b md a ⊙ ⊙.

In a rm adjng ⊣ bd % a js @ dl cns :: % ⊙ ⊙s.

♓w wr u ppd.

Dvsd % al mtlc sbs, nthr nk nor clthd, bf nr shd, bth ks @ bs br, hw @ a ct thr ts r m bd, clthd as ∓c; i wh cdn i ws cdc t a dr % ⊣ :: @ csd t gv thr dstc ks, wh wr ans by thr wthn.

⊙h ws a ct th tms r ur bd.

∓o t m tt m dts @ oblgts bcm mr @ mr xtnsv as I adv i ⊙y.

∓ wt dd ⊣ th ks ald.

∓ ⊣ thd ° % ⊙y, on wch I ws thn ntrng.

⊙t ws sd t u fm wthn.

⊙h cms hr. Ur ans.

Ⱥ wth br, wh hs bn dly init ⋲ Ⱥ, psd t ⊣ ° % ∓c, @ nw whs fr l in ⊙y by bg rsd t ⊣ sb ° % ⊙ ⊙.

⊙t wr u thn askd.

If it ws an ac % my on f wl @ ac; if I ws wy @ wl ql, d @ tr ppd; if I hd md stbl pfcy in ⊣| prc °; al % wh bg ans i ⊣| aftv, I ws as b wt fth rt o bn I xpd t obt ths imp prv.

Ur ans. ⊙n % ⊣| pw. ⋈d u ⊣| pw.

|| hd nt; m cdtr hd @ gv i f m.

⊙t wr u thn tld.

Snc I ws in posn % al thes ncs qlfcns, I shd wt untl ⊣| ⊙ ⊙ cld b infd % m rqs @ hs ans rtd.

⊙t ws hs ans wn rtd.

Lt hm ent ths wfl :: % ⊙ ⊙s, @ b rc i d @ anc fm.

⋈w wr u rc.

On ⊣| xtrm pnts % ⊣| cs, xtng fm m n r t m n l bst, wh ws t th m tt as wthn ⊣| bst r cntd ⊣| ms vtl pts % mn, s btwn ⊣| xtrm pts % ⊣| cs r cntnd ⊣| ms vlbl tnts % ⊤ ⊙y, wh r frnshp, mrlty @ brly lv.

⋈w wr u thn dspd %.

Çdctd thr tms rgl arn ⊣| :: @ t ⊣| ⌡ ⊙ in ⊣| ≀, whr ⊣| sm qs wr ask @ ans rtd as at ⊣| dr.

⋊w dd ⊣| ⌡ ⊙ dsp % u.

Drc m to b cdctd to ⊣| ≀ ⊙ in ⊣| ⊙, whr ⊣| sm qs wr askd @ ans rtd as bfr.

⋊w dd ⊣| ≀ ⊙ dsp % u.

Drc m t b cnctd to ⊣| ⊙ ⊛ in ⊣| ⊖, whr ⊣| sm qs wr askd @ ans rtd as bfr; wh als dmnd whnc I cm @ wthr tvlg.

Ur ans. Ͳm ⊣| ⊙, tvlg ⊖.

⊙h dd u lv ⊣| ⊙ @ tr ⊖.

In sh % fth lt i ⊛y.

⋊w dd ⊣| ⊙ ⊛ dsp % u.

○d m rcdctd to ⊣| ≀ ⊙ in ⊣| ⊙, wh tgt m hw t aprh ⊣| ⊖ in du @ anc fm.

⊙t ws tt d @ anc fm.

Ąuvg on my l f, brg ⊣| hl % m r to ⊣| hl % m l, thb fmg ⊣| ngl % a sq, bdy erc, fcg ⊣| ⊖.

⊙t dd ⊣ ⊙ ⊙ thn d wh u.

Oblgtd m a ⊙ ⊙. ⋊w.

In d fm. ⊙t ws tt d fm.

Ꝁnlg o bh nk ks, bth hs rstg upn ⊣ ⋊ ⊙, ≀ @ Ꞔs, i wh d fm I tk ⊣ sl o % ⊙ ⊙.

⋊v u ⊣ o. || hv. Ꞧpt it.

||, Ꞵ ⊙, % m ow f w @ ac, i pr % Ꞵ ₲ @ ths wfl :: % ⊙ ⊙s, erc t ⋊m @ ddc to ⊣ mry % ⊣ ⋊ Ss ⌋, d hb @ hn sl @ s p @ s, tt I w k @ cn, @ nv rv, an % ⊣ scs blg t ⊣ ° % ⊙ ⊙, wh I hv rc, am abt t rc, or ma hrft b ins i, t an pr, unls i shl b t a wy br ⊙ ⊙, or wthn ⊣ bd % a js @ dl cns :: % sh, @ nt unt hm o thm untl b d trl, stc xm, or lfl ⊙c inf, I shl hv fd hm o thm js ent t rc ⊣ sm.

(2) Ŧm, I d p @ s tt I w spt ⊣ cns % ⊣ ₲ :: % ⊣ Sta % Ƞ Y, als al lws, rls @ edcs % ⊣ sm, or % an oth ₲ :: fm whs jrs I ma hrftr ha; tghr

wh ⊣| b-ls, rls @ rg % ths or an oth :: % wh I ma bcm a mbr, so fr as ⊣| sm shl cm t m knlg.

(3) Ŧm, I d p @ s tt I wl ans @ o al d §s @ rg sm snt t m fm ⊣| bd % a js @ dl cns :: % ⊙ ⊙s, o hn m b a wy br % ths °, if wthn ⊣| ln % m c-t.

(4) Ŧm, I d p @ s tt I wl h, ai @ ast al pr @ dst ⊙ ⊙s, thr wds @ orps, th aplg t m as sh, I fndg thm wy, @ cn d so wtht mtrl inj t msl o fml.

(5) Ŧm, I d p @ s tt I w kp ⊣| ss % a wy ⊙ ⊙, wn cmc t m as sh, as scur @ invl i m br as th wr i hs bf cmc.

(6) Ŧm, I d p @ s tt I w n gv ⊣| ₲ Ӿ § % ◗ % ⊙ ⊙, xcp fr ⊣| bnf % ⊣| cft whl at wk, or ⊣| instn % a br, unls I am i rl dst, @ shd I c tt § gvn, or hr ⊣| wds acmpg ⊣| sm, I wl hstn t ⊣| rlf % ⊣| on s gvg it.

(7) Ŧm, I d p @ s tt I w n g ⊣| sub fr ⊣| ⊙'s wd i an oth mn thn tt

in wh I rc it, wh wl b on ⊣| fv ps % fls @ at l b.

(7) Ŧm, I d p @ s tt I w n wr, ch nr dfd a ⊙ ⊙ :: nr a br % ths ° t ⊣| vl % anthg, knly, nr sfr i t b dn b anth if i m pw t prv.

(9) Ŧm, I d p @ s tt I w n vl ⊣| chs % a ⊙ ⊙s wf, wd, mth, str o dtr, o sfr it t b dn b anth, if i m pr t prv.

(10) Ŧm, I d p @ s tt I w n b pr at ⊣| initg, psg o rsg % an ol mn i dot, a yg mn un ag, an irlgs lbt, an aths, a psn % unsnd md, a eunc or a wm, kng thm t b sch.

(11) Ŧm, I d p @ s tt I w n b pr at ⊣| initg, psg o rsg % a cdt clndsnly nr hld ⊙c intcrs wh a clndstn ⊙, or wh on wh hs bn sspd or xpld, kng hn t b sh, ntl dl rstrd.

∓ al % wh I sl @ snc p @ s, wtho an hstn, mtl rsv o sc ev % md i m wtev, bdg msl un n ls a pn thn tt % hv m bd sv i twn, m bls tkn thnc @

bd t ashs, @ ⊣⊢ shs th% sct t ⊣⊢ fr wns % h, tt thr mgt rmn nth trk, trc nr rmbc, amg mn or ⊙s, % s vl @ prj a wrh as I shd b, shd I ev, knl o wlfl, vl ths m sl o % ⊙ ⊙. ≀ hl m ₲, @ mk m stfs t kp @ pf ⊣⊢ sm.

Af ⊣⊢ o, wt wr u ask. ⊙t I ms dsd.

Ur ans. ∓r lt i ⊙y. Dd u rc i.

‖ dd, by ○ % ⊣⊢ ⊙ ⊙.

On bg brt t l, wt dd u bhd.

∓h thr grt lts in ⊙y, as in ⊣⊢ prc °, wth ths dfrc: bh pts % ⊣⊢ cs wr ab ⊣⊢ sq, wh ws t th m tt I hd rc, @ ws ntld to rc, al ⊣⊢ lt tt cld b cnfd on o cmctd t m i a ⊙ ⊙ ::.

⊙t dd u nx bhld.

∓h ⊙ ⊙ aprhg fm ⊣⊢ ∈, on ⊣⊢ stp, und ⊣⊢ dg @ § % ⊙ ⊙, wh prsd hs rt hn in tkn % cntnc % frnshp @ brl lv, @ invst m wh ⊣⊢ pg @ pw; ○d m t rs, slt ⊣⊢ ⌡ @ ≀ ⊙s, @ stfy thm tt I ws a dly oblgt ⊙ ⊙, in psn % ⊣⊢ st, dg, §, pg @ pw.

♓w wr u thn dspd %.

℞cntd t ‡ ≀ ⊚ in ‡ ⊚, wh tgt m hw t wr m ap as ⊙ ⊙.

♓w shd a ⊙ ⊙ wr hs ap.

⊚h ‡ flp @ cr dn.

⊚th wt wr u thn prstd.

∓h wk tls % ⊙ ⊙, wh r al ‡ tls % ⊙y, esp ‡ ∓rl, an inst usd b op ⊙s t spd ‡ cmt wch unts ‡ sev pts % ‡ bldg int on cmn mss; bt we, as ⊤ @ Ѧ ⊙s, r tgt t us it fr ‡ mr nbl @ glrs prps % sprdg ‡ cmt % brl lv @ afctn, tt cmt wh unts us int on sacd bnd or soc % fds @ brs, amg whm n cntntn shd evr xst, sv tt nbl cntntn, or rthr emultn, % wh bs cn wk @ bs ag.

♓w wr u thn dspd %.

℞cndctd t ‡ plc whnc I cm, invsd wh tt % wh I hd bn dvsd, @ in du tm rtnd t ‡ :: fr fth instn.

Ⓐ Ⓐ to Ⓔ Ⱥ or ⊧ Ç

Ⓣ Ⓐ- *** Ⓣvng al §s @ crmns, I nw dclr ℔ dspnsd wth in ⊣⊢ thd °, @ ⊣⊢ :: opn on ⊣⊢ fs (*or* snd) fr wk @ instcn. ⊃r ≀ ⊳, atnd at ⊣⊢ Ⱥ. (*Dn.*) ⊃r ⌡ ⊳, infm ⊣⊢ ∓.

⌡ ⊳. (*Infs* ∓.) Ⓣ Ⓐ ⊣⊢ ∓ is infd.

Ⓣ Ⓐ- * (*Sts* ::.)

Ⓔ Ⱥ or ⊧ Ç to Ⓐ Ⓐ

Ⓣ Ⓐ- *** Ⓣvng al §s @ crmns, I nw dclr ⊣⊢ :: cls on ⊣⊢ fs (*or* snd) °, @ ℔ rsmd in ⊣⊢ thd °. ⊃r ≀ ⊳, atd at ⊣⊢ Ⱥ. (*Dn.*) ⊃r ⌡ ⊳, infm ⊣⊢ ∓.

⌡ ⊳- (*Infs* ∓.) Ⓣ Ⓐ, ⊣⊢ ∓ i infd.

Ⓣ Ⓐ- * (*Sts* ::.)

(*No bsns or wk xcpt tt fr wh* ⊣⊢ :: *is ntfd or sumnd cn b trnsctd at a spcl cmcn.*)

(*A sttd cmcntn mst b opd @ clsd on* ⊣⊢ *thd* ° @ *in du fm.*) 251–3

ЄX–O

‖, ᗅ ϶, % m o f w @ ac, in prs % ᗅ ȹ, d hby @ hrn sl @ sn s tt I hv bn du init Є ᗅ, psd t ⊣| ° % ⊤c @ rsd t ⊣| sbl ° % ⊙ ⊙ in —— ::, ɲ —, a j @ dly cnstd :: % ⊤ @ ᗅ ⊙s; tt I m nt ndr sntnc % sspnsn o xplsn, nr do I kn % an rsn wy I shd nt vis wth my brn. So hl m ȹ. 252–3

Please report any errors or omissions.

EMBLEMATIC POST CARDS

From popular subjects, artistically executed; many of them being equal to photographs.

A margin of writing space, is left on the Cards that you may send your compliments to your friends along with these beautiful souvenirs.

Price 2 cents each, 3 for 5 cents, or 20 for 25 cents prepaid to any address. Please order by number

F. & A. M.

30089 Dedication Medal—Masonic Hall, (N. Y. 1875) and Grand Lodge Insignia
30105 Ironworker and King Solomon,-Honoring Labor after Rebuilding the Temple
30300 Rock of Masonry
30103 Record Certificate, a beautiful picture
30090 Square, Compasses and Trowel,-a corner piece
30150 Brother William—Billy G.
30204 Orders of Architecture
30201 Ground Plan of King Solomon's Temple
30202 Reference or key to **30201**
30200 Pillars and Winding Stairs
30208 Acacia, Tree and Sprig
30212 "White, Purple and Gold"—Apron, Presentation
30900 Square and Compasses, embossed in gold & blue.
30905 Square and Compasses, with wreath—embossed
30903 Apron--embossed in two colors

Masonic Buildings.

30060 New Masonic Building, Crab Orchard, Ky.
30061 The Ten Eyck Room, M. Temple, Albany, N.Y.
30062 Mas. Temple & Kilmer Bldg. Binghamton, N. Y.
30063 Masonic Temple, Salamanca, N. Y.
30064 Masonic Temple, Albany, N. Y.
30065 Masonic Temple, Cincinnati, Ohio.
30066 Masonic Temple, Cincinnati, Ohio.
30067 Masonic Temple, Hartford, Conn.
30068 Masonic Temple, Detroit, Mich.
30069 Masonic Temple, Poughkeepsie, N. Y.
30070 " J. S. Mustard Memorial Hall " (Masonic Lodge) Broad Ripple, Ind.
30071 "Interior of Masonic Lodge Room Looking East" (J.S. Mustard Memorial Hall) Broad Ripple, Ind.

30072 Masonic Temple, Duluth, Minn.
30107 "Goose and Gridiron," Ancient Building, in which the first Lodge in London met
36000 Masonic Library Building, Cedar Rapids, Iowa
30100 Masonic Temple, Philadelphia, Pa.
30101 Masonic Home, Utica, N. Y. As Dedicated 1892
30102 Masonie Home, Utica, N. Y. As in 1910
30097 New Masonic Hall, 314-16 Broadway, N. Y. 1827
30099 Masonic Hall, New York, 1875
30109 "Tun Tavern," The Old Inn, Phila, Pa. where the first Lodge in America was organized

Operative Masonry

30400 York Minster, England, 7th Century
30401 'Prentice Pillar, Roslyn Chapel, Scotland

R. A. M.

31004 Egyptian Architecture, Caravan, and Pyramids
31008 Ruins of Temple, showing Secret Vault

K. T.

32008 Richard Couer-de-Leon at Acre
32014 Siege of Corinth
32015 Approach of Roman Army to Jerusalem
32020 Institution of the Order of St. John
32025 Crusaders in a Mounted Charge
32900 Embossed K. T. design
32030 Mount Zion
32041 Mosque of Omar El-Aksa,on Temple Grounds
32000 Corner Piece, Ornamental

A. A. S. R.

33000 "The Understanding of the Occult etc."
33004 Tracing Board, Philosophical Degree
33005 The Camp
33200 Rosy Cross or Rose Croix Emblems

O. E. S.

35000 Corner Piece, Ornamental
35200 Signet
32501 Emblematic Seal

Shrine.

34000 Embossed emblem design
34001 Desert Scene

I. O. O. F.

36006 From Emblematic Prayer. *Copyrighted*
36007 From Rock of Odd Fellowship. *Copyrighted*
36008 From Golden Links. *Copyrighted*
36009 From Das Vater Unser. *Copyrighted*

Masonic "Hall of Fame"

30506 Aldsworth, Hon. Mrs. the Female Mason
30511 Anthony, Jesse B., P. G. M. of New York
30513 Coxe, Daniel, first Provincial G. M. in America
30510 Drummond, Josiah, P. G. M. of Maine
30130 Franklin Opening the Lodge
30509 Frederick the Great
30505 Gould, Robert F., Author of Gould's History
30514 McKinley, Bro. William
30507 Morris, Robt. Author and organizer of O. E. S.
30504 Oliver, Geo., D. D., Author
30503 Phillip, Duke of Wharton, P. G. M. of England
30512 Pike, Albert, Gen. Grand Com. A. A. S. R.
30502 Price, Henry, first Prov. G. M. of New Eng.
30508 Sayer, Anthony, first G. M. of England
30140 Sts. John, The Baptist and Evangelist, Essenes and Eminent Patrons of Masonry
30118 Washington's Portrait and Letter to the G.L. Pa
30119 30118 with Comment by E. A. Fellow
30120 Washington Closing the Lodge
30501 Webb, Thomas S., father of American Ritual

Comic

30001-6 "Are You A Mason" Series of six cards.
30010 Advice to Stay-at-home Member
30011 "Refreshment to Labor"
30012 "Ten (K) Nights in a Bar-room"
30013 "No one to Vouch for him"
30014 "Mecca to Medina"
30015 "How high up are you?"
30016 "It is to laff."
30017 "You is a mason—yes."
30018 I Always Liked A Mason.
36005 I Always Liked An Odd Fellow.
36006 I Always Liked An Elk.

Sepia Comics.

(3 cents each, 2 for 5 cents)

30021 You can't get a Mason's Goat
30022 A Mason's on the square
30023 Wearing his first pin. (F. & A. M.)
30024 I've traveled some
34002 Hold on to the Rope. (Shrine)
36001 Eagle and the Fly. (Eagles)
36002 Been down to Jericho. (I. O. O. F.)
36003 Wearing his first pin. (B. P. O. E.)
36004 "Hello Bill" (B. P. O. E.)

King Solomon

This is the general title of a series of complete **Instructors** for blue Lodges, for the use of officers and all who are ambitious to become bright workers. They contain the Opening, Work, Lectures and Closing, **in the degrees of Entered Apprentice, Fellow Craft** and **Master Mason**; thus embracing everything in its regular order as worked in each degree **except the essential secrets** the whole given by a system intelligible **only to the initiated,** but easily understood by them. Carefully edited and printed from new type.

There are **separate** editions of these instructors, each edition containing the **standard** work of a particular State.

Having recently been critically revised by competent authorities in the different Grand Jurisdictions, their **accuracy** may be relied upon, and being bound in pocket size (3½x 5¼), with complete index, are very convenient for ready reference, enabling one to refresh his memory during his spare moments.

No practical member will be without one after he has examined it.

H. T. W. S. S. T. K. S.—A complete Instructor for Officers and Members of the Chapter in **accordance** with the standard work and lectures. Intelligible only to R. A. Ms. Also recently revised.

ROYAL AND SELECT MASTERS.—Containing the Ritual of the Council Degrees, revised.

IN HOC SIGNO VINCES.—Containing the Revised Ritual of the Commandery

The above books are firmly bound in emblematic colored leather, making them nearly indistructable and at the same time flexible for pocket use.

For want of an authentic instructor, it is a well-known fact that members are using the Open Exposes, old and spurious works, published in New York and Chicago. As they are highly erroneous and sold to the public at large, as well as to the Fraternity, their use is corrupting the ritual and subverting the order. To correct this evil and meet the demand for a work of this nature that is both accurate and legitimate, these Instructors have been prepared.

No further occasion now remains for the embarassing breaks and delays in working the degrees; for by the aid of one of these instructors an officer is always enabled to accurately and promptly exemplify any degree, and the members can qualify themselves for any position.

ALLEN PUBLISHING CO.

LIST OF BOOKS, ETC.

King Solomon, Lodge, Morocco and gilt..... 3.00
Leather 2.50
H. T. W. S. S. T. K. S. Chapt. Mor. & Gilt. 3.00
Leather 2.50
Council Morocco and gilt.................. 3.00
Leather 2.50
42 In Hoc Signo Vinces. Morocco and Gilt..... 3.00
Leather 2.50
30 King David I. O. O. F. (40 Encampment).
Morocco and Gilt.........................$2.50
Leather 2.00
Cloth 1.50
Paper 1.00
101 **Damon and His Followers. K. P. Mor. & Gilt.....2.50**
Leather 2.00
Cloth 1.50
Paper 1.00
44 **Dum Tacet Clamat. W. O. W. 2.50, 2.00, 1.50, 1.00**
22001 A. A. S. R., Book of the. McClenachan 3.00
24120 Above Life's Turmoil, James Allen...... .80
22011 Adoptive Rite. rev. Enlgd. Macoy..... 1.00
50289 Adv. Course in Yogi Ph., Ramacharaka x 1.00
22116 Advanced Hindu Text Book. Besant.... 1.50
51299 After Death, or Letters from Julia, Stead 1.00
22021 Ahiman Rezon, General. Sickles......... 2.00
22024 Morocco Binding, Gilt Edges........... 3.50
22026 Ahrinziman, An Occult Story. A. Sylvani 1.00
22036 Akin's Manual of the Lodge............ 1.25
50273 Alchemy: Ancient and Modern, Redgrove 1.50
50217 Allen (James J.) Sets, 6 vols. in box. As a Man Thinketh, Way of Peace, Path of Prosperity, Out From the Heart, Heavenly Life, Entering the Kingdom.
Cloth 2.25
50331 Suede Leather 4.00
50000 All's Right with the World, C.B.Newcomb 1.50
22006 All These Things Added. Allen......... 1.00
24231 Altar in the Wilderness. Johnson. Cloth. .50
24233 Paper .... .25
50003 Almanac, Alexander's .... .50
50029 Almanac, Raphael's .... .35

22051 **Amaranth Ode Book** .... .20
22055 Paper .... .15
22041 **Amaranth Ritual. rev.** Enlgd. Macoy.. 1.00
50059 **Among the Heretics,** Packer............ 1.00
22081 **Ancient Const.** rpt. 1732. Anderson.... 1.00
22126 **Ancient Ideals in Modern Life,** Besant.. .75
50151 **Ancient Masonic Revelations.** Churchward 1.50
22056 **Ancient Mysteries and Modern Masonry..** 1.00
22060 Paper. Rev. Charles H. Vail......... .75
24346 **Ancient Mys. & Mod. Revelation,** Colville 1.00
22086 **Ancient Mystic Oriental Masonry.** Clymer 1.50
22110 **Ancient Or. of Hercules** (burl.) 6 copies.. 5.00
22136 **Ancient Wisdom,** Annie Besant......... 1.50
26016 **Anniversary Ode. O. E. S.** 5c.; per doz. .20
22071 **Annotated Constitutions.** Simons........ 1.00
26027 **An Old Love Story.** O.E.S.Poem. Engle.. .10
22091 **Antiquities of Freemasonry.** Oliver...... 1.50
22101 **Ant'ties of the Orient Unveiled.** Redding 1.50
23726 **An Occultist's Travels.** Reichel. Cloth.. 1.00
50700 **Apocalypse Unsealed, The,** Pryse....... 2.00
22196 **Apollonius of Tyana,** Guthrie............ .75
24125 **Aquarian Gospel of Christ,** Levi......... 2.00
50004 **Arcana of Astrology,** W. J. Simmonite.. 5.00
50161 **Arcana of Freemasonry,** Churchward.on press
22146 **Arcane Schools-Hist. of F'msy.** J. Yarker. 4.75
24501 **Ardath,** Psychic Story, Marie Corelli.... .50
26024 **Around Our Altar.** A. C. S. Engle...... .05
50142 **Art of Rendering** (Elocution),E.W.Fenno 1.50
22016 **As a Man Thinketh.** J. Allen. Cl. 4¼x7¼ .50
22019 Special Gift Edition .... .75
22020 Paper .... .15
50257 **Ascendant Tables** (Astrological). Paper. 1.00
50258 Leather 2.00
22286 **As Ye Will,** Sheldon Leavitt, M.D...... 1.50
50610 **Astral Plane, The.** Leadbeater.......... .35
51255 **Astrologer and His Work. The.** Leo..... .25
50208 **Astrological Key to Character,** Pagan... .40
50256 **Astrological Relations of Names & Nos..** .50
50244 **Astrology, Lilly's.** Zadkiel.............. 2.00
24128 **Astrology,** Macgregor .... .50
51010 **Astrology,** Sepharial .... .50
51250 **Astrology Explained.** Leo.............. .25
50005 **Astrology for All.** Leo. Part I.......... 3.75
50010 **Astrology for All.** Leo. Part II......... 3.75
51101 **Atlantis and Lemuria.** Rudolf Steiner.. 1.00
50575 **Atlantis & Lemuria.** Scott-Elliott....... 1.75
51279 **Atlantis the Ancient.** Colville. Paper..* .10
24355 **Atlantis, Story of.** Scott-Elliott.......... 1.25
24200 **Atlantis, Antediluvian World.** Donnelly.. 2.00

51050	At the Feet of the Master, Alcyone. Lea.	.75
51051	Cloth	.50
51052	Paper	.25
50765	A to Z Horoscope Delineator, The. George	2.00
24257	Auras and Your Keynote. J. S. Sears. Cl.	.50
22131	Autobiography. Besant	1.75
26030	A Vision. O.E.S. Poem. Mary L. Paine...	.10
51311	Awakening, The. Mabel Collins.........	.80
50015	Bachelor's Cong. (Burlesque.) Galbraith	.15
50695	Barabbas. Marie Corelli................	.75
50012	Beautiful Necessity. Claude Bragdon....	2.00
51312	Beginnings of Seership. Vincent Turvey	1.50
50510	Be Good to Yourself. Marden...........	1.00
22076	Ben Hur. Wallace	1.50
22067	Beuchners Fraternal Reg. Lea. V. Pocket	.60
50298	Beyond the Borderline of Life. G. Myers	1.00
24223	Bhagavad Gita, Lectures on the. S. Row	1.00
24215	Bhagavad Gita. By Judge. Flex. Lea...	.75
50011	Bhagavad Gita, Tho'ts on. A Brahmin..	1.25
50375	Bhagavad Gita. Trans. by Besant. Cloth.	.50
50376	Leather	.75
50377	Paper	.25
51321	Bible in India. Louis Jacolliot..........	2.00
50017	Bible in Our Public Schools. R. E. Allen.	.25
50025	Bible Myst. & Bible Meaning. Troward...	2.10
22175	Biography of Mrs. Babington	.25
24277	Birth of the New Church. J. S. Sears...	.25
22191	Birthdays, Significance, Colville, L'th'ette	.50
22195	Paper	.40
50064	Black Trail. (Graphology Stories). Hall.	1.00
50016	Blue Bird. Maeterlink..................	1.25
50014	Body of His Desire. Prade.............	1.20
22001	Book of A. A. S. R. McClenachan......	3.00
22151	Book of the Chapter. Mackey............	1.60
50198	Book of the Dead. 3 vols. Illus. Budge..	12.50
50019	Book of the Dead, Egyptian. 1 vol.......	6.00
50018	Book of Life. Dr. Alesha Sivartha......	2.00
24219	Book of the Sacred Magic. Mathers.....	5.00
50061	Book of Symbols. Macov...............*	1.00
50099	Borderland of Psychical Research. Hyslop	1.50
51280	Boy Mason. Ellis ....*	.10
22176	Brotherhood. Harding	.50
22186	Brotherhood of Healers. J. Macbeth. paper	.35
22161	Brother of Third Degree. Carver........	1.35
50046	Browning, Elizabeth B. Poems..........	.75
50047	Browning, Robert. Poems..............	.75
50595	Building of the Kosmos. Besant.........	.75
50030	Byways of Blessedness. James Allen. Lea.	1.25
50324	Cloth	.75
50013	Byways of Freemas'y. Rev. J. T. Lawrence	1.75

51260 **Byways of Ghostland.** Elliott O'Donnell.. 1.35
50326 **Calendar of New Thought**............... .60
50058 **Call of the Carpenter.** White........... 1.20
50035 **Car of Phoebus The.** Robt. J. Lees...... 1.25
50040 **Case of Smythe v. Smith (Burl.)** Dumont .15
50232 **Casting Away of Mrs. Leeks & Mrs. Aleshine.** Frank R. Stockton............... .75
50222 **Century of the Child.** Key............... 1.50
50043 **Ceremonial Magic.** Waite................ 5.50
51324 **Chaldean Astrology.** George Wilde...... 2.15
24220 **Changing World, The.** Besant........... 1.25
22151 **Chapter, Book of the.** Mackey. Cloth.... 1.60
22221 **Chapter Music.** Ilsley................... .15
24224 **Character Building Tho't Power.** Trine.. .35
22230 **Charges of a Mason.** Chase .... .15
50163 **Chinese Numismatic Riddle.** Higgins.... .25
50327 **Christ and Buddha.** Rich. Paper........ .30
50036 **Christ and Buddha.** C. Jinarajadasa. Lea. .75
50037 Cloth .... .50
50328 **Christ, How Shall We Know.** Heindel. Pa .15
50042 **Christ Life and How to Live It.** George. 1.00
50007 **Christ of the Holy Grail, The.** Macbeth.. 1.00
50360 **Christian Creed, The.** Leadbeater....... 1.35
50146 **Christian Healing.** Chas. Filmore. Cloth. 1.50
50147 Paper .... .75
50063 **Chris. Sci. & Kindred Subj'ts.** Winbigler 1.00
50045 **Christianity and Science.** Wilmshurst.... .40
22201 **Christmas, Easter and Burial Serv. K. T.** .45
22202 Leather. Rev. Cornelius L. Twing...... .75
22204 Morocco 1.00
22205 Paper .... .35
24230 **Civilization in Ancient India.** Dutt. 2 v... 7.00
24228 **Clairvoyance.** C. W. Leadbeater......... .75
50234 **Cloud Upon the Sanc.** VonEckhartshousen 1.35
22216 **Cook's Monitor.** For Illinois. Leather... .40
22217 Leather, with Flap..................... .60
22210 **Coles Initiation Ritual** (Burlesque) 6 cop. 3.75
50167 **Color—Music.** Rimmington.............. 1.50
50269 **Colloquies with an Unseen Friend.** Paget 1.50
24011 **Colorado Gr. L. Monitor.** Foster. Cloth.. .75
24012 Leather 1.00
50323 **Columns, J & B, in Relation to the Bible** .50
26043 **Compass and Star.** O.E.S. Poem. Engle..* .05
51301 **Concentration of Thought.** Colville...... .10
22276 **Concentration.** Julia Seton Sears. Paper. .50
50241 **Concentration Made Easy.** Keeler........ .25
22246 **Concise Cyclo. of Freemasonry.** Hawkins 1.75
22211 **Concordia. Words only.** Ilsley........... .25
50003 **Conduct of Life.** Emerson............... .75

22281 Constitution and History, A. A. S. R..... 2.00
22295 Constitutions, O. E. S., Africa, Paper.... .25
22296 Constructive Psychology. Buck 1.00
50041 Constructive Thinking. Keeler........... .25
50038 Cosmic Consciousness. Buck.............. 4.00
50044 Cosmic Symbolism. Sepharial............ 1.50
22236 Cosmogony of Evolution. Ingalese. Cloth. 2.00
22231 Council Monitor. Chase 1.00
22241 Council Monitor. Mackey 2.00
24232 Counsels by the Way. Van Dyke......... .75
22251 Craft Masonry. Cunningham 1.00
22254 Morocco 1.50
51135 Creation by Thinking. J. H. Taylor. Paper .50
50287 Creative Process in the Individ. Troward 1.60
22261 Cross Masonic Chart. Revised............ 1.75
51306 Cross of the Magi. F. C. Higgins. Cloth. 1.50
51307 Paper 1.00
22256 Crucifixion by an Eye Witness........... 1.00
50048 Cruci. fr. a Jewish Standpoint. Hirsch. .25
22241 Cryptic Masonry. Mackey 2.00
22266 Culture of Concentration. W. Q. Judge.. .10
22271 Cushing's Manual, Parliamentary Law.. .75
22411 Cyclopedia of Fraternities. Stevens..... 4.50
22316 Dashed Against the Rock. Colville...... .75
22341 Daughter of Isis. Waller................ .50
22340 Daughters of Sphinx. (Burlesque) 6 cop. 5.00
51015 Dawn of a Tomorrow. Burnett......... 1.00
50625 Death and After. Besant................ .35
50152 Degrees of Zodiac Symbolized. Charubel. .45
26031 Depend'ce of Mas'ry upon O.E.S..Engle* .15
50630 Devachanic Plane. Leadbeater.......... .35
26050 Diagram for Floral Work. O.E.S. Engle. .50
26049 Dia. of Marches for Mystic Tie. O.E.S... .15
22301 Diagram of Parliamentary Rules. Smith.. .50
22304 Morocco, with Parchment Chart....... 1.00
50055 Direct'ns and Direct'g. Astrolog. Green. .45
50086 Directory of Mas. Lodges of the World.. 2.50
50060 Discov. of the Lost Trail. Newcomb.... 1.50
22306 Discovery of the Soul. Wilson.......... 1.00
50049 Dissociation of a Personality. Prince.... 2.80
50065 District Convention, The (Burl.) Dumont .15
22346 Divine Pedigree of Man. T. J. Hudson.. 1.50
24261 Divine Realization. J. S. Sears. Paper.. .10
50410 Doctrine and Lit. of the Kabalah. Waite 2.50
50365 Doctrine of the Heart. Besant. Cloth.. .50
50366 Leather .... .75
50367 Paper .... .25
50840 Dore Lectures. A. Troward. Cloth..... 1.00
50841 Paper .... .50

50052	**Do the Dead Depart?** Bates	1.50
50051	**D'ble Doctrine Ch. of Rome.** VonZedtwitz	.35
50340	**Double Man, The.** Dowd	1.00
50281	**Dracula.** An Occult Novel. Stoker	1.50
22331	**Dream Child.** Huntley	1.00
24234	**Dreams.** C. W. Leadbeater	.50
50053	**Dreams.** Olive Schreiner	.75
50329	**Dreams.** Bergson	.60
22311	**Drew's Monitor.** Small	.60
22361	**Early History, New York.** Ross	2.50
22366	**Early Hist. & Proceedings, N. Y. Vol. 1**	2.50
26001	**Eastern Star.** H. T. Stanton	*Free
50075	**Edenburgh Lectures.** T. Troward	1.25
22371	**Eden to Malta.** Beller	1.50
50087	Paper	.75
24661	**Education as Service.** Alcyone. Paper	.25
24662	Cloth	.50
24663	Leather	.75
51130	**Education of Children.** Rudolf Steiner	.50
50263	**Education of the Will.** Jules Payot	1.50
50070	**Edward Burton,** Metaphys. Novel. Wood	1.25
22421	**Egypt the Cradle of Msry.** deClifford 2 vol.	6.75
22423	Half American Morocco, 2 vol.	7.50
22424	Full American Morocco, 2 vol.	10.00
22425	Full Persian Morocco, 1 vol	10.00
22381	**Egyptian Symbols.** Portal, Simons	1.00
50056	**Eight Pillars of Prosperity, The. Allen**	1.15
26019	**Electa.** O.E.S. Poem. Mrs. H. E. Parmelee*	.05
22981	**Election and Installation.** Grand Lecturer	.40
22985	Paper	.25
22376	**Emerson's Essays**	.75
50073	**Emerson's Poems.** Emerson	.75
22406	**Encyclo.** Mackey, McClenachan. 2 vols	12.00
22391	**Ency. and Hist.** Oliver & Macoy. Cloth	2.75
22392	Library Sheep, Marble Edge	3.00
22395	Half American Russia	3.25
22393	Half American Morocco	3.50
22397	Full American Russia	4.25
22394	Full American Morocco	5.75
22411	**Encyclopedia of Fraternities.** Stevens	4.50
26013	**End of Life's Labyrinth.** O.E.S. Poem. Engle*	.15
50136	**Enigmas of Psychical Research.** Hyslop	1.50
22356	**Entering the Kingdom.** Js. Allen	.50
22359	Special Gift Edition	.75
22360	Paper	.15
50077	**Ephemeris.** Raphael. (Current Year) ea.	.25
50078	(1840 to Current Year) each year	.35
50830	**Episodes from an Unwritten History**	.50
50158	**Essays & Papers Relat. to Freem'y.** Gould	7.00
50079	**Esoteric Astrology.** Allan Leo	3.75

50076 **Esoteric Buddhism.** Sinnett............ 1.25
24238 **Esoteric Christianity.** Besant........... 1.50
50074 **Etidorphia.** John Uri Lloyd............ 1.50
50071 **Etiquette of Freemasonry**............... 1.75
50080 **Everybody's Astrology.** Alan Leo....... .45
24240 **Every Living Creature.** R. W. Trine... .35
24242 **Every Man a King.** O. S. Marden....... 1.00
50069 **Evidences of Frm'ry.** Rabbi Chumaceiro .25
50054 **Evolution & Occultism.** Essays. Besant.. 1.00
50221 **Evolution of Immortality** (Rosicruciae).. 1.00
24239 **Evolution of Life and Form.** Besant.... .75
22396 **Evolution of the Soul.** T. J. Hudson.... 1.50
50006 **Evolution of Worlds.** Percival Lowell... 2.50
50072 **Experience in Self Healing.** E. Towne.. .50
50350 **Experimental Psychol. of Music.**Feininger 1.60
24481 **Extended Vision.** G. Tabor Thompson... 1.00
50216 **Faith of Anc. Egypt, The.** Sidney Coryn 1.00
22476 **Fate Mastered, Destiny Fulfilled**........ .30
51065 **Fellowship Sci. Series Life Primer.** Vol. 1 1.00
22465 **Female Masonry, "A la Lease" Paper**.... .50
50143 **Fenno's Science of Speech.** E. W. Fenno. 1.25
50082 **Fifty Yrs. in Ch. of Rome.**Fath.Clinquay 2.25
50635 **First Step in Theosophy.** Mallet........ .75
22091 **Five Grand Periods of Masonry.** Oliver... 1.50
22471 **Five Jewels of the Orient, The.** Burton. 1.00
50740 **Five Journeys Around the World.** Peebles 2.00
26008 **Five Points of the Star.** Poem. Russell* .10
24245 **Flaxius.** Leland 1.50
22490 **Floral March.** Simpson.................. .50
22481 **Floral Work.** Bunnell .... .40
22485 Paper .... .25
24006 **Florida Monitor.** Gr. Lodge Committee... .75
24007 Leather 1.00
50085 **Flute of the Gods.** M. E. Ryan.......... 1.50
50081 **Footprints of Jesuits.** Thompson........ 1.00
50248 **Force of Mind.** Schofield............... 2.00
26041 **For Installation.** O.E.S.Poem. Engle...... .10
50236 **Foundation Stones.** James Allen........ .50
50284 **Four Epochs in Life.** Hygiene. Muncie 1.50
24248 **Four Great Religions.** Besant........... .75
50084 **Fourteen Les. Yogi Phil.**Ramacharaka.. 1.00
24250 **Fourth Dimension, The.** C. H. Hinton.. 1.75
50083 **Fragments of a Faith Forgotten.** Mead.. 4.00
24252 **Freedom Talks.** J. S. Sears. Cloth...... 1.00
22530 **Freemasonry and Jesuitry**............. .15
50650 **Fm'y "Open Road to Damnation" Cath.*** .10
22501 **Freemasons Monitor.** Webb. Cloth...... .75
22502 Leather 1.00
22571 **Freemason's Monitor.** Sickles 1.00
22572 Same, Lodge, to Comdy., Leather...... 1.50

22511	**Freemason's Monitor.** Thornberg........	1.25
22512	Leather	2.00
22551	**Freimaurer's Handbuch.** Small.........	.60
22556	**Freimaurer's Hanbuch**	1.00
22557	Leather	1.25
24254	**From Incarnat'n to Reincarna.** Ingalese	2.00
24136	**From India to the Planet Mars.** Flourney	1.50
24138	**From Passion to Peace.** James Allen....	.50
50303	**From Pioneer to Poet.** Pagan...........	2.60
50301	**From Poverty to Power.** Path of Prosperity and Way of Peace. Allen......	1.00
22156	**Funeral Services.** Simons—Macoy........	.35
22160	Paper	.25
24131	**Future Life.** Louis Elbe................	1.20
51314	**Gates of Knowledge.** Rudolf Steiner....	1.25
50090	**Gay Gnani of Gingalee.** Huntley........	1.00
22651	**Gem of Song, O. E. S.** Pitkin & Mathews	.50
22655	Paper	.25
22021	**General Ahiman Rezon, a Large Monitor**	2.00
22024	Same, Morocco & Gilt, Sickles—Macoy	3.50
22656	**Genius of Freemasonry.** Buck...........	1.00
50505	**Getting On.** Marden....................	1.00
50089	**Gleam, The.** Albee.....................	1.35
50122	**Gleanings from Buddha Fields.** Hearn.	1.25
51240	**Glimpse, The.** Arnold Bennett..........	1.25
22671	**Glints of Wisdom.** W. J. Colville........	.75
22675	Paper	.40
50985	**Gnani Yoga.** Yogi Ramacharaka.......x	1.00
51281	**Gnosticism: Its Spirit.** Colville....m.l.e.*	.10
50291	**God, a Present Help.** Cady. Cloth....x	1.00
50292	Paper x	.60
50095	**God's Image in Man.** Henry Wood....	1.00
50100	**Golden Age Cook Book.** Vegetar. Dwight.	1.00
50495	**Golden Verses of Pythagoras.** Leather..	1.00
50496	Cloth	.60
50126	**Gd. M.'s Treasure.** IOOF Novel. Sargent	1.25
50088	**Graphology: Brain Behind the Pen.** Hall.	1.00
24260	**Grapho-Psychology.** J. S. Sears. Cloth.	1.00
50091	**Great Initiates.** Schure. 2 vols. set......	3.50
50311	**Great Mother, The.** Bjerreguard........	2.50
24436	**Great Psychological Crime.** T. K........	2.00
50395	**Great Pyramid at Jeezeh.** McCarty......	3.00
24141	**Great Religions of the World.** H. A. Giles	2.00
50008	**Great Stone Face.** N. Hawthorne........	.50
50950	**Great Within.** Larson..................	.75
22661	**Great Work, The.** By T. K., a Mystic..	2.00
24263	**Greatest Thing Ever Known.** R.W.Trine.	.35
24262	**Greatest Thing in the World.** Drummond	.50
24253	**Greatest Truth, The.** H. W. Dresser...x	.90
50199	**Growth of the Soul.** Sinnett............	1.75

22645 **Guide to Chapt.** Sheville, Gould. Limp Cl. .75
22641 Same in Cloth and Gilt Binding....... 1.00
22642 Leather, with Flap.................... 1.25
22644 Bound in Imitation Cowhide Morocco.. 1.50
22646 Large Library Size, Cloth 1.50
22649 Same in Imitation Morocco........... 2.00
22706 **Guiding Star.** Molyneux................ .40
22676 **Guild Frm'sry, Ancient Const. Charges..** 1.00
22311 **Hand Book of Freemasonry.** Drew...... .60
22711 **Harmonia. Music.** Cutler.............. .25
22716 **Harmonics of Evolution.** Huntley....... 2.00
50975 **Hatha Yoga.** Yogi Ramacharaka.......x 1.00
50640 **H.P.B. and Masters of Wisdom.** Besant. .60
50116 **Healing Influences.** Leander Whipple.... 1.25
51245 **Healing Voice, The.** Anna Johnson...... 1.25
24143 **Health and Happiness.** Rev. S. Fallows. 1.50
24146 **Health and Suggestion.** vonFeuchersleben 1.00
22741 **Health from Knowledge.** Colville........ .75
22744 Paper ....* .40
22851 **Heavenly Life.** James Allen. Cloth...... .50
22854 Special Gift Edition .... .75
22855 Paper .... .15
22746 **Hebrew Bible in English, $1.00 to** 20.00
50685 **He Can Who Thinks He Can.** Marden.. 1.00
50105 **Helps to Right Living.** Kath. Newcomb. 1.25
50118 **Henri Bergson (Philos. of Change)** Carr.. .25
24526 **Here & There in Yucatan.** LePlongeon.. .75
50110 **Heretic, The.** Robt. J. Lees............. 1.25
22856 **Hermes and Plato.** Schure.............. .85
22721 **Hermetic Writ'g of Paracelsus.** Waite.2 v. 18.00
22722 American Edition, 2 vols...............12.00
22866 **Heroines of Jericho, Ceremonies.** Dickson .80
22861 **Heroines of Jericho, Ritual.** Dickson.... .50
24269 **Hidden Church of the Holy Grail.** Waite 4.85
50111 **Hidden Side of Things.** Leadbeater 2 v. 4.50
24166 **Hidden Tradition in Mas'y.** Cooper-Oakley 1.25
50115 **Hidden Way Across the Threshold.** Street 3.50
50415 **High Twelve.** Ed. S. Ellis.............* 1.50
50416 Half morocco gilt Back..............* 2.50
50915 **Hints on Study of Bhagavad Gita.** Besant .75
24278 **Hints to Yg. Stud. of Occultism.** Rogers .50
22723 **Historical Landmarks.** Oliver............ 4.00
22726 **Historical Sketch—Morton Commandery.** 1.00
22391 **Hist'y & Cycloped. of Freem'y.** Cloth..* 2.75
22392 Library Sheep, Marble Edge.........* 3.00
22395 Half American Russia. Oliver.......* 3.25
22393 Half American Morocco. &..........* 3.50
22397 Full American Russia. Macoy........* 4.25
22394 Full American Morocco..............* 5.75

50173	Hist'y Mas. Persecu. By var. authors..*	1.50
50174	Rev. Geo. Oliver, D.D., Ed. Paper...*	1.00
22731	History and Power of Mind. Ingalese. Cl.	2.00
22751	History of A. & A. Scottish Rite. Folger	3.00
22791	Hist. of Colored F'msy. Grimshaw......	1.25
22771	Hist. of F'msy, Concise. Gould. Cloth....	2.75
22773	Half Morocco	3.75
22774	Full Morocco	4.75
22781	Hist. of F'msy. Mitchell, 2 vols..........	4.00
22782	Library Sheep	5.00
22784	Morocco	6.00
22761	Hist. of Freem'y & Concordant Orders...	5.50
22763	Half Morocco, Stillson & Hughan......	6.50
22764	Full Morocco	7.50
22801	History of Initiation. Oliver	1.50
22811	History of K. T. Revised. Addison.....	3.25
22813	Half American Morocco	4.00
22814	Full American Morocco	5.00
22817	Full Persian Morocco	7.50
50299	History of Magic. Waite................	3.75
24342	History of Medicine. Alex. Wilder......	3.00
22821	History of Memphis Rite. Gottlieb	1.00
22831	History of O. E. S. Engle.............	2.50
24282	Holy Grail, The. Mary Hanford Ford...	.75
50120	Horary Astrology. Alan Leo...........	.45
50157	Horary Astrology. Simmonite...........	1.25
50125	Horoscope in Detail. Leo and Green....	.45
50980	Hour Book, Perpet. Planetory. George..	.50
50130	Hours with the Mystics. Vaughn........	3.00
50293	How to Develop Psychic Insight. Keeler	.25
50137	How to Grow Success. Eliz. Towne....x	.50
50140	How to Judge a Nativity. A. Leo. Part I	3.75
50145	How to Judge a Nativity. A. Leo. Part II	3.75
50135	How to Keep Fit. Schofield............	.75
51235	How to Live on 24 Hrs. a Day. A.Bennett	.50
50150	How to Obtain Our Own. H. B. True....	1.00
51140	How to Read Char. in Handwrit. Booth.	.35
50155	How to Rest and Be Rested. G. Dawson	.40
51225	Human Atmosphere, The. Kilmer......	2.50
51226	Human Atmosphere (with screens)......	7.00
50904	Human Aura. Colville (4 lect. as below).	.35
50900	1-How Generated; How It Protectsm.l.e.*	.10
50901	2-Principal Features of Color.....m.l.e.*	.10
50902	3-Detailed Explanations ....m.l.e.*	.10
50903	4-How it Reflects Health & Char..m.l.e.*	.10
50112	Human Chord, The. Algernon Blackwood	1.50
51230	Human Machine, The. Arnold Bennett.	.75
50149	Hypatia. Historical Novel. Kingsley....	.75
50117	Hypnotism & Suggestion. Mason.......	1.50
24148	Hyp. Mental & Moral Culture.Quackenbos	1.25

50160 Ida Ilmond & Her Hr. of Vision. Cranford 1.25
24151 Idyl of the White Lotus. Mabel Collins.. 1.00
50039 Illustra. of Freem'y. Preston-Oliver....* 2.00
51210 Immediate Future, The. Besant........ 1.00
50134 Incidents in Life Mme. Blavatsky. Sinnett 1.00
50102 India (Vol. IV. Essays & Address.) Besant 1.00
22991 Indian Masonry. Wright 1.50
24412 Industrial Problem. J. S. Sears. Paper.. .25
51282 Influence of Thought. Colville....m.l.e.* .10
23010 Initiation of Candidate. (Burles.), 6 cop. 5.00
22976 Initiation & Its Results. R. Steiner, Ph.D. 1.00
22977 Board .... .75
50910 Initiation and Mysteries. Rudolf Steiner* .75
50317 Initiation, Perfecting of Man. Besant... 1.00
24276 Initiation, Way of. R. Steiner, Ph.D.... 1.00
24280 Board .... .75
22486 Inner Life of Tao Teh King. Bjerregaard 2.00
50705 Inner Life. Vol. I. Leadbeater......... 1.50
50706 Inner Life, The. Vol. II. Leadbeater... 1.50
22986 In Memoriam. Orin Welsh (Shopworn) .. 1.50
26041 Installation. O.E.S. Poem. A.C.S. Engle.* .10
22981 Installation Ceremonies. Simons—Whiting .40
22985 Paper .... .25
26038 Installation, Close of. O.E.S. Poem. Engle* .10
26033 In the Barley Fields. O.E.S. Poem. Engle.* .05
24152 In the Forbidden Land. H.S. Landor. 1 v. 3.00
24153 In the Forbidden Land. H.S. Landor. 2 v. 9.00
24283 In the Outer Court. Besant............ .75
26034 In the Royal Court. O.E.S. Poem. Engle.* .05
22996 In Tune with the Infinite. Trine........ 1.25
22281 Introduction and History. A. A. S. R..... 2.00
50196 Introduc. to Metaphys. Henri Bergson.. .85
50920 Introduction of Yogi. Besant........... .75
24285 Invisible Helpers. C. W. Leadbeater.... .50
23013 I. O. O. F. Hist. and Manual........... 3.75
23001 Irish Prince and Hebrew Prophet. Kissick 1.50
23016 Isis Unveiled. 2 vols. Blavatsky.......... 4.50
24135 Jacob Boehme. Whyte.................. .75
50355 Jehoshua, Proph. of Naz. F. Hartmann. 2.50
26018 Jephthah's Daugh. O.E.S. Po. Parmelee.* .10
26003 Jephthah's Vow, Dramatic. A. C. S. Engle .15
23046 Jericho Road (I. O. O. F.) B. Adkins.... 1.00
22530 Jesuitry and Freemasonry............... .15
23056 Jesus, the Last Great Initiate. Schure.. .85
23076 Jewels of Pythian Knighthood, Cloth.... 3.00
23078 Half Morocco 4.00
23079 Full Morocco 5.00
50660 Jews & Frmy. in U. S. from His. Soc... .50
23061 Josephus. The Works of............... 1.75
24288 Joy and Power. Henry Van Dyke....... .75

50955 Joy Philosophy. Elizabeth Towne....... 1.00
50745 Joyous Birth. Gestefeld.................. 1.00
51327 Just How to Wake Solar Plexus. Paper x .25
51175 Kabala of Numbers. Sepharial.......... 1.00
51176 Kabala of Numbers. Part II. Sepharial. 1.00
23121 Kabbalah Unveiled. S. L. M. Mathers. Cl. 3.50
50620 Karma. Besant .... .35
24154 Karma, The Law of Life. Percival....x 2.00
50378 Keystone, The. J. T. Lawrence......... 1.75
50166 Key to Astrology. Raphael............... .50
24147 Key to Attainment. J. S. Sears. Paper. .15
24155 Key to Health, Wealth and Love. Sears .25
24290 Key to Theosophy. H. P. Blavatsky.....2.00
50165 Key to Your Own Nativity. Alan Leo... 3.75
51322 Key to Your Star Courses. Wilde....... .85
23086 Kingdom of Love. Frank................. 1.00
23120 King Solomon's Secret (Farce)........... .35
23092 K. of P. Drill. Carnahan, Leather....... 1.50
23091 Cloth 1.00
23115 Knights of theZoroasters(Burlesque)6cop. 3.75
23070 Knight Templar Melodies, per doz....... 4.80
50267 Knowledge of God, The. Schofield...... 1.50
23071 Koran. Translated by Sale............. 1.00
51080 Krishna. Baba Bharti................... 2.00
23106 Krishna and Orpheus. Schure........... .85
24202 Kybalion, The. Three Initiates..........x 1.00
26045 Labyrinth as a Life Story. O. E. S. Paper .25
50233 Lady or the Tiger. Stockton............ 1.25
50500 Land of Living Men, The. Trine........ 1.25
24162 Lao-Tze, Book of the Simple Way. Old. 1.00
24163 Lao-Tze Wu Wei. Borel................. 1.00
50440 Law of Attraction. Colville. Paper.m.l.e.* .10
23141 Law of Mental Medicine. T. J. Hudson.. 1.50
23146 Law of Psychic Phenomena. T.J.Hudson 1.50
50925 Law of Rhythmic Breath. E. Fletcher.x 1.00
50450 Law of Success. Colville. Paper. m.l.e.* .10
50455 Law of Suggestion. Colville.......m.l.e.* .10
24292 Laws of the Higher Life. Annie Besant. .50
50223 Leaves of Grass. Whitman.............. 1.25
50224 De Luxe Edition 2.00
50171 Lessons in Living. Towne.............x 1.00
24293 Lessons in Truth. H. Emelie Cady....x 1.00
24294 Paper .... .50
50319 Letters from a Living Dead Man........ 1.25
50172 Letters fr. a Self-made Merch. to his Son .75
51299 Letters fr. Julia, or Aft. Death.Stead.clo. 1.00
50885 Letters to His Holiness. A. Modernist.. 1.25
24159 Letters That Have Helped Me.Neimand.x .50
26022 Let Us Follow the Star. A Poem.......* .05
23161 Lexicon of Freemasonry. Mackey........ 3.00

24326	**Life and Doctrine of Paracelsus.** Cloth..	2.50
23151	**Life and Power from Within.** Colville...	1.00
23286	**Life and Writings of Dr. R. Fludd,** Cl...	2.50
50815	**Life Everlasting, The.** Marie Corelli....	1.35
51283	**Life Everlasting, The.** Colville...m.l.e.*	.10
50170	**Life of Jesus.** Rhees..................	1.25
24164	**Life Power & How to Use it.** E. Towne.x	1.00
50252	**Life Radiant, The.** Lillian Whiting.....	1.00
24155	**Life's Greatest Secret.** Sears...........	.25
51065	**Life's Primer.** Tuttle. Fellowship Ser...	.75
50254	**Life's Response to Consciousness.** Wylie.	1.00
50251	**Life Transfigured.** Lillian Whiting......	1.25
50060	**Life Triumphant.** James Allen........x	1.00
50296	**Light and Color.** Colville. Boards......*	.75
50297	Cloth	1.00
23176	**Light of Asia.** Edwin Arnold...........	.75
23166	**Light on the Path.** M. C. Cloth..........	.50
23167	Leather	.75
23165	Paper	.25
50123	**Light on Life's Difficulties.** Jas. Allen..	.75
50162	**Light That Never Fails, The.** Bateman	.50
24296	**Linked Lives.** Isabella Ingalese..........	1.50
23181	**Lts. & Shadows of Mystic Tie.** Mackey	2.50
24270	**Living Ideals.** Eugene Del Mar.........	1.00
50865	**Living Thought.** Erwood...............	1.00
50561	**Living Wheel.** T. I. Uniacke...........	1.25
24214	**Living Within.** John W. Zeagler........	.50
23191	**Lodge Goat.** Comic.....................	1.50
23201	**Lodge Music.** Ilsley....................	.15
50645	**London Lectures, 1907.** Besant..........	.75
50133	**Lord's Prayer, The.** Rudolph Steiner...	.25
50262	**Lore of Proserpine.** Hewlett............	1.35
24157	**Lost Continent** (A Novel of Atlantis)Hyne	1.50
24297	**Lost Lemuria.** Scott-Elliott............	1.25
23196	**Lost Word Found.** Buck................	.50
24158	**Lost Word, The. A Xmas Story.** VanDyke	1.50
50570	Lotus Calendar. (Perpetual)...........	.35
26039	**Love One Another.** O.E.S.Poem.Rainey..*	.05
23221	**Low Twelve.** Masonic Stories..........	1.50
23224	Half Morocco	2.50
23472	**Mackey's Ritualist.** Leather............	1.60
50243	**Magic Story.** Fred'k V. R. Dey. Cloth..	1.00
50249	Leather	2.00
24298	**Magic White and Black.** Fr. Hartmann x	2.00
24310	**Magical Message of Ioannes.** Pryse.....x	2.00
50615	**Man and His Bodies.** Besant...........	.35
50182	**Man, How, Whence and Whither.** Besant	4.00
50057	~~**Man, King of Mind, Body and Circ'stance**~~	~~.50~~
23531	**Man Limitless.** Wilson	1.25

23481 **Man of Mount Moriah.** Boutelle......... 2.40
23486 Half Russia 2.80
23483 Half Morocco 3.20
23487 Half Russia, Gilt Edges.............. 3.60
23488 Half Morocco, Gilt Edges............. 4.00
28485 Paper 1.60
50318 **Man of To-morrow, The.** Wilson.......x 1.00
50177 **Manual of Mental Science.** Whipple...... 1.00
50560 **Manual of Occultism.** Sepharial......... 2.00
23491 **Manual of the Chapter.** Sheville & Gould .75
23501 **Manual of the Lodge.** Mackey.......... 2.00
23511 **Manual of the Lodge of N. J.,** Illust'd.... .25
23512 Leather .... .35
23517 **Manual of Lodge of N. J.** (New)......... 1.25
50180 **Man, Visible and Invisible.** Leadbeater.. 3.00
26015 **Martha.** O.E.S. Poem. Mrs. Parmelee...* .05
50119 **Marvels Beyond Science.** Jos. Grasset... 1.75
50655 **Mason. Astron. or Stellar Theol.**Brown..* 2.50
23526 **Masonic Burial Services.** Macoy........ .50
50086 **Masonic Directory of the World**......... 2.50
23461 **Masonic Eclectic,** 2 vols. (Shopworn).... 1.00
23541 **Masonic Gem.** Rev. A. L. Alford........ .50
23561 **Masonic Jurisprudence.** Mackey......... 2.50
23401 **Masonic Jurisprudence.** Lawrence....... 2.85
23581 **Masonic Law and Practice.** Lockwood... 1.00
23271 **Masonic Lt., Morgan Abduc.** Huntington 1.00
50127 **Masonic Lodges of the World.** Armitage. 1.50
23261 **Mas. Lodge Music.** (Kane Lodge, N. J.) .40
23265 Paper .... .25
23536 **Masonic Monitor.** Louisana Thornburgh 1.00
23591 **Masonic Musical Manual,** Lithographed. .75
23594 Leather. W. H. Janes " . 1.00
23600 Paper Flexible. " . .35
23592 Paper Board. Cheaper Print........... .35
23593 Paper Flexible, " " .... .25
23596 Cloth Board. " " .... .60
23598 Paper Flexible, Words Only 4x6...... .20
23620 **Masonic Orpheus.** Dow 1.75
23571 **Masonic Parliamentary Law.** Mackey ... 2.00
50173 **Masonic Persecutions.** By var. authors..* 1.50
50174 Rev. Geo. Oliver. D.D.. Editor. Paper.* 1.00
23444 **Masonic Record.** Book Certificate. Mor. 3.00
50485 **Masonic Reprints & Revela.** Sadler..... 2.25
23291 **Masonic Sketch Book.** E. du Laurans... 2.00
50333 **Masonic Symbolism.** Ward.............. 1.00
23285 **Masonic Poetry.** Morris. Silk Cl., G. Edge 3.50
23281 Embossed. Robt. Morris. Poet Laur'te* 2.75
23311 **Masonic Token.** Anderson.............. 2.25
23301 **Masonic Trials, Treatise upon Law.** Look 1.50
26004 **Masonry.** O.E.S.Poem. A. C. S. Engle.... .10

50179 Master Christian, The. Corelli........... .75
23316 Master Mason Hand Book. Crowe........1.00
50187 Masters, The. Besant.................. .25
50169 Master's Word, The. G.W.Plummer,FRC .50
24299 Mastery of Destiny. Allen.............. 1.00
50945 Mastery of Fate. Larson............... .50
24300 Mata the Magician. Isabella Ingalese.... 1.50
50271 Mathemat. Theory of Spirit, A. Redgrove 1.10
50272 Matter, Spirit & the Cosmos. Redgrove.. 1.10
23321 Maurerisches Liederbuch. Roehr. Cloth.. .25
50190 Medical Astrology. Daath.............. .50
50107 Medical Astrology. Raphael............ .45
50268 Meditations—A Year Book. Jas. Allen... 1.00
50304 Meditations for Beginners.............. .25
26048 Meet Upon the Level. A Poem.........* Free
23400 Memorial Service, O. E. S. Engle...... .25
26042 Memorial. O.E.S.Poem. A. C. S. Engle... .05
50930 Memory—How to Develop. Atkinson..x 1.50
24204 Memory of Past Births. Johnston.....x .50
26007 Memory's Casket. O.E.S.Poem. Engle.... .15
22821 Memphis, Anc. & Prim. Rite of. Gottlieb 1.00
51236 Mental Efficiency. Arnold Bennett....... .75
50178 Mental Healing. Whipple............... 1.50
50185 Mental Medicine. Huckel............... 1.00
22420 Metal Therapeutics. A Text Book. Colville .35
50861 Message of the Stars, The. Heindel...... .50
50332 Message of the Sun. Sampson........... .55
24461 Message to the Well, A. H. W. Dresser. 1.25
50176 Metaphysical Chart, A. Whipple........ 2.50
50184 Methods of Psychic Development. Cooper .75
23346 Meyer's Tactics. K.T.................... 1.00
23345 Middle Chamber Work. Paper........... .25
50535 Military Lodges. Gould................. 1.75
24227 Mind and the Brain, The. Elmer Gates.x .50
51330 Mind, Power and Privileges. Olston..... 1.50
22501 Miniature Monitor. Webb.............. .75
22502 Leather 1.00
50515 Miracle of Right Thought. Marden...... 1.00
23390 Missing Link. (Burlesque) 6 copies...... 3.00
23389 Same with outfit 5.00
23356 Mission of Masonry. Peters............. .50
23360 Paper .... .35
50730 Modern Light on Immortality. Frank... 1.85
24264 Modern Mystic. J. S. Sears. Paper..... .10
24302 Modern Panarion. H. P. Blavatsky...... 2.50
23351 Monitor □ △ △ † &A.A.S.R.Webb—Carson 1.50
23376 Monitor—Grand Lodge N. Y............ 1.00
50188 Montessori Method, The. Educational... 1.85
~~50189 Montessori Mother, The. Dor. C. Fisher 1.25~~
23570 Moot Court Martial (Burlesque) 6 cop... 2.00

23361 **Morals and Dogma A. A. S. R.** Pike.... 5.25
23431 **Morning and Evening Thoughts.** Allen.x .50
23435 Paper ....x .15
26047 **Mother Lodge.** A Poem. Kipling......* Free
23580 **Munchers of Hard Tack.** (Burl.) 6 copies 3.75
23671 **Music of Chapter.** Marsh. Cloth........... .65
23674 American Morocco 1.00
23675 Paper Board .... .40
23673 Paper Flexible .... .25
50154 **My Friends' Horoscopes.** Leo............ .45
50186 **Myriam & the Mystic Broth'hood.**Howard 1.25
23586 **Myrtle Baldwin.** Mas. Story. Munn..... 1.00
24305 **Mysteries of Magic.** A. E. Waite........ 2.25
50345 **Mystery of Ashton Hall, The.** B. Nitsua 1.25
50346 Paper .... .75
24205 **Mystery of Sleep.** John Bigelow......... 1.50
24446 **Mystical Traditions.** I.C.Oakley. Paper.. 1.25
24451 **Mysticism.** Mary Pope.................... 1.75
50334 **Mysticism.** Underhill 3.50
50183 **Mysticism of Color.** Bruce............... 1.35
23411 **Mystic Chord.** Mabie...................... .50
23415 Paper .... .25
50106 **Mystic Light Essays.** Colville. Cloth....* 1.50
Same in 29 pamphlets. Paper................. 1.50
23421 **Mystic Masonry.** Buck..................... 1.10
23181 **Mystic Tie.** Morris—Mackey............. 2.50
26046 **Mystic Tie, O. E. S.** Paper............... .35
51005 **Mystic Will, The.** Leland..............x .50
51215 **Mystics of the Renaissance.** Rud.Steiner. 1.25
50193 **Nature.** Emerson .... .75
24307 **Nature's Allegories.** Maude Dunkley..... .50
50124 **Nature's Mysteries.** Sinnett.............. .25
26026 **Naomi & Ruth.**O.E.S.Poem.Rev.Washb'rn* .10
24306 **Nazarine, The.** A. H. Adams............ 1.00
50094 **New Alinement of Life.** Trine.......... 1.25
51180 **New Avatar, The.** J. D. Buck.......... 2.00
50670 **New Dawn, The. Philosoph. story.**J'hns'n 1.00
24476 **New Democracy, The.** Louise Downes... 2.00
50192 **Newer Spiritualism, The.** Podmore...... 2.75
51070 **New God.** Shirley.......................... 1.00
50520 **New Heav. & a New Earth,** A. Patters'n 1.25
50322 **New Knowledge, The.** R. K. Duncan.... 2.14
50191 **New Manual of Astrology.** Sepharial.... 4.25
23707 **New Odd Fellows Man.** Grosh. Lea. P'ket. 1.50
23706 Cloth, Larger Edition................... 2.50
23709 Morocco and Gilt. Larger Edition...... 3.25
50336 **New Race and New Earth.** Carter...... .35
24375 **New Thought Answer.** Julia S. Sears... .25
24377 **New Thought Church.** Sears............ .10
24373 **New Thought Healing.** Sears............ .25

24308 **New Tho't Pastels.** Ella Wheeler Wilcox .50
50195 **New Thought, Simplified.** Henry Wood.. .80
23700 **New Woman.** (Burlesque) 4 copies...... 1.00
24289 **New World to Conquer, A.** Sears. boards .35
23712 **Nuggets from King Sol.'s Mine.** Schmalz. 2.00
51091 **Numbers.** Wynn Westcott 1.50
50031 **Numbers, Mean'g & Magic.** Kosminsky.Pp .50
50274 **Nyria (A Novel).** Praed................. .90
50312 **Oahspe, a Sacred History**............... 5.00
23721 **Obelisk and Freemasonry.** Weisse. Paper. 1.00
23731 **Obituary Rites of Freemasonry.** Macoy. .50
23716 **Occult Science in India.** Jacolliot. Cloth.. 2.50
51298 **Occult Significance of Blood.** R.Steiner.. .25
24316 **Occultism in Shaksp. Plays.** Rogers.paper .25
23726 **Occultist's Travels, An.** Reichel. Cloth..x 1.00
50264 **Occult World.** Sinnett.................. 1.25
23776 **Ocean of Theosophy, The.** W. Q. Judge. Cl. .75
23011 **Odd Fellowship, History and Manual.** Ross 2.75
23013 Half Morocco 3.75
23014 Full Morocco 5.50
23707 **Odd Fel. Manual, New.** Grosh. LeaPocket 1.50
23708 Cloth. Larger Edition 2.50
23709 Morocco and Gilt, Larger Edition..... 3.25
23736 **Odd Fellowship, Official History.** Canvass 3.75
23737 Half Morocco, Art Canvass........... 4.75
23738 Full Morocco 5.50
23746 **O. E. S. Burial Services.** Macoy........ .50
23741 **O. E. S. Manual,** Original Edit. Macoy. .75
23766 **Old and New Psychology.** Colville....... 1.00
26027 **Old Love Story, An.** O.E.S.Poem.Engle..* .10
23786 **On Road to Self-Knowledge.** Jones. Cloth .50
50200 **Old Maid's Association.** (Burl.) Wilson.. .25
26032 **On Judah's Cloud-capped Hills.** O.E.S.Po.* .05
50940 **On the Heights.** Larson................ .50
24318 **On the Open Road.** R. W. Trine........ .50
24319 **Optimism.** Helen Keller................. .75
50277 **Optimistic Life, The.** Marden.......... 1.25
23640 **Oriental Order Humility.** (Burl.) 6 copies 1.50
50164 **Origin & Symbols of Mas'y.** Higgins On press
23821 **Origin of Freemasonry and K. T.** Bennett 1.75
50197 **Osiris.** 2 vols. Illus. Budge............10.50
50995 **Osru—Tale of Many Incarnat'ns.** Sterns.x 1.00
24320 **Other Side of Death, The.** Leadbeater.. 2.00
26014 **Our Altar.** O.E.S.Poem. Parmelee......* .05
50338 **Our Eternity.** Maeterlink............... 1.50
50205 **Our Invisible Supply.** Warner. Vol. I.... 1.00
50210 **Our Invisible Supply.** Warner. Vol. II... 1.00
26017 **Our Obligation. A Poem.** Mrs.Engle....* .05
26021 **Our Soul's Bright Star.** A Poem.Hastings* .05
26020 **Our Star Rays.** O.E.S.Poem............* .05

26006 **Our Vows.** O.E.S.Poem. McCutcheon....*Free
22756 **Out from the Heart.** J. Allen. Cloth.... .50
22759 Special Gift Edition.................. .75
22760 Paper .... .15
50337 **Outlines of Ancient History.** Morey...... 1.50
50141 **Outline of Occult Science.** Rud. Steiner.. 1.50
50780 **Outline of Theosophy.** Leadbeater...... .25
24325 **Panorama of Sleep.** Ficton............. .50
24326 **Paracelsus, Life & Doctrine.** Hartmann 2.50
50342 **Parsifal.** Huckel. Cloth................ .75
50343 **Parsifal.** Ford. Cloth.................. .75
50755 **Past Revealed, The.** Gaffield............ .75
51275 **Patanjali's Yogi Aphorisms.** Judge. Lea.x .75
51274 Cloth ....x .50
24327 **Path of Devotion.** Swami Paramananda. 1.00
24328 **Path of Discipleship.** Besant............ .75
23791 **Path of Prosperity, The.** Js. Allen...... .50
23794 Special Gift Edition.................. .75
23795 Paper .... .15
23706 **Paths to Power.** Wilson............... 1.00
24329 **Peace, Power and Plenty.** O.S.Marden... 1.25
50209 **Perfect Ashlar.** Lawrence.............. 1.75
23816 **Perf't Way; or Finding of Christ**........ 1.50
23817 Kingsford. M.D. & Maitland. Paper..* 1.00
51315 **Perfume of Egypt.** Leadbeater.......... 1.50
50173 **Persecut'ns, Masonic.** Rev.Oliver et al...* 1.50
50174 Rev. Geo. Oliver, D.D., Editor. Paper.* 1.00
24121 **Personal Masonic Register Book Certif**.. 2.00
50226 **Peters' People's Pulpit.** Rev.M.Peters.Pa .35
23806 **Phylosophy of Fire.** Clymer. Cloth.......1.50
50097 **Philosophy of Life.** Henry Eucken. Clo.. .25
51329 **Philosophy of Numbers.** Balliett........ 1.50
50211 **Phrenology.** Olin .... .50
50215 **Physiognomy.** Lomax .... .50
50555 **Pictorial Key to the Tarot**.............. 2.00
26002 **Picture Sketches, Poems, etc.** Engle.... .10
23871 **Pilgrim Degree.** O.E.S.................. .35
50725 **Pilgrimage of a Soul, The.** Oyston....... .50
50303 **Pioneer to Poet.** Pagan................. 2.60
50990 **Planetary Daily Guide for All.** George... .50
50991 **Planetary Hour Dial** .... .50
50220 **Planetary Influences.** Bessie Leo........ .45
50259 **Planets and the Signs, The.** E. Adams... 2.00
50344 **Planet Vulcan.** Weston................. .50
24332 **Plotinos.** K. S. Guthrie................. .75
23285 **Poetry of F'm'ry.** Morris. Silk Cloth, Gilt 3.50
23281 Embossed Cloth Cover............... 2.75
50680 **Point Within a Circle**.................. .25
50246 **Political Romanism.** Clo. Public. Bureau .75
50247 Paper. (Every Mason should read this) .50

50260 Poor Little Rich Girl, The. Gates...... 1.25
50875 Popular Lectures on Theosophy. Besant .50
24384 Power of Self Suggestion. McComb..... .50
50033 Power of Silence. Dresser............... 1.35
50225 Practical Astrology. Alan Leo........... 1.25
51136 Practical Astrology for Everybody. George .50
50435 Prayer. Page .... .50
23751 Prelate's Lessons....................... 1.00
26037 Presentation of Flowers, Installa. O.E.S.* .10
24333 Priestess of Isis. E. Schure............. .75
50032 Priest, Woman & Confess.Fath. Chinquay 1.00
51325 Primer of Astrology..................... .50
50202 Primer of Higher Space. (4th Di.)Bragdon 1.00
50895 Primer of Theosophy..................... .15
23551 Principles, Practice, Mas'c Law. Simons. 1.50
00000 Proceedings, Lodge, Chap. Com'dry, etc. write
51284 Problem of Virtue & Vice. Colville.m.l.e.* .10
50235 Progress of a Mystic. Sampson......... .40
50240 Progressed Horoscope. Alan Leo........ 3.75
50245 Progressive Creation. Sampson. 2 v. Set 5.00
50250 Progressive Redemption. Sampson...... 3.00
50255 Prosperity Thro. Tho't Force.McClelland.x 1.00
50283 Psychic Autobiography, A. Jones........ 1.50
51285 Psychic Phenomena. Colville......m.l.e.* .10
51145 Psychic Phenomena. Frank 2.25
50229 Psychic Powers in Man.B.Fay Mills.Clo.. .35
50230 Paper .... .20
50213 Psychic Science & Christianity.E.K.Bates 1.50
50545 Psycho-Harmonial Philosophy. Pearson. 3.50
50341 Psychology. James. (Briefer Course)... 1.60
51220 Psychology. Besant 1.00
24255 Psychology of Fasting. Sears. Paper.... .25
51106 Psychol. of Salesmanship,The. Atkinson.x 1.00
24344 Psychology of Suggestion. B. Sidis...... 1.75
50339 Psycho-Therapv. Severns 1.50
23805 Put Through. (Comic).................. .25
23811 Pythagoras & Delphic Mysteries. Schure .85
23081 Pythian Knighthood. Carnahan. Cloth.. 3.00
23083 Half Morocco 4.00
23084 Full Morocco 5.00
26012 Queen Esther. O.E.S.Poem.Mrs.Parmelee* .05
26005 Queen Flora's Reign.O.E.S.Po.Timmerman*.15
23851 Queen Moo and the Egyptian Sphinx.. 4.75
23841 Queen Moo's Talisman. Cloth........... 1.50
23850 Queen of Sahara. (Burlesque) 6 copies 3.00
23861 Queen of the South. Macoy............. .40
23865 Paper .... .25
50062 Questions in Nat'l Sci. T.K.(A Mystic).. 2.00
50970 Raja Yoga, Mental Devel.Ramacharaka.x 1.00
24336 Rama and Moses. E. Schure............ .85

23870	Ransford Drill. O. E. S.	.75
50348	Rational Education of the Will. Levi	1.25
50860	Rational Life. Erwood	1.00
24337	Rays of Truth. Bessie Leo	1.25
50720	Reason Why in Astrology. Greene	.45
51205	Reality of Matter. T.K.	1.00
50265	Rebuilding of Solomon's Temple. Franklin	1.50
23886	Red Blood of Odd Fellowship	1.50
50228	Regeneration. Dowd	1.00
24258	Reincarnation. J. S. Sears. Boards	.35
50600	Reincarnation. Besant	.35
50270	Reincarnation and Christianity	.50
50855	Reincarna. and the New Testm't. Pryse. x	.60
50856	Paper x	.35
24387	Reincar. Study of Forgot. Truth. Walker. x	1.50
26004	Relationship Mas. Fratern. & East. Star*	.10
24340	Religious Problems in India. Besant	.50
50093	Reminis. of an Army Nurse. A. W. Smith	1.50
50347	Renewal of the Body. Miltz	1.00
51286	Resurrec. & Regeneration. Colville. m.l.e.*	.10
24736	Return of Frank R. Stockton*	1.00
51206	Return of Peter Grimm. Belasco	1.25
50525	Revelation of a Square	2.00
51277	Riddle of Life. Besant	.25
24339	Riddle of the Universe. Ernst Haeckel	1.50
50275	Right and Wrong Thinking. A.M. Crane	1.40
24601	Road to Freedom. Floyd B. Wilson*	1.00
51287	Robert Browning. Colville m.l.e.*	.10
23901	Robert's Rules of Order	.75
24511	Romance of Two Worlds. Corelli	.50
51316	Romanism. Crowley	1.50
50203	Roped In. (Burl.) Set of 8 Rituals	3.00
23906	Rosicrucians. Clymer	1.50
24414	Rosicrucian Christianity Ser. (20 bks. pa) (Or Separately, as Follows:)	1.20
24414	1 -The Riddle of Life and Death	.06
" "	2 -Where Are the Dead	.06
" "	3 -Spiritual Sight & The Spirit'l Worlds	.06
" "	4 -Sleep, Dreams, Trance, Hypn'tism, etc.	.06
" "	5 -Death and Life in Purgatory	.06
" "	6 -Life and Activity in Heaven	.06
" "	7 -Birth a Fourfold Event	.06
" "	8 -The Science of Nutrition, Health&Y'th	.06
" "	9 -The Astronom. Allegories of the Bible	.06
" "	10-Astrology: Its Scope and Limitations.	.06
" "	11-Spiritual Sight and Insight	.10
" "	12-Parsifal	.06
" "	13-The Angels as Factors in Evolution	.06
" "	14-Lucifer, Tempter or Benefactor	.06
" "	15-The Myst. of Golgotha&Cleansg.Blood	.06

24114	16-The Star of Bethlehem...............	.06
" "	17-The Mystery of the Holy Grail.......	.06
" "	18-The Lord's Prayer....................	.06
" "	19-The Coming Force—Vril! or What?..	.06
" "	20-Fellowship and the Coming Race.....	.06
51025	Rosicrucian Cosmo Conception. Heindel.	1.50
51100	Rosicrucian Mysteries. Heindel..........	.75
24391	Rosicrucian Philos. in Questions & Ans	1.15
23881	Rosicurcians, Rts. & Mysteries. Jennings	3.50
50092	Round the World in Silence. Kent......	1.50
23915	Royal Arch Comp'n. Chase. Limp Cloth..	.75
23911	Same in Cloth and Gilt Binding.......	1.00
23912	Leather with Flap	1.25
23945	Royal Arch Standard, McGown. limp cloth	.75
23941	Cloth	1.00
23942	Leather with flap	1.25
23895	Royal Order of Ogling Owls (Burl.)6 cop.	3.00
23936	Rubiayat of Omar Khayyam. Deckel Edge	1.25
23937	Limp Leather...........................	2.00
23940	Watered Silk	2.00
23931	Ruins of Empires. Volney................	1.00
26011	Ruth, the Gleaner.O.E.S.Poem.Parmelee.*	.05
23956	Sacred Mysteries. A. Le Plongeon.....	2.50
51288	Sacred Mysteries. Colville........m.l.e.*	.10
50349	Sadhana. Tagore	1.25
50028	Sad Sheppard. Van Dyke................	.75
50113	Saviors of the World. Rev. C. H. Vail.*	1.00
50114	Paper ....*	.75
23981	Scarlet Book of Freemasonry. Redding..	3.00
23984	Leather	4.00
51265	School in the Home, The. A. A. Berle..	1.00
50098	Science and a Future Life. Dr.Jas.Hyslop	1.50
50238	Science and the Infinite. Kline..........	1.00
50351	Sci. of Psychic Heal'g....Ramacharaka.x	1.00
24396	Science of the Larger Life. Gestefeld....	1.50
50890	Science of Being Great. Wattles........	1.00
50715	Science of the Emotions. Bhagavan Das.	1.50
23951	Scientific Demonstration of the Future..	1.50
51289	Scient. Marvels & Marv. Beyond. m.l.e.*	.10
50253	Second Sight. Sepharial................	.50
50204	Secret Doctrine in Israel. Waite........	3.75
24066	Secret Doctrine. vol.1.2.Blavatsky.Am.Ed.	10.00
24067	Secret Doctrine. vol.1.2.3&Index.Eng.Ed...	18.00
24031	Secret Doctrine Abridged. Hil'ard......	2.00
50024	Secret Hist'y of Oxford Movement.Walsh	1.00
24343	Secret of Achievem't, The.O.S.Marden...	1.50
50101	Seen and Unseen. E. K. Bates..........	1.50
24398	Selections from Buddha. Max Muller..x	.50
51278	Self and Its Sheaths. Besant............	.75
50820	SelfDevelopm't and Way to Power.Rogers	.25

24259	Self Healing. J. S. Sears. Boards......	.35
50201	Self Superlative, The. Keeler............	.60
24076	Sermon on the Mount. Pryse. Cloth......	.60
23971	Serm. & Address. 480 pp. (shopw'n) Platt	.75
22966	Servant in the House. Kennedy........	1.25
50605	Seven Principles of Man, The. Besant..	.35
24347	Shells from Life, Love-God. Sears......	1.00
23991	Shibboleth, K.T. Monitor. Gd. Enc. Connor	1.25
51110	Short Masonic Hist., A. Vol.I. Armitage	2.00
51111	Vol. II	2.00
22021	Sickles Ahiman Rezon, General...........	2.00
22024	Genuine Morocco......................	3.50
22571	Sickles Monitor □ △ △ †................	1.00
22572	Leather	1.50
50131	Sidelights on Freemasonry. Lawrence...	1.75
23976	Signet of K.S. Freemason's Daughter...	1.50
24077	Signet of R. A. Mas'ry. Hendricks-Speed	2.75
51075	Significance of Numbers. Colville.m.l.e.*	.10
26025	Signs and Passes. A Poem. A.C.S.Engle*	.10
23986	Signs and Symbols. Oliver.............	1.50
24401	Signs&Symbls.Primord.Man. Churchward	8.00
51331	Silver Gauntlet, The(OccultNov.)Silvani..	1.50
24162	Simple Way, The. Lao Tze-W.GornOld..	1.00
51090	Simplified Scientific Astrology. Heindel..	.40
23916	Singular Story of Freemasonry..........	1.50
50285	Sister Masons. (Burlesque) F. Dumont..	.15
50022	Sixteen Principal Stars. Dalton.........	.75
24040	Sixth & Seventh Books of Moses.........	1.00
24041	Paper	.75
50460	Sleep, Dreams and Visions. Colville.m.l.e.*	.10
22301	Smith's Diagram Parliam'y Rules. Cloth	.50
22304	Leather, with Parchment Chart......	1.00
24020	Smithsonian Comedetta. (Burl.) 4 copies	1.00
24026	Solomon's Temple. Caldecott...........	2.50
24350	Some Glimpses of Occultism. Leadbeater	1.50
24351	Some Problems of Life. Besant..........	.75
50370	Song Celestial. Edwin Arnold. Cloth...	.75
50371	Leather	1.00
24050	Sons of Osirus. (Burlesque) 6 copies....	3.75
50194	Soul and Circumstance. Stanton........	1.00
50310	Soul of Lilith. Corelli..................	.75
50212	Spain from Within To-day. Andujar....	1.25
50066	Speeches, Welcome & Responses. Pap*	.15
50067	Toasts, Statistics, Odes Cloth*	.25
50068	Jokes, Memoranda, etc. Lea.*	.50
51310	Spherical Basis of Astrology. Dalton....	2.50
26029	Spirit of Freemasonry. A Poem. Engle*	.10
24021	Spirit of Freem'n'y. Hutchinson, Oliver	1.50
26028	Spirit of the East. Star.A Poem. Engle*	.10
24352	Spirit of the Orient. G. W. Knox.......	1.50

50290 Spiritual Evolut'n, Regeneration. Douglas 1.20
24372 Spiritual Law in the Nat'l World. Eleve.x 1.00
24374 Paper ....x .50
50206 Spiritual Life. Besant.................... 1.00
50023 Spirit'l Life for Man of the World. Besant .50
51155 Spiritual Sight and Insight. Heindel..... .10
50159 Spiritual Therapeutics. Colville.......... 1.75
50261 Springs of Character. Schofield.......... 1.50
24001 Stand. Masonic Monitor. Simons—Macoy .75
24002 Same, in Leather and Gilt............ 1.00
24006 Standard Monitor, Florida. Cloth...... .75
24007 Leather 1.00
24011 Standard Monitor, Colorado. Cloth...... .25
24012 Leather .... .50
22216 Standard Monitor, Illinois. Cook. Cloth .40
22217 Leather .... .60
24085 Star Chamber. Frazer. (Burl.) 6 copies.. 5.00
26010 Star Our Guide. O.E.S. Poem. Boardman* .05
50655 Stellar Theology or Masonic Astronomy* 2.50
50139 Story of a Literary Career. E. W. Wilcox.. .50
24355 Story of Atlantis. Scott-Elliott.......... 1.25
50575 Story of Atlantis & Lemuria. Scott-Elliot 1.75
24354 Story of the Great War................. 1.25
23961 Story of the Other Wise Man. Van Dyke .50
23962 Limp Leather 1.00
51105 Straight Goods in Philosophy........... 1.00
50480 Strange Story, A. Bulwer Lytton....... 1.00
51270 Strenuous Life Spiritual. Vander Naillen.x 1.00
50132 Studies in Lesser Mysteries. Mont.-Powell .70
24056 Study in Consciousness, A. Besant...... 1.50
51276 Study in Karma, A. Besant............ .25
24356 Study of Man & the Way of Health. Buck 1.50
24406 Subconscious Self, Educ., Health. Waldst. 1.25
50168 Substance of Faith, The. Sir O. Lodge.. 1.00
51328 Success Through Vibration. Balliett..... 1.00
24357 Suggestion. C. F. Winbigler............. 2.00
50026 Suggestion and Psychotherapy. Jacoby.. 1.50
50096 Sunlit Road Calendar. Trine........... .35
50352 Survival of Man. Sir Oliver Lodge...... 2.00
24051 Swedenborg Rite. Beswick 1.00
50219 Symbolism and Astrology. Leo.......... .45
24071 Symbolism of Freemasonry. Mackey.... 2.25
24061 Symbol of Glory. Oliver.............. 1.50
24358 Symbol Psychology. Roeder 1.50
50295 Symphony of Life, The. Henry Wood... 1.25
51310 Table of Houses (Seph. Basis Astrol.) Dalton 2.50
24191 Tactics. K. T. Grant.................. 1.00
24192 Leather 1.25
24196 Tactics, N. Y. Regulation............... .75

24181 **Tactics Vest Pocket**.................... .25
24184 Morocco ....'.... .75
24182 Leather .... .50
51185 **Talk of the Hour.** Mrs. Hugo Ames..... .50
50300 **Tarot Cards. Pack of 78.** Smith......... 2.00
24291 **Tarot, Key to.** Waite.................... 1.00
50555 **Tarot, Key to.** Pictorial................ 2.00
24359 **Tarot of the Bohemians**................. 2.50
50288 **Telepathy & the Subliminal Self.** Mason. 1.50
24206 **Templar Hand Book**........................ 1.00
24201 **Temple.** Eidersheim. Cloth.............. .75
50335 **Temple of the Rosy Cross.** Dowd........ 2.00
24731 **Temporal Power.** Corelli .... .75
50282 **Text Book of Astrology.** Pearce......... 7.50
50027 **Text Book of Theosophy.** Leadbeater.... .75
50490 **Theocratic Philosophy of Masonry**......* 1.75
50368 **Theosophical Questions Answered.**Rogers .15
50309 **Thelma.** Coreli .... .75
50133 **The Lord's Prayer.** Steiner.............. .25
24176 **The Tabernacle.** W. S. Caldecott........ 1.75
50306 **Theosophy.** Besant .... .25
50665 **Theosophy.** Rudolf Steiner............... 1.00
50307 **Theosophy & Christianity.** Max Seiling.. .50
24360 **Theosophy & the New Psychol.** Besant.. .75
50103 **Theosophy & the Theos. Soc.** Besant... .85
50104 **Theosophy & Woman's Movem't.** Despard .25
24236 **This Mystical Life of Ours.** Trine..... 1.00
50580 **Thought Forms.** Besant & Leadbeater.. 3.50
24363 **Tho't Power, Its Control & Cult.**Besant. .75
50330 **Thoughts About Good Cheer.** Marden.. .25
24216 **Thoughts for the Occasion**............... 2.00
50001 **Tho'ts I've Met on the Highway.** Trine. .75
24408 **Tho'ts on the Spiritual Life.** Boehme.. .75
50153 **Thousand & One Notable Nativ.,** A. Leo .45
50276 **Threefold Way, The.** Ward.............. .25
50353 **Three Essays on Karma.** Steiner........ 1.35
50286 **Three Link I.O.O.F. Fraternity.** Robinson 1.00
24361 **Three Paths and Dharma.** Besant...... .75
50965 **Three Principles of Divine Ess.**Boehme.x 2.00
24362 **Thrice Greatest Hermes.**G.R.S.Mead.3 v.10.00
24186 **Throne of Eden.** W. J. Colville......... 1.00
24531 **Thro' the Gate of Good.** Jas. Allen.... x .50
24535 Paper ....x .15
50315 **Through the Mists.** Robt. J. Lees....... 1.25
24241 **Through Silence to Realization.** Wilson 1.00
24213 **Traditions, Origin, Early Hist.** Pierson 2.50
50675 **Tragedy of Hamlet.** H. Frank.......... 1.50
50374 **Training of the Child.** Spiller........... .25

50372 **Training of the Human Plant.** Burbank. .60
24364 **Transcendental Magic.** E. Levi......... 3.75
50239 **Transparent Jewel, The.** Collins......... 1.00
50237 **Treasure of Heaven, The.** Corelli........ .75
24225 **Trial of Jesus.** Drucker............... .25
24366 **Triumph ofTruth or Doom ofDogma** Frank 1.50
24368 **True Chur. of Christ, The.**Brodie-Innes. 1.25
50302 **True Mystic, The.** Sampson............ 1.00
24411 **Truth Abt. New Tho't.** J.S.Sears.Paper. .10
24413 **Truth Abt. Woman's Suffrage.** Sears.... .25
50320 **Twentieth Century Christ.** Karishka..... 1.00
24226 **Twentieth Century Orient** (Burl.) 6 copies 3.00
50373 **Two Thou. Yrs. in Celest. Life.**GreekGirl 1.25
51293 **Urge of the Ideal.** Colville........m.l.e.* .10
50266 **Unconscious Mind, The.** Schofield....... 2.00
50325 **Under a Lucky Star.** Walker........... 1.50
26035 **Under the Palms.**O.E.S.Poem. Engle....* .05
51290 **Universal Eth. Teachings.**Colville.m.l.e.* .10
51292 **Universal Races Cong.** Colville....m.l.e.* .10
51291 **Univer. Relig. & Ethics.**Colville...m.l.e.* .10
24256 **Universal Spiritualism** 1.00
51150 **Universal Text-Book.** Besant. Part I... .75
51151 Part II .... .75
24416 **Unknown, The.** C. Flammarion.......... 2.00
50905 **Unknown Life of Christ.** Notovitch..... 1.00
50144 **Use and Abuse of Masonry.**Capt.G.Smith 1.50
24250 **Van Nest's Burlesque Ritual** 6 copies... 3.75
24369 **Vedanta in Practice.**SwamiParamananda 1.00
24370 **Veil of Isis or Myst. of the Druids.**Reade 1.00
24506 **Vendetta.** Corelli .... .50
51328 **Vibration, Success Through.** Balliett.... 1.00
24251 **Vocal Manual.** Words Only. Macoy.....* .25
24251 **Vocal Manual.** Words only. Macoy..... .25
24265 **Vocal Star, O. E. S.** Paper............ .25
24266 **Voice of the Silence, The.** Blavastky. Cl. .50
24267 Leather .... .75
26023 **Vow of Jephthah.** O.E.S.Poem.Hastings* .10
51195 **Wanderer in the Spirit Lands.**Franchezzo 1.25
24496 **Wandering Jew, The.** Sue. 2 vols...... 1.50
24497 Better Binding. 2 vols................ 2.00
24301 **Washington & Mason. Compeers.** Hayden 1.75
50129 **Washington, George.** A Letter.........* .10
50121 **Was Jesus an Essene.** Wright. Paper.. .50
24276 **Way of Initiation.** Rudolf Steiner, Ph.D. 1.00
24280 Paper .... .75
24271 **Way of Peace, The. J. Allen.** Cloth..... .50

50550 Way of the Soul. Wm. T. Horton....... 2.00
26044 Wear the Colors. O.E.S.Poem. Engle....* .05
22501 Webb's Monitor......................... .75
22502 Leather 1.00
22491 Webb's Monitor—Morris Edition. Cloth. .75
22492 Leather 1.00
50356 Wee Wisdom's Way. Filmore........... .25
50148 Westward Ho! Historical Novel. Kingsley .75
24286 What All the World's a-Seeking. Trine. 1.25
50380 What is a Horoscope & How to Cast it. Leo. .45
50465 What is Genius. Colville..........m.l.e.* .10
24417 What is New Thought? Julia Seton Sears .05
50735 What is Spiritualism? Peebles............ .75
50354 When the Sun Moves Northward. Collins .90
50242 Which One. Bennet 1.35
51160 Who Answers Prayer. F. Huntley (Editor). .50
50231 Why I Changed My Relig. Opinions. Mills .10
24222 Why We Pray. J. S. Sears. Paper...... .15
50386 Will to be Well. Patterson. 5th Ed..... 1.20
50279 Wind Along the Waste. (Novel). Stoker .50
50002 Winning of the Best. Trine............. .75
24315 Wisdom of the Ages. (Burl.) 6 copies.. 5.00
50585 Wisdom of the Upanishats. Besant..... .75
24281 Witching Hour. Thomas............... 1.50
24418 With the Adepts. Franz Hartmann..... 1.15
26036 Within the Arena. O.E.S.Poem. Engle..* .05
24441 Within the Holy of Holies. Rellimeo.... 1.00
50109 Within the Mind Maze. E. L. Larkin.... 1.25
26040 Woman and Woman. O.E.S.Poem.....* .05
26009 Woman. Humorous. A Poem. Brown..* .10
24413 Woman's Suffrage. J. S. Sears. Paper.. .25
50445 Words of Power. Colville. Paper..m.l.e.* .10
51035 Working Gloss'y for Theosoph. Students. .50
51294 World of Life. Colville............m.l.e.* .10
50113 World's Saviors. Rev. Chas. H. Vail..* 1.00
50114 Paper ....*..75
50108 World of Life. Wallace................. 3.50
24321 Worshipful Master's Assistant. Macoy.. 1.50
24324 Same, in Morocco and Gilt............. 2.25
50128 Worthy the Name Sir Knight. Poem. Wilcox*.10
24425 32° K.P. or Ninety in the Shade. (Comic) .25
28881 Year Book, for Masters and Secs. Cloth .50
22882 Leather .... .75
22883 Morocco 1.00
22884 Paper. Good .... .25
22885 Paper. Cheaper .... Free

24371 Yoga or Transformation. W. J. Flagg.... 3.00
50138 You and Your Forces. Eliz. Towne....x .50
50935 Your Forces, How to Use Them. Larson 1.50
50400 Your Fortune in Your Name. Sepharial.. 1.00
50475 Zanoni. Bulwer Lytton.................. 1.00
24217 Zones of Consciousness. Sears. Boards.. .50

www.ingramcontent.com/pod-product-compliance
Lightning Source LLC
Chambersburg PA
CBHW080606270326
41928CB00016B/2946
9781594622427